Cross Lane

The first pub to open on Cross Lane was the **Dog and Partridge** at Richmond Place, which was the name given to the area at the beginning of the lane, next to New Windsor. The first licence was granted to Richard Ellor in 1803 and at that time virtually all the land south of Broad Street and west of Cross Lane was still covered by fields.

The pub was renamed the **Weavers Arms** about 1816, then in 1823, when Peter Thomason was the licensee, it was known as the **Two Greyhounds**. In the September it was advertised for sale along with 2,000 square yards of land. There was another auction at the pub in 1824, when a nearby house, barn, some cottages, a dyeworks and about fifteen acres of land were sold. Ten years later Ellor Street had been laid out at the side of the pub and rows of houses were being built on the land.

The Two Greyhounds was renamed the **Grapes Hotel** soon after the sale and the licensee until about 1830 was Thomas Phillips. Later tenants included William Hawthornthwaite in the 1830s and John and Alice Hope in the 1840s-50s. During this period the Grapes was owned by Joseph Bleackley of the Sun Brewery, Ardwick.

Thomas and then John Canavan had the licence from about 1857 to the 1880s. Abraham Garside took over in the 1890s, advertising dinners, teas and well aired beds for overnight visitors, with good stabling for their horses. The

The Grapes, Cross Lane, in 1961

Grapes also had a room suitable for 'balls, conversaziones and parties'. The next licensee, James Ward, had a few minutes of fame when Wombwell's travelling circus was set up on land nearby. Lion tamer Mustang Ned took Mr Ward into the lions' den, where he drank a glass of champagne and smoked a cigar.

By then the Grapes was owned by the Manchester Brewery Company and they renovated the building, giving the ground floor a facing of coloured tiles.

Licensees in the twentieth century included George and Rose Hill, James Kelly in the 1920s, Charles Cliffe in the 1930s, Clarence Wilkes in the 1940s and Edward and Annie Taylor in the 1950s-60s.

Ownership of the Grapes passed from the Manchester Brewery to Walker & Homfray and then Wilsons. Martin and Joan Browne were the tenants when it closed in 1966. Before the building was demolished a local firm bought the furniture, fixtures and fittings with a view to exporting mahogany doors, acid-etched windows and other items to America. Another feature of the Grapes survived a few more years. In 1970 the licence was formally given up by Wilsons when the Woodman was opened on the Ellor Street development.

In an account of a journey on the Liverpool & Manchester Railway, published in 1833, the writer describes a stop at Cross Lane bridge: '...a flight of several steps leads to a neat village inn, which conspicuously displays its whitewashed walls on a lofty eminence to the right.' The 'village inn' was Cross Lane's second licensed house, the **Railway Inn**, first recorded as the **Railroad Tavern** in 1829. At the time it was the only building on the east side of the lane south of Liverpool Street. Elizabeth Oldham was the licensee in 1829 and subsequent tenants included James Hughes in the 1830s, Cornelius Hope in the 1840s, and Robert and then Harriet Madeley in the 1850s-70s.

John Higham took over about 1880 and at that time the London & North Western Railway Company had plans to build a cattle station nearer to Cross

The London & North Western in the 1920s

Lane market than their sidings at Ordsall Lane. A new cutting would be made for lines into sidings alongside Windsor Street and this meant the Railway Inn would have to be demolished. In 1886 the company obtained permission to build a new hotel 27 yards to the north of the original inn, at a cost of around £5,000. The new site measured 1,180 square yards, more than twice the area of the original.

When it was completed, John Higham moved his family into the new **London and North Western Railway Hotel**. Sarah Higham took over after her husband died and their daughter Florence had the licence at the time of the First World War. In 1891 Mrs Higham proudly advertised 'The Prettiest and Best-conducted Concert Hall in Lancashire'. She engaged the 'best professional talent' and there was a change of artistes every week. At that time the pub was the headquarters of Salford Football Club.

Ten years later Mrs Higham claimed that the upstairs concert room was attracting over 1,500 people a week. There was some open space at the back of the pub and she had plans to build a music hall there, with seats for 520 people in the pit and 225 in the circle. The planning application was turned down and Mrs Higham and her successors had to make do with the concert room, which remained a popular venue for many years. When Thomas Worsley was in charge in 1930, he was advertising regular concerts with good artistes and 'refinement at all times'. By then the London and North Western was owned by Threlfalls Brewery; in Mrs Higham's day McEwan's and Burton ales were advertised.

Later licensees included William Lyth in the 1930s, John Quinlan in the 1940s, Lewis Stewart in the 1950s, Joseph and Florence Wagner in the 1960s and Samuel and Margaret Boardman in the 1970s. It became a Whitbread pub and underwent the first of a series of makeovers in 1981. When it reopened in October, the Salford City Reporter announced that a 'dirty, dingy, nicotine-stained Victorian pub' had been transformed into the **Norwest**, a 'trendy disco bar' aimed at the under-30s. There was another reopening in April 1983, when landlord Jackie Richmond reintroduced live entertainment, with Frank Foo Foo Lamarr top of the bill. Two years later the Norwest became **The End**. By November 1989 the building was derelict and it was pulled down in 1990.

The Cross Lane Cattle Market opened in 1837 and soon afterwards two public houses - the Cattle Market Hotel and the Butchers Arms - opened nearby. The 1840 directory lists Abraham Whittaker at the **New Cattle Market Hotel** and the 1848 map shows the building with sheep and cattle pens on one side and the gardens of Oak Hall on the other. The hall, its gardens and an adjoining chemical works disappeared a few years later when the market was enlarged.

The 'New' had been dropped by 1843, when James Whittaker was listed at the **Cattle Market Hotel**. Thomas Goodwin took over in the 1850s and he was still there in the 1880s. Mr Goodwin served as a Salford councillor and he was a founder of the soap works on Ordsall Lane which later became Colgate-Palmolive. About 1870 he obtained a special licence to cater for cattle dealers arriving in town for the

Tuesday markets - the hotel was allowed to stay open until 1.00am on Tuesday mornings, then open again three hours later.

James Fletcher Whittaker was the licensee in the 1890s, then Thomas Goodwin Whittaker until about 1920. Brewers Groves & Whitnall bought the pub in 1921 and their tenants included Fred Arnold and Thomas Woodward in the 1930s, Leonard Burton in the 1940s and Herbert Court in the 1950s.

In 1958 the pub was modernised and the name was changed to the **Red Rose Hotel**, the red rose having been the brewery's trademark since about 1950. A 'first-class concert room' was fitted out downstairs, whilst upstairs there was a ballroom with a cocktail bar called the Windsor Suite, which according to the publicity could accommodate a five-piece band and three hundred dancers in evening dress. The suite could be hired for eight guineas an evening.

In December 1964 the suite was modernised and renamed the Bamboo Bar. The Red Rose eventually closed in 1971.

The **Butchers Arms** on the corner of Unwin Street, midway between the Grapes and the Cattle Market Hotel was first listed as a beerhouse in 1840. The tenant was a house agent called Edward Eden and by 1843 he had managed to get a full licence.

John and Emma Walley took over about 1860 and in August 1867 they advertised an unusual attraction - 'the largest hog pig in the world' was to be seen free of charge at the pub. Freak animals which had been brought to the market were sometimes exhibited in the yards of nearby pubs to bring in curious customers.

Later licensees included Timothy Henshall in the 1870s and John Barlow about 1890. Cardwell's Brewery of Hulme acquired the pub on a six-year lease in 1894 and this was taken over by Wilsons Brewery in 1899. By 1902 Groves & Whitnall were listed as the owners and John Murray was the licensee. Ten years later the pub belonged to the North Cheshire Brewery. In December 1922, only a few months after the first radio broadcast from Manchester, the Butchers was the venue for a show of this modern wonder. The pub advertised a 'free wireless demonstration' for half an hour on three evenings a week.

John Johnson became the tenant in the 1930s and the Butchers was run by members of his family for over twenty years - Elsie Johnson took over in the 1940s, John Alfred about 1950 and Emily a few years later.

The Red Rose (formerly the Cattle Market Hotel) in 1962

The Butchers was owned by Ind Coope, which became part of the Allied Breweries group in 1961. The pub closed about 1967 and the last licensees were William and Edith Hutchinson.

Across the road from the three-storey, purpose-built Cattle Market Hotel was the much smaller **Cattle Market Tavern**, a beerhouse which opened a few years before the hotel. The building is shown on the 1831 map, part of a row of houses set back from the roadway, with front gardens that were later covered to provide a pull-in for horse-drawn traffic.

William Burgess was the licensee in 1836, followed by Henry and Elizabeth Leater until about 1863. Two years later John Green was in charge and the beerhouse had been enlarged by taking over the shop next door. In August 1867, when 'the largest hog pig in the world' was on show at the Butchers Arms, Mr Green advertised a rival attraction, 'the greatest wonder out. To be seen alive, a calf with six perfect legs.'

John and then Ann Windley had the licence in the 1870s, followed by John Beahan in the 1880s. The beerhouse was acquired by Messrs Watson & Woodhead of the Bolton Street Brewery, who in 1895 leased it to Cardwell's of Hulme. Wilsons Brewery took over the last few years of the lease in 1899 and after that Walker & Homfray were the owners.

A well known local figure, Tom Connors, became licensee of the Cattle Market Tavern in 1898. He was a wrestler and he promoted matches at a ring on Liverpool Street as well as

The Cattle Market Tavern in 1951

putting on events on some open land behind the beerhouse. In 1905 he was advertising 'splendid grounds' where customers could practise 'quoit brasses and jumping'.

Ellen Connors took over from Tom and she was still there in the 1920s. By then some of the old houses on either side had been taken down and replaced by shops up to the pavement line. Walker & Homfray rebuilt the tavern in line with the shops, giving it a frontage of cream-coloured tiles and a new name - the **Cattle Market Wine Tavern**. It was licensed to sell beer and wine only until about 1960, when the then owners, Wilsons Brewery, obtained a spirits licence.

Licensees after the Connors included

Thomas Johnson in the 1930s, Vincent Chilton in the 1940s and Albert Heap in the 1950s. The pub was included in the Windsor Extension compulsory purchase area and closed in 1966. Wilsons also owned some garages at the back, which had been built on the site of three houses on Partington Street.

Another beerhouse had opened opposite the Salford Cattle Market by the early 1840s. The **Craven Heifer** was on the corner of Richmond Street and was kept by Robert Crossley until about 1850. John Shaw was there a few years later and Sarah Drummond was in charge in 1863, when the hotel was granted a full licence.

Thomas Bullock took over about 1865 and in 1872 he applied for a special licence to extend his opening hours from 11.00pm to 1.00am on Tuesday mornings (market days), then reopen at 4.00am rather than 6.00am, which was the usual opening time for pubs in those days. He explained that many cattle men, especially those from Cheshire and Ireland, arrived late on Monday or early on Tuesday and he was in danger of losing customers because Mr Goodwin had been granted a special licence for the Cattle Market Hotel across the road. The application was turned down, with the magistrates sympathising with Mr Bullock and saying it was a pity Mr Goodwin's licence had been granted.

Sarah and then Matthew Bullock ran the pub in the 1870s, when the owners were listed as the executors of brewer John Mayor Threlfall. A new Craven Heifer seems to have been built around this time, replacing the original pub, which was set back from the road. John Davies had taken over by 1880 and Elizabeth Davies was there in the early 1900s. Joseph Sinclair took over in

The Craven Heifer in the 1920s

1913, advertising Threlfalls' Liverpool and Salford Ales and a billiard table 'in A1 condition'. Four years later Stafford Sinclair was the manager and he advertised that the hotel had been redecorated throughout. Dinners could be had for 1/3d in his large dining room.

Later licensees included Sydney Brookes in the 1930s, Lilian Etchells in the 1940s, Sydney Hall in the 1950s and Ernest Dale in the 1960s-70s. The pub was included in the Windsor Extension compulsory purchase area in the 1960s, but it survived and in 1973 the building was renovated by Whitbread and reopened as the **Golden Gate**.

The brewery's first choice of name was the 'Barbary Coast', but this was rejected by the Council. The old nickname for Cross Lane and Trafford Road was not suitable, because it was 'a reminder of when the dockland area was full of fights and slums.' The Golden Gate was fitted out with two lounges and a cabaret restaurant on the first floor called the San Francisco room.

The pub eventually closed in mid-1995, when the owners were Discovery Leisure, and about five years later it became the Windsor Minimarket.

In the 1830s a retired Manchester publican called Samuel Popplewell built a block of houses - Popplewell's Buildings - between the Craven Heifer and Tontine Street. These houses were set back from the road, but within a few years the two at the Tontine Street end had been extended forward and the one on the corner became the **Corporation Inn**. It is first recorded in the 1848 directory, when the licensee was John Whiteley. Subsequent tenants

included Maria Brentnall in the 1860s, Ward Whiteley in the 1870s-80s and Mary Alice Hall in the 1890s. In 1864 the beerhouse was listed as the **Apollo Inn**, but this may have been a mistake in the directory.

At the beginning of the twentieth century the Corporation was owned by the Manchester Brewery Company, who leased it to Messrs Kay & Whittaker of Hulme. Wilsons Brewery took over the lease in 1904, then the following year the owners obtained permission to rebuild the 'cramped and insanitary' beerhouse, taking in the greengrocer's shop next door. By then, most of Mr Popplewell's houses had been replaced by shops fronting Cross Lane and the Corporation was rebuilt alongside these, with the ground floor frontage adorned with coloured tiles in Manchester Brewery style.

Albert Clare was the licensee at the time, then in 1915 James Clampitt took over. Mr Clampitt was a rugby international who had played for Broughton Rangers since 1906 and became team captain in 1910. Later tenants included John Barker in the 1920s and William and Emily Johnson in the 1930s-40s.

Ownership passed from the Manchester Brewery to Walker & Homfray, then when Robert Smethurst was there in the 1950s, the Corporation was once again a Wilsons house. The building was included in the Windsor Extension compulsory purchase area in 1966, reprieved, then ten years later it was reported that Salford Council had agreed to buy the building for £31,000. The deal didn't go through and the pub survived. Tenants in the 1960s-70s included Francis and Kathleen Arnold and Clifford and Lilian Lightfoot. After

a few periods of closure from about 1995, it was put up for sale by the Nomura company and at the beginning of 2002 the building had become an Indian takeaway.

In the mid-nineteenth century, across Tontine Street from the Corporation and where Macdonald's is today, there were some cattle sheds which had been erected following the opening of the Cross Lane Cattle Market. A beerhouse called the **Drovers Arms** opened next to the sheds and this was first listed in 1850, when the licensee was John Edwards.

The beerhouse and the sheds were let together - an advertisement from April 1857 mentions 'shippon room for more than 100 cows.' The next tenant was James Leater; George Holehouse was listed there in the 1860s and at that time the Drovers was owned by Benjamin Joule of the local brewing family.

The last recorded licensee was Henry Robinson in 1874. A few years later Pendleton Unitarian Chapel had been built at the Windsor Bridge end of Cross Lane and a row of three shops stood on the site of the Drovers Arms.

Another beerhouse listed in the 1850 directory was the **Cross Lane Tavern**. It was part of Windsor Terrace, four houses with long front gardens which had been built in the 1830s at the top of Ellor Street, across from the Grapes Hotel. When the premises were converted into a beerhouse, the entrance was made on the Ellor Street side and the address became No.1 Ellor Street.

The earliest licensees included James Hulme and William Times in the 1850s and John Knott in the 1860s. When Enoch Teece was in charge in the 1870s, the name had been changed to the **Horse and Jockey**. Frederick King and James Kelly were there in the 1880s. Mr Kelly was a former sergeant major, so he may have been the man responsible for the next change of name, to the **Fusiliers**. In September 1888 he was advertising the beerhouse as 'the only house in Manchester and district where you can practise with military rifle, Winchester repeating rifle and revolver.' The range was in the cellar and it was well lit. Above ground, there was a skittle alley on the old front garden.

Ten years later the Fusiliers was owned by brewer J G Swales and it was in a poor state of repair. At the brewster sessions in August 1898 the tenant, Elizabeth Bainbridge, said the building was 'practically tumble-down' and her family had to live in the cellar. The owners wanted to rebuild the beerhouse on the open land

The Corporation in 1961

fronting Cross Lane (the site of the Windsor Terrace gardens), but permission was refused.

Swales applied again in 1899 and 1900, when tenant Edward Grace complained that the place was insanitary and the smells in the cellar were very offensive. It could also get flooded after a heavy rainstorm. The magistrates suggested that he move upstairs to live in the bar parlour, to which Mr Grace replied, 'If the bar parlour is not altered soon it will be in the cellar!' After yet another unsuccessful application to rebuild on Cross Lane in February 1904, Swales put forward an alternative plan to enlarge the Fusiliers by extending into three cottages fronting Ellor Street. In 1905 the plan was modified to add just one of the cottages, whose cellar was already part of the beerhouse.

The brewery must have been allowed to make some changes, since the old Fusiliers remained standing for another thirty years. Tenants during this period included William O'Brien, Mary Cooke and, in the 1930s, Daniel and Agnes Sanderson. Swales eventually obtained permission to build a £12,000 hotel on Cross Lane in 1937 and two years later the full licence of the Royal Veteran on Stanley Street was transferred to the new pub. Licensees in the 1940s-50s included Norman Marsland, John Clerk and Henshaw Spilsbury.

In December 1959 Swales refurbished the Fusiliers to provide an entertainment venue 'with a standard as high as the established Manchester

clubs.' The interior was decorated in white and gold, with a star-studded ceiling. Manager John Cairns had a staff of 25, there was waiter service on show nights and entry was by ticket only. Draught beer and spirits prices were not increased, but the brewery put a penny on the price of bottled beer. Lita Roza was famously the first star to appear at Cross Lane's new venue, and the Dallas Boys were advertised as a forthcoming attraction.

The Fusiliers was altered again about 1970, when the pub was redecorated on a horse racing theme and renamed the **Paddock**. It became a Boddingtons house and has seen a few changes since then, but it is still going in 2003.

On the other side of Cross Lane, a beerhouse opened in the row between Tontine Street and Richmond Street (Popplewell's Buildings) in the mid-1850s. It was then seven doors along from the Corporation Inn and, like the Corporation, this beerhouse and the shop next door had been extended up to the pavement line. William Bennett was listed there in 1858 and William Atkinson in the 1860s. The 1864 directory lists the beerhouse as the **Original Three Pigeons Inn**, then later records show it was called the **Sportsman Inn**.

Joseph Mills was there in the 1870s, Ralph Parkinson in the 1880s and John Wild in the 1890s. Dyson Broadbent was in charge in the early 1900s, when the Manchester Brewery Company were the owners and they tried to get permission to rebuild the beerhouse and the shop next door. Jonas Smith

took over about 1905 and after his death in 1910, there was a move to close the Sportsman on the grounds that the premises were structurally unsuitable and no longer needed. The brewery appealed, claiming beer sales of up to six barrels a week, and more rebuilding plans were submitted by their new tenant, James Greenwood.

The licence was renewed, but the beerhouse was not rebuilt. Jane Greenwood had the licence after her husband and Herbert McHale was there in 1928, the year the Sportsman closed.

The last beerhouse to open on this part of Cross Lane was the **Royal Oak**. In 1863 two shopkeepers, George Pimblett and Elizabeth Cunliffe, are listed next to the Craven Heifer Hotel. By about 1870 Mr Pimblett's premises were described as dining rooms and the shop next door was occupied by a beerseller called Elizabeth Wilde. In the 1880s the two shops had been combined to form the Royal Oak beerhouse. John Lowe, a drill instructor with the Rifle Volunteers, had the licence in 1881, William Nicoll was there in 1886 and James Melia in the 1890s.

The property was acquired by Wilsons Brewery and in 1899 the company obtained permission to rebuild. The old house was set back from the road and it was described as being in a ruinous state. The new Royal Oak was completed in 1900, in line with the rebuilt Craven Heifer next door. The plans for the rebuilding show a wide lobby on the right hand side, with the bar at the far end. The room at the front on the left was the tap room and behind this was the parlour. Arthur Warham had the licence in 1905 and later tenants included Walter Fishwick in the 1920s-30s, Eileen Kelly in the 1940s, Walter Bentley in the 1950s and finally Stanley and Winifred Worrall from about 1960.

The Royal Oak closed in 1970, when it was part of the Windsor Extension compulsory purchase area.

The beerhouses further along Cross Lane, between Liverpool Street and Regent Road, opened in the 1850s-60s. One of the first building developments in this area was Wilton Terrace, three rows of houses at the corner of Liverpool Street. One row - the North Wing - faced Liverpool Street, which on the 1848 map is shown with gates across the end. The houses were set back from Cross Lane and gardens were laid out in front of them. As a select residential development, Wilton Terrace was soon in the wrong place and two of the rows were demolished in the 1860s. The third, the South Wing, was in use as the Wilton Fever Hospital in the 1880s-90s.

The Paddock in the 1990s

Rows of smaller houses and shops were built on the site of Wilton Terrace and its gardens, and the shop on the Liverpool Street corner was licensed as the **Wilton Arms** in 1862. Thomas and Alice Clarke were listed as the tenants a few years later, Joshua Amphlett in 1870 and Thomas and Mary Jane Nicholls in the 1880s.

Arthur Walters had the licence in the 1890s and early 1900s and by then the property was owned by brewers Watson, Woodhead & Wagstaffe. When Walker & Homfray took over this company in 1912, they acquired the Wilton and two adjoining shops. The shop next door was incorporated into the beerhouse and the ground floor frontage of the enlarged building was given a facing of coloured tiles.

Charles Farrell was running the Wilton in the 1920s and later tenants included Alfred Middleton in the 1930s, William Mottershead in the 1940s, William Hayhurst in the 1950s and Alfred and Josephine Walker in the 1950s-60s. By then it was a Wilsons pub. The property was included in a clearance area in the 1960s and a Compulsory Purchase inquiry was held in 1971. Four years later the Council paid the then owners, the Grand Metropolitan group, £20,000 for the Wilton and the snack bar next door.

The **Buck Hotel**, on the other side of Cross Lane from the Wilton, was built as a public house by Edwin Done. In the 1860s he was an agent for two Scottish manufacturers of sail cloth and sacking, with an office in Manchester and a house in Seedley. By 1869 he had become a beer retailer at the Buck, or **Bucks Head**, and began applying for a full licence. There was some local opposition - the Rev Clarke, who lived nearby in Park Place, said there were already too many public houses and beerhouses on Cross Lane - but the licence was granted in 1871.

Soon after that Mr Done moved out and the next owners seem to have been Taylor's Eagle Brewery. Joseph Newsham was the tenant until about 1880, and William and then Agnes Twist for about twenty years from 1890. George Wilkinson took over about 1920 and he obtained permission to incorporate a disused ground floor room into the licensed area, despite opposition from a local temperance organisation. Mr Wilkinson said the Buck was a busy house and the customers were tumbling over one another.

Tom Wall was at the Buck for a few years in the 1920s, then from the 1930s to the 1950s his daughter and son-in-law, Nellie and Samuel Stonehouse, were at the pub. It was owned by the Openshaw Brewery Company during that period, then after a series of company mergers the Buck became a Bass Charrington pub.

James and Nellie Hindle took over about 1970 and they were the Buck's last tenants, since by then the pub was in an area scheduled for redevelopment. Nellie was Tom Wall's granddaughter and when the Buck closed in January 1975 her mother, 73-year-old Vina Lewis, was still pulling the pints. Vina had worked in the pub when her dad was there in the 1920s and so she was one of the longest serving barmaids in the city. At the end of 1975 the Council agreed a purchase price of £47,000 for the property.

Further along Cross Lane and on the same side as the Buck, the **Globe Inn** was on the corner of Lord Duncan Street. It was first listed in the 1858 directory, with Thomas Wilkes the licensee. When it was advertised to let in February 1861, it was described as a 'respectable beerhouse in a healthy neighbourhood', three doors from Cross Lane Station. The last recorded licensee was Benjamin Porter in 1865.

The **Falcon Inn** was next door but one to the Globe, on the corner of Hodge Lane. Hannah Huddart was listed there in 1861, then Robert Hyde a few years later and William Hyde and John Nichols in the 1870s. By this time the beerhouse had been extended into the

shop next door and the property was owned by the London & North Western Railway.

The company had plans to widen the railway cutting at Cross Lane Station to accommodate new lines leading to cattle sidings between Cross Lane and Windsor Street. This meant that Hodge Lane had to be realigned and half of the Falcon (the bar and kitchen) demolished. Since the company also owned the former Globe Inn next door, this was converted into a new vault for the Falcon.

Henry Thornhill was the licensee in the 1880s and Mrs Alice Thornhill was there in the 1890s and early 1900s. In the 1890s the beerhouse was leased to a Hulme brewery, Henry Cardwell & Company, then Wilsons Brewery took over in 1899. In 1918 their tenant, David Allardyce, was advertising 'Wilsons noted ales and stout in fine condition. Cigars and cigarettes of all the choicest brands.'

Wilsons bought the Falcon and six cottages in Lord Duncan Street from the railway company in 1921. They remodelled the beerhouse in contemporary style, giving the whole building a cladding of cream-coloured tiles. Charles Beswick was the licensee about this time; Edwin and Alice Barrett were there in the 1930s, William Watmough in the 1940s-50s,

Passers-by pose for the photographer outside the Wilton about 1900

John and Elsie Fielding in the 1950s-60s and Cyril and Lavinia Higgins in the 1960s-70s. The pub eventually closed in the summer of 1979.

The other Wilsons beerhouse on this part of Cross Lane, the **Wellington Inn**, was also given a tiled frontage in the 1920s. The Wellington was bigger than the Falcon, a three-storey building, and it opened on the corner of Myrtle Street in 1851. It had probably been built as a public house, but didn't become fully licensed until about 1960.

The first licensee was Henry Barlow and he was followed by his son-in-law, Richard Williams, in 1864. Matthew Bradshaw took over in 1866, advertising 'choice mild and bitter ales, London and Dublin porters, etc.' Like his predecessors, Mr Bradshaw applied for a full licence. At the brewster sessions in August 1866 he said a spirits licence was needed because there had been a great increase in traffic past the Wellington since the toll bar at the Eccles New Road end of Cross Lane had been removed. The following year he pointed out that Cross Lane would become even busier once the proposed road to Old Trafford (Trafford Road) had been built. In his last application in 1868, he said that thirty-seven trains a day stopped at Cross Lane Station and a new public house was needed because the Railway Inn was about to be pulled down.

Unfortunately for Mr Bradshaw, the railway company had their own plans to replace the Railway Inn and when it was eventually pulled down in the

The Falcon in 1961

1880s, they built the London & North Western Hotel.

Later tenants at the Wellington included Samuel Millward in the 1870s and John Chetham in the 1880s. During this period the beerhouse was owned by Salford councillor Thomas Goodwin. Watson Pidd had the licence in the 1890s and Mrs Ann Pidd in the early 1900s. The beerhouse was bought by Wilsons Brewery and given its tiled frontage in the 1920s, complete with a 'Sign of Quality' draughtboard

trademark set above the corner window. Naomi Rhodes was the licensee from the 1920s to about 1935. Subsequent tenants included David and Josephine Harrison, Walter Green in the 1950s and George Gilfillan in the 1960s-70s.

Like the Falcon, the Wellington closed in the summer of 1979.

On the other side of Cross Lane, near the railway line, there were two Groves & Whitnall beerhouses, the Station Hotel and the Railway Inn. Both opened under different names. Before it was rebuilt, the **Station Hotel** was called the **Star Inn**. It was described in an 1858 advertisement as an 'old original beerhouse opposite the railway station,' although it wasn't that old, since the row of property was built about 1850 and the earliest recorded licensee was Joseph Bird in 1858.

Thomas Norbury was there from the 1860s to the 1880s and Joseph Wharf in the 1890s. Groves & Whitnall became the owners of the Star in 1891 and rebuilt it as the Station Hotel in 1898. The tenant at the time was Alfred Hind and he stayed on until about 1910. James Higginbottom took over at the time of the First World War and was still there in the 1940s. Later tenants included William and Annie Johnston in the 1950s-60s and Stanley and Ada Bootes in the 1960s-70s.

The Station became a Greenall Whitley pub and it closed early in 1979. The building was pulled down a few months later.

At the other end of the row, the **Albion Inn** opened on the corner of West

The Wellington in 1965

Albert Street in the late 1860s. The earliest recorded licensee was Robert Seddon in 1870. William Hampson was there a few years later, Joshua Whittaker about 1880 and Elizabeth Keenan in 1890.

The beerhouse was renamed the **Railway Inn**, probably following the demolition of the first Railway Inn in the 1880s, and it was bought by Groves & Whitnall in 1898. The brewery also acquired the two remaining shops between the Railway Inn and the Station Hotel. When it was built, the row comprised six houses; the rebuilt Station covered the sites of two of them and at the other end, the Railway had been extended into the house next door. In the 1920s Groves & Whitnall gave the Railway a cladding of cream-coloured tiles, similar to Wilsons' Falcon and the Wellington across the road. The shop next door was given the same treatment, so the brewery was probably considering extending the Railway into this building as well.

Licensees of the Railway in the twentieth century included Henry Wharf before the First World War, Elizabeth Allmark in the 1920s, Thomas and then Catherine Grant from the 1930s to the 1950s and Norman and Dora Wilkinson in the 1950s-60s. It became a Greenall Whitley pub and closed at the beginning of August 1979. The shop next to the Station Hotel was the first of the row to be demolished, then the Station, then finally the Railway and the former tobacconist's shop next door. The coloured, leaded windows depicting railway locomotives remained intact right up to the end.

The Railway in the 1970s

The **Church Inn** was part of a row of shops near the Regent Road end of Cross Lane. Matthew Bradshaw was listed as a shopkeeper there in 1863, then a few years later he had become a beer retailer. John Halsall (or Hassall) had the licence in the 1880s and Charles Dewhurst around 1890. At this time the Church Inn consisted of a front room vault, with a parlour behind and a kitchen and scullery at the back. By the early 1900s the beerhouse had been extended into a former milk shop next door, then in 1906 an extension was built in the backyard so that the smoke room could be enlarged. In return for permission to make the alterations, the owners - the Rochdale

& Manor Brewery - agreed to give up the licence of the Tyrone Castle on Arlington Street.

The licensee at the time was Peter Jones and Mrs Ann Alice Jones continued to run the Church Inn in the 1920s. George Baddeley was there in the 1930s, Isaac Bradley in the 1940s and Joseph and Emma Maxwell in the 1950s-60s. By then the Church was owned by Sam Smith's Brewery.

Like the Railway Inn nearby, the Church Inn closed in August 1979. The last tenants were William and Edith Hutchinson.

Four months after the Church closed, Cross Lane gained a new pub, the **Ship Inn**, named after the old Ship Hotel which stood at the corner of Eccles New Road and Cross Lane. It was built near the corner of Liverpool Street for Wilsons Brewery, by then part of the Grand Metropolitan group, and opened on 14th December 1979. The first licensee was Sam Fawcett. In the early 1990s the pub was acquired by Vaux Breweries.

In its beery heyday there were nineteen pubs on Cross Lane, if you count the Ship Hotel, which strictly speaking was on Eccles New Road. Directories for the 1830s-50s show that there were other, short-lived beerhouses, probably at the Windsor Bridge end. The site of only one of these can be identified, but its name, if it had one, isn't known. Between 1845 and 1852 Luke and Ann Crowther were listed at Windsor Place, which was the name given to some big houses between Broad Street and the Grapes at the top of Ellor Street. This beerhouse closed when a three-storey block of shops was built on the Broad Street corner.

The Church Inn and adjoining shops on Cross Lane in the 1970s

Windsor and Wallness

The first public house in this part of Salford was the **Windsor Castle Inn**. It was licensed in 1791 by Thomas Alsop, who moved here from the Spread Eagle in the heart of the old town. Work on cutting the Manchester, Bolton & Bury Canal began the same year and in 1796 passengers embarked at the Windsor Castle for the first packet boat trip to Bolton.

William Dakin took over from Mr Alsop and about 1808 he had the franchise for running the passenger boats. John Beeston was the licensee in 1813 and ten years later he opened the Rose and Crown on Broad Street. William Dakin took over again and was at the Windsor Castle for another twenty years.

In February 1842 the pub was to let. The advertisement mentions 'a commodious brewhouse, stabling, and yard adjoining, and a good supply of excellent spring water.' The house was near the new Cattle Market on Cross Lane, and it was 'well frequented by the most influential of the cattle salesmen, as well as the butchers.'

Peter and Rebecca Kay were listed there in the 1840s, Thomas Jordan in the 1850s and John Moffitt in the 1860s. Thomas Wagstaffe took over about

The Windsor Castle in 1961

1870 and in 1876 he transferred the licence to John Rhodes Wagstaffe, who ran the pub until about 1900. They were related to John Wagstaffe, owner of the Lion Brewery in Hulme, and when this company merged with Salford brewers Watson & Woodhead in 1898, the Windsor Castle was one of the properties taken over. It passed to Walker & Homfray in 1912.

Licensees in the twentieth century included George Whitaker about 1910, John Bamber in the 1920s, James Clampitt and Ernest Brotherton in the 1930s, Anne Bentham in the 1940s, John Donachie and then Leslie Bell in the 1950s.

The Windsor Castle was a Wilsons pub when it closed in 1976. The building was pulled down for the Albion Way development.

The Windsor Castle was on the corner of New Windsor (later just Windsor) and West George Street. The area's second public house was at the other end of the same row, on the corner of Albion Street. This was the **George the Fourth**, opened in 1825 by Thomas Stephens and run by him and then Maria Stephens until the 1840s. Robert Crossley and James Leigh were there in the 1850s, then Elizabeth Brown in the 1860s. In June 1866 Mrs Brown advertised wines, spirits, refreshments, tea and beds, all at moderate charges, and she had good accommodation for visitors to Peel Park.

James Bailey was running the pub in the early 1870s, then in 1873 the last licensee, Benjamin Mawdsley, took over. In August 1885 he applied to transfer the licence to the Clarence beerhouse on Whit Lane, because the George the Fourth was about to be demolished to make room for the new Lancashire & Yorkshire line to Hindley and Wigan, which was to run under a widened Windsor Bridge next to the Bolton line. The transfer was refused and the pub and other buildings at the top of Albion Street were demolished.

One of the first beerhouses to open at New Windsor was the **Founders Arms**, kept by Arthur Spence in the 1830s. It was on the south side of the road, part

George Hanson at the door of the Founders Arms, Windsor, in the 1920s

of a row of houses between the Windsor Castle and Cross Lane. Subsequent licensees included William Kay in the 1840s, William Marsh in the 1850s-60s, James Chapman and Samuel Greenwood in the 1870s and Samuel Bardsley in the 1880s.

The Founders was acquired by Walkers Brewery and in 1901 they applied, unsuccessfully, to extend into the house next door. They had problems in February 1905, when the magistrates refused to renew the licence because the tenant, Sarah Ellis, had been convicted of running a disorderly house. The brewery managed to get the decision overturned at the Quarter Sessions, but they had to defend the licence again in 1907. The police reported that the nearby pubs - Windsor Castle, Grapes, Corporation and Fusiliers - were all doing better and they wanted the Founders closed. Walkers were able to show that the Founders was selling four or five barrels of beer a week, trade was increasing and they expected it to do even better once the Staff of Life across the road closed. This beerhouse was referred for compensation at the same sessions.

Licensees around this time included James Hulme and Thomas Cobb, who took over in 1913 after running a beerhouse called the Flower Pot in Crumpsall. The Founders eventually closed in 1925, after the police reported that it was no longer needed and the Corporation building inspector said the only living room on the ground floor was a kitchen and scullery

measuring twelve feet by ten feet. Walkers tried to have the licence transferred to a grocer's shop on Ross Street so that it could become an off-licence, but they had picked the wrong shop. Temperance campaigners said that Ross Street was in a slum area and there were already thirty 'off' and five 'on' licences within a few minutes' walk. The last licensee of the Founders was George Hanson.

The 1845 directory lists John Trow as a butler living at Windsor Place, Cross Lane. Three years later he had moved to premises near Windsor Bridge, facing the Windsor Castle, and become a brewer and beer retailer. The beerhouse was called the **Bridge Inn**, or the **Windsor Bridge Inn**. The career change evidently suited Mr Trow, as he continued to run the business until the 1880s. Advertisements from the 1870s show that he leased another beerhouse, and maybe some more, and that the Windsor Bridge Brewery sold 'family beer' in half or quarter casks. Burton and Scotch bitter ales were also available.

The brewery was probably a casualty of the widening of Windsor Bridge to accommodate the Lancashire & Yorkshire line through Pendleton to Hindley and Wigan, but the beerhouse survived. John Wood was the licensee in 1890 and John Turner in the early 1900s. The property was now owned by the railway company and leased to Boddingtons Brewery.

The Windsor Bridge Inn was on the closure list in 1906, when the police

reported there were never more than three people in the place. There was a new licensee, Ernest Hadfield, who said that he had cleared out all the old customers and got a respectable class instead, and he was now selling three barrels of beer a week. The police agreed that he did 'clear a lot of rabble out' and the licence was renewed. The Windsor Bridge Inn survived for another two years and closed in 1908. The last licensee was George Palmer.

About halfway between the Windsor Bridge Inn and the Windsor Bridge Tavern at the beginning of Broad Street, there was a beerhouse called the **Staff of Life** on the corner of Vulcan Street. It was recorded in the 1861 directory, with James Titterington the licensee. William Andrews was there for about ten years from 1864 and George Waterhouse from the 1870s to the 1890s.

By then the Staff of Life was owned by Broadbent's Steam Brewery of Chorlton-on-Medlock. This firm was acquired by the Manchester Brewery Company in 1899, but the beerhouse didn't have much of a future. At the 1907 brewster sessions the police reported there weren't many customers. The rooms were 'most rambling in plan' and difficult to supervise, and the billiards and concert rooms were dilapidated. The licence was surrendered for permission to make alterations at another former Broadbents pub, the Tanners Arms on Oxford Street. The last tenant was Joseph Francis.

The **Prince of Wales Feathers** was on the other side of Windsor Bridge, next to Wallness Lane (now University Road). In 1863 this was a confectionery shop run by Frederick Bowling. He probably sold beer as well, because he had previously had a licence on Wallness Lane. The premises were certainly licensed two years later, when Elizabeth Bowling was in charge. She was listed as a confectioner and beerseller until the 1870s and then as a beerseller only until the 1880s, when her step-daughter, Clara Chatterton, took over.

Frederick Jackson had the licence by 1890 and the following year the beerhouse, two adjoining houses and others in Wallness Road were bought by Wilsons Brewery. Charles and Ann Kirton were their tenants in the early twentieth century. Some alterations were made in 1912, when Mrs Kirton obtained permission to enlarge the upstairs clubroom. It was the meeting place for the Buffs and the Oddfellows and 'it got crowded'.

Later licensees included Mary Willoughby in the 1920s-30s, John Chaloner in the 1940s and Herbert

A photograph taken at Windsor Bridge about 1905. The building on the left is Bradford's engineering works and next to it is the Staff of Life

Jackson in the 1950s. The Prince of Wales Feathers was included in the Wallness clearance area and a compulsory purchase order was issued in 1960. It closed in May 1965 and the last licensee was Jimmy Parkinson.

Albion Street

The **Railway Inn** on the corner of Tontine Street and Albion Street can be traced back to 1860, when the beerseller was Sarah Croft. She probably had a licence before that, but directories in the 1850s list her only as a shopkeeper. Earlier, from 1838 to 1845, Joseph Brown was listed as a beer retailer on Albion Street and this may have been the same place.

James and then Emma Taylor had the licence in the 1870s-90s and by 1900 the beerhouse was owned by Hardy's Crown Brewery. At the brewster sessions in August 1901 the premises were described as 'tumbledown and not safe', so the brewery was given permission to build a new Railway, taking in the cottage next door. Later licensees included Thomas Hebblethwaite about 1910, Walter Boon in the 1920s, John Vause in the 1930s-40s, Thomas Wordsworth in the 1950s and finally Harold and Margaret Batty in the 1960s-70s. For its last few years the Railway was a Bass pub and it closed in 1975.

In 1888, when the Freemasons Arms on Spaw Street was due to be pulled down, Boddingtons Brewery had the licence transferred to a shop they owned on the corner of Albion Street and Harrogate Street. The shop became

the **Red Cow** beerhouse and the shopkeeper, John Luty, its first licensee.

Ernest Luty took over from John about 1920 and he ran the Red Cow until the 1930s. Stanley and then Ethel Cliffe were in charge in the 1940s-50s and Charles and Florence Roberts in the 1960s. In the 1960s and 1970s many of the remaining beerhouses in the city became fully licensed. The Red Cow was one of the exceptions and when it closed for the building of Albion Way in August 1980, it was the last Salford beerhouse. Lilian Wood was the last landlady.

Tontine Street

Tontine Street went from the Corporation Inn on Cross Lane to the Railway Inn on Albion Street. Between the two there was another beerhouse, on the end of a row of houses called Pikes Buildings, which fronted Partington Street. Charles, Elizabeth and then Mary Holden were listed as beersellers there in the 1830s-40s. Other Holdens in the area were in business as dyers, which may account for the beerhouse being called the **Dyers Arms**.

Thomas Leater had the licence in the 1860s and Robert Ramsden in the early 1870s. John Farrell took over in 1873 and around that time the Dyers was given a new name, the **Bee Hive Inn**. Subsequent licensees included John and Ann Mellor, Robert Besson in 1880, Timothy Rotherham about 1890 and William Hitchen in 1905.

In February 1910 licensee James Eckersley was cautioned by the police for opening at 10.30am on a Sunday. Colliers had been catching trams from Pendlebury and arriving at Windsor Bridge on Sunday mornings to take advantage of the law which allowed drinks to be served to 'bona fide travellers' outside normal licensing hours. Other beerhouses in the neighbourhood were beginning to cater for the same trade and the police decided to put a stop to it. The colliers may have been travellers, but their motives were not really 'bona fide'.

Brewers J W Lees owned the Bee Hive by this time. They rebuilt some walls because they were dangerous and in August 1910 obtained permission to take over the site of a cottage in Partington Street so as to extend the kitchen and build some lavatories.

The last licensee was Harry Clarke, who took over in 1912. Five years later beer sales had declined because it was wartime and the police reported that Mr Clarke had an average of only seven customers, when there were over twenty in nearby houses. There were six other 'on' licences within a hundred yards. The Bee Hive closed the following year and J W Lees received £750 in compensation for the licence.

Wallness Lane

About fifty yards down Wallness Lane from Windsor Bridge there was a short row of houses fronting Hall Street called Albert Terrace. The shop on the corner became a beerhouse called the **Royal Oak** and Frederick Bowling was listed there in 1861. Two years later Mr Bowling had moved up the lane to the Prince of Wales Feathers and Thomas Hargreaves had taken over. Thomas Hanson was there by 1865 and after he died in 1871 the last licensee, James Collins, took over.

Within twelve months, Mr Collins seems to have lost his licence and for a few years afterwards he was listed as a shopkeeper. He tried to get another licence in 1875 after the Peel Tavern on Hulme Street closed, but the transfer was opposed by the trustees of Christ Church School, who were the owners of his shop.

From Windsor Bridge, Wallness Lane ran alongside the canal for about a hundred yards and then turned right towards Wallness Farm. From there, the lane followed the edge of Peel Park to some cottages at Wallness Bank, below Strawberry Hill. By 1845 a beerhouse called the **Peel Park Cottage Inn** had opened here. Walter Scott was the licensee in that year, John Cooper was there in the 1850s and Henry and Harriet Birkby in the 1860s.

Prince of Wales Feathers, Windsor Bridge, in the 1950s

A farm worker called James Shore had the licence by 1870 and in 1884 it was transferred to William Grimshaw. John Walker was in charge in 1900 and at the brewster sessions that year the Wallness was said to be in a bad state. The owners wanted to pull down the old property, which was made up of four cottages knocked into one, and replace it with 'a pretty building', suitable for visitors to Peel Park.

The rebuilding was eventually carried out, probably by Walkers Brewery, and the Peel Park Cottage Inn was renamed the **Wallness Hotel**. Edgar Briggs was the licensee in 1910 and Frederick Atherton a few years later. The beerhouse almost closed in 1919, when trade had dropped from six to just over two barrels of beer a week because of the First World War. Mr Atherton's licence was renewed and he continued to run the Wallness until about 1930. However, the building was almost a casualty of the Second World War, when it was damaged during an air raid which destroyed houses at Strawberry Hill.

Edith Redford was at the Wallness from the 1930s to the 1950s and Lilian Barrett in the 1960s-70s, when it was a Tetley pub. In 1983 Salford University Students' Union took a lease on the property and it reopened after refurbishment in the September. The pub is still going in 2003.

Strawberry Hill

The **Grove Inn** was on the end of Strawberry Hill Terrace, one of the rows of houses above Wallness Lane. The earliest recorded licensee was James Pearson, who was there from the 1870s to the 1890s. At the beginning of the twentieth century, the whole row was owned by brewers Watson, Woodhead and Wagstaffe and their tenant at the beerhouse was Sarah Ann Redford.

In later years the Grove was a Walker & Homfray house and the last licensee was Elizabeth Wilkinson. The licence was not renewed in 1936, when the building was described as structurally unsuitable.

The Wallness about 1930

The Old Pubs of Pendleton

Pendleton's earliest licensing records show that there were six alehouses in the whole of the district in 1629. Two hundred years later there were still fewer than ten, but just forty years after that, in 1869, the area had well over a hundred public houses and beerhouses. Someone born in a cottage on Ford Lane at the beginning of the nineteenth century would have witnessed the transformation of Pendleton from village to industrial town. He would have seen the building of some of the first terraces along Broad Street and bigger houses in their own grounds near Eccles Old Road. Railway lines were built, cotton mills and other industries developed and eventually rows and rows of houses covered the rest of the land from Brindleheath in the north to Eccles New Road in the south.

When he was 18, the Ford Lane resident had the choice of the two Broad Street pubs, the Horse Shoe and the Hare and Hounds, as his local. Further up the road was the Woolpack, and in the other direction there was the Windsor Castle at Windsor Bridge. By the time he was 65, a walk round the perimeter of St Thomas's churchyard would have taken in six licensed houses, and a stroll down to the Windsor Castle another ten or so, and that was without venturing into Hanky Park.

A map of 1786 shows the line of Broad Street and Bolton Road, with the road to Eccles branching off to the west near St Thomas's Chapel, and Ford Lane leading to the Broughton Ford on the north side. Also shown are Whit Lane, Sandy Lane, Tanners Lane, Height Lane (Claremont Road) and Weaste Lane. That year, there were seven alehouses in Pendleton's licensing records...

The one with the longest recorded history was the **Pack Horse**, Irlams o'th'Height. The Irlam family farmed land near the junction of the old roads to Lancaster and Bolton in the sixteenth century and they gave their name to this part of Pendleton. When Thomas Irlam made his will in 1600, he described himself as an innkeeper, so the Pack Horse was certainly in business by then. The last member of the family to have the licence was Martha Irlam, who left about 1769.

Thomas Cheetham ran the inn until 1798 and the next long serving licensee was James Brooks, who took over in 1817 and was still there in the 1840s. The Pack Horse of this period was recalled by a Mr Nicholls: 'The house stood in divisions with an entry of about eighteen inches between them.

The old part fronted towards Manchester and the other part in the Swinton Road. The old part was covered in the old heavy (thick slate). The inn sign was suspended on a beam with hinges and it swung to and fro as the wind blew it.'

The pub was bought by Holts Brewery in 1867, when Joseph Valentine was the licensee. Later photographs show a plain, two-storey brick frontage with a central doorway. There was a door in the gable end on the Claremont Road side and next to this was a gentlemen's urinal, with a lamp fitted to the wall above it to show the way on dark nights.

In the 1870s the pub was run by Joseph and Mary Hindley, and they were followed by Thomas Hodgson. Mr Hodgson also bred show horses and 1881 was a good year for him. His stallion Columbus won first prize at shows at Skipton, Halifax and St Helens.

The Pack Horse in 1949

Throughout its history part of the Pack Horse was in Pendlebury and part in Pendleton. After the First World War, closing time in Salford was 10.00pm, but since the Pack Horse was licensed by the County magistrates, it stayed open until 10.30 - the only Salford pub that could do so.

In May 1902 the tradition of walking the Pendlebury boundary by township officials was revived. The party left the Pack Horse through the smoke room window and on their return 'partook

of welcome refreshment' provided by landlord William Jackson. The bill for fourteen dinners, drinks and cigars, plus three dinners for boys, came to £2.14.5d.

The Pack Horse was rebuilt by Holts in 1934 in 'Tudor' style, with stonework round the doors and the upper part of the building rendered and decorated with strips of wood. The licensee at the time was Alfred Derbyshire. John McCluskey was there in the 1940s and Stanley Brookes in the 1950s. The pub

closed on 14th September 1975 and it was pulled down for the making of the Height roundabout. The last licensees were Joseph and Gladys Brown.

Also at the Height was the **Flower Pot**, built by James Johnson on land he leased from the Bridgewater Estates. His first licence was granted in 1781. Esther Johnson was in charge in 1787, followed by Thomas Johnson from 1788 to 1796. James Merrick came next, then about 1812 the licence seems to have lapsed.

Between 1817 and 1820 a **Joiners Arms** appears in the Pendleton records, kept by George Johnson and then Richard Dawson. This may have been another name for the Flower Pot, since the title deeds show that Mr Dawson went on to rebuild the Flower Pot and reopened it as the **Waggon and Horses** in 1823. He kept the pub for over twenty years and was followed by Edmund Clegg in the 1850s, David Clarkson in the 1860s and Thomas Alcock in the 1870s.

Holts Brewery acquired the Waggon and Horses in 1899 and the following year the company obtained permission to construct a new frontage, because the original projected too far out on to the footpath. The pub was run by Annie Wilks in the early 1900s, Samuel Goldsmith in the 1920s-30s and John Connor in the 1940s-50s. Later tenants included Thomas and Cicely Berry in the 1950s-60s.

The three-storey building on the corner of Bolton Road and Queen Street was demolished in 1981 and a new Waggon and Horses was built, set further back. The carving of a waggon and horses from above the door of the old building was preserved in the new pub.

The Waggon & Horses, Bolton Road, in the 1970s

The **Woolpack Inn**, at the junction of Eccles Old Road and Bolton Road, was kept by Benjamin Ingham in 1786 and licensing records show that members of the Ingham family were tenants here in the 1750s. In the 1820s Jacob Chatterton was in charge and one of his advertisements provides an impression of Pendleton in those days. The advertisement announced the opening of his bowling green and tea gardens in May 1829 and ladies and gentlemen of Manchester were invited to visit the 'pleasant retreat from the toils of business and family care'. The gardens were 'laid out in a very tasteful manner,' the air was 'extremely salubrious' and the view from the Woolpack was 'not to be exceeded in extent and beauty'. Mr Chatterton provided 'the very best wines and spirits, London bottled and draught porter and excellent home brewed ale'.

Joannah Chatterton had the licence in the 1830s, then in 1840 the inn was advertised to let, complete with brewhouse, bowling green, cottages and stables. It was advertised again two years later, 'pleasantly situated between turnpike roads leading to Bolton and Eccles'. A map of this time shows a triangle of land with the Woolpack and its outbuildings on the corner facing Broad Street. The bowling green was behind them and behind the green, on the Bolton Road (then called North Road) side, there were gardens. On the Eccles turnpike side was Halton Bank - two residences set back from the road in their own grounds. Across the Eccles turnpike (then called Sandy Lane) were more

big houses in their own grounds. The toll gates for the Eccles turnpike were next to the inn and there was another set of gates on North Road.

John, Samuel and Reuben Lord ran the Woolpack in the 1840s-50s, followed by Jeremiah and Nancy Kemp until about 1870. Samuel Derrington was there in the 1870s and George Bagnall in the 1890s.

A photograph taken at the beginning of the twentieth century shows the Woolpack was a combination of two buildings. The older, three-storey inn was on the Bolton Road corner, with a two-storey extension on the Eccles Old Road side. Signboards advertised 'Hardy's Celebrated Ales'. This changed in 1905, when brewers Walker & Homfray were the owners and they gave the place a facelift. Windows were altered, the whole of the ground floor frontage was tiled and the upper part was rendered and adorned with timber for a black-and-white effect. The licensee was local footballer Robert Valentine, who was then playing for Manchester United. Mr Valentine relaid the bowling green and built a new bowl house behind the pub to replace the original one on the far side of the green.

Photographs taken a few years later show the Woolpack with sky signs advertising Walker & Homfray wines, spirits and home brewed ales. The bowling green was still being used but there was nothing left of the gardens. A row of houses had replaced the Halton Bank residences and Halton Bank School covered the rest of the land.

John Wilson was the tenant in the 1920s-30s and William and Kathleen Roth were there in the 1940s-50s.

The Woolpack became a Wilsons pub and it closed on 28th September 1966. The last licensees were John and Emily Malone. The site is now part of the Bolton Road and Eccles Old Road junction. A new Woolpack opened in 1970, part of the Ellor Street development.

The **Horse Shoe Inn** on Broad Street was kept by William and Mary Fish from 1774 until 1780, then by Samuel Chantler from 1781 to 1820. The inn stood on a prominent site at the top of Tanners Lane (later Church Street) and across from Pendleton Church. A map published in 1831 shows it was a sizeable property, with a bowling green, stables and other outbuildings. Directories from the 1820s to the 1850s list it as the **Horse Shoe and Bowling Green Inn**.

John and then William Hobson were the tenants in the 1820s, followed by Thomas and Mary Barlow in the 1830s. One of the Horse Shoe's notable licensees was John Greenwood in the 1840s. Several years before, when Mr Greenwood was the Pendleton toll bar keeper, he started a horse-drawn omnibus service between Pendleton and Manchester. These first buses were used by businessmen who lived in the big houses of Eccles Old Road and the Height. Many years later a writer recalled seeing the small vehicles turn out from stables near the church between 8.00am and 9.00am and run up to the toll gates next to the Woolpack. About half a dozen gentlemen would be waiting and they paid sixpence each to be conveyed to town. Since the service operated from the Manchester side of the gates, there were no tolls to pay and the gentlemen didn't have the expense of bringing their own carriages through the gates. So as well as starting one of England's first bus services, Mr Greenwood was a pioneer of park'n'ride.

Mr Greenwood opened a coach office next to the Horse Shoe on the corner of Church Street and the 1848 map shows more buildings behind the inn - stables and coach sheds for his growing business. He was remembered as a very stout man who was usually to be seen in his office or seated on a form outside, smoking a long clay pipe. He wore yellow corduroy knee breeches and white shirts, had a loud voice and 'a fairly extensive vocabulary of expressive words.'

The next licensee of the Horse Shoe was Charles Richard Earle, who took over in 1850 and stayed until the 1870s. In his advertisements he styled himself 'The Earle of Pendleton': 'Pure home-

The Woolpack in the 1960s

brewed ales' from the Horse Shoe brewery were a shilling a gallon and Bass and Allsopp's ales, Dublin stout and London porter could be bought from his ale and porter stores in casks and in bottles.

When Mr Earle left the Horse Shoe, most of the streets of Hanky Park had been laid out. The bowling green was still there and Mr Greenwood's offices were being used by the Manchester Carriage Company. Threlfalls Brewery acquired the property and in 1896 they obtained permission to redevelop the site. A new Horse Shoe and two shops were built fronting Broad Street, between Church Street and Pine Street, and rows of houses in Pine Street covered the bowling green. The tenants during this period were Harry and Mary Strafford.

The new pub was a typical three-storey Threlfalls house of the period. In 1915 the licensee, Walter Willsdon, was advertising the pub's billiard room (two tables) and a dining room which provided four-course lunches for 1/6d. Later licensees were Robert Hargreaves in the 1920s, Thomas Parkin in the 1930s and Charles Carter in the 1940s-50s.

The Horse Shoe had been built to last, but in the 1960s, when Broad Street was carrying more traffic than Mr Greenwood could ever have imagined, it had to go. Compulsory purchase orders were issued in 1963, but the brewery wanted to keep the pub in some form or other - it was a 'large house doing a tremendous trade' and since they still owned the land at the back, there was room for an extension or replacement.

The Kings Arms, Whit Lane, about 1930

The Council had other plans, but the Horse Shoe stayed open for a few more years, run by James and Ethel Lennon. In September 1965 it was advertised as 'Salford's Palace of Variety', promising 'all-star variety' every night. The pub closed in 1969 and the site became part of the widened road on the Eccles Old Road side of the roundabout at Pendleton Church.

The fifth Pendleton alehouse recorded in 1786 was the **Grapes**, kept by John Yates. He was listed there in the two previous years and was followed by Thomas Cheetham and then John Boardman. In 1798 and 1804 Mr Boardman was listed at the **Strawberry Gardens**, which seems to have been the same place, and from 1805 until the final entry in the licensing records in 1812 it was listed as either the Grapes

or the **Sandy Lane Tavern**, run by William Lazenbury.

The 1786 map shows buildings at two places on Sandy Lane - on the turnpike, near where Langworthy Road crosses Eccles Old Road today, and on the lower part of the lane, where it joins Langworthy Road today. The Grapes may have been at one of these locations before Belmont, Prospect Hill, Ashfield and other residences for the local gentry were built between Eccles Old Road and Seedley Road. An 1815 plan of the fields in this area shows a 'Strawberry Field' next to Prospect Hill, then the home of cotton merchant John Walker.

The sites of the other two 1786 Pendleton alehouses are unknown. One was the **Golden Lion**, sometimes listed as the **Red Lion**, and kept by Sarah Holden from 1778 to 1792. James Holden was the last licensee in 1795. In 1776-77 Sarah was recorded at the **Plume of Feathers**, which could have been the same place. This can be traced back to 1768, when it was kept by John Holden, and it was also known as the **Crown** or **Irish Crown**.

The **Sun**, or **Rising Sun**, is listed between 1776 and 1786, with licensees Joseph Smithson, James Fletcher and Peter Travis.

Two Pendleton alehouses are named in the records before 1786. These are the **Robin Hood**, also known as the **Green Man**, kept by Thomas Worsley from 1770 to 1777, and the **Eagle and Child**, kept by William Hamer from 1771 to 1773. Their locations are not known.

A few Pendleton alehouses opened between 1786 and 1830 and one, the **Fox and Goose**, seems to have had a very brief existence. It appears in the records for just one year, 1805, when the licensee was Charles Heaton.

The Horse Shoe, Broad Street, in the 1920s

The **Hare and Hounds** on Broad Street was kept by Thomas and Elizabeth Mellor from 1788 until 1795. They were followed by Thomas, Mary and then Joseph Coupe, who was there until the 1840s. The pub was one of the first houses to be built on the north side of the street and it stood at an angle to the road, nearly opposite Hankinson Street.

Joseph and Mary Statham ran the Hare and Hounds for over twenty years from 1850 and later licensees were Charles Penwarden in the 1870s-80s and Charles B Mills in the 1890s. By then the pub was owned by J G Sykes, a Liverpool liquor merchant, and it subsequently passed to Higsons Brewery of Liverpool. John Leigh was the tenant in the 1930s-40s, then Percy Gee in the 1950s.

The last licensees were Stanley and Annie Ogden, who had been there six years when the pub closed in 1959. Interviewed in August 1959, Mr Ogden said the pub had five rooms along Broad Street, with low, arched-roof cellars beneath them. The back of the building had a wide entrance and bow windows and he wondered if many years ago this had been the front of the house.

Between 1806 and 1815 a **Kings Head**, kept by William Ledsome, is listed in Pendleton's records. There is no indication of the site, but it may have been the same as the **Kings Arms**, which is first listed in 1824 with James Lang as the licensee. George Heyward was there in the 1830s, John Thorpe in the 1840s and Charles and Charlotte Stringfellow from the 1850s to the 1880s.

The Rose & Crown, Broad Street, in 1970

The Kings Arms was on Whit Lane, between Union Street and Back Union Street and at the 1899 licensing sessions it was described as being over sixty years old and in a bad state of repair. John Lavery was the tenant at the time, so when the Worsley Brewery Company built a new pub on the same site he saw a dramatic improvement in his living conditions.

Later licensees included William Haworth in the 1920s, Thomas Baines in the 1930s-40s, Douglas Taylor in the 1950s and Alfred and Bessie Willetts in the 1960s. The Kings Arms became a

Walkers, then a Tetley pub and survived the Charlestown redevelopment of the 1960s-70s. It closed in the early 1990s, when it had been renamed **Jolsons Bar**. The building later became the Kings Court care home.

From 1807 to 1809 there was a licensed house on Frederick Street called the **Bowling Green Inn**, kept by Nathaniel Nunnerley. The street is shown on the 1815 map of Pendleton, connecting Broad Street with Bedlam Lane (later Strawberry Road), but there is no clue as to the exact location of the alehouse, or its bowling green.

By 1830 a variety of houses and shops lined the south side of Broad Street. The lower part, from Cross Lane to Pimlot Street, was called New Richmond and the first pub to open on this section was the **Rose and Crown** on the corner of Booth Street. The first licensee was John Beeston, who moved here from the Windsor Castle about 1823. William Hilton was in charge in the 1830s-40s, Henry Holder in the 1850s-60s and John Mitchell in the 1870s.

In 1889 the building was looking dilapidated and at the licensing sessions that year, the new owners, brewers Hardy & Sons, were given permission to pull it down and build a new pub. The work was completed in 1891 and this date was set in the brickwork on the corner of the three-storey building. Hardys also rebuilt the shop next door, which was later used as the offices of the Salford City Reporter.

Licensees in the twentieth century included William Burke in the early

The Maypole, Ford Lane, in 1961

1900s, George Morris in the 1920s, Frank Hutchinson in the 1930s, William Dudley in the 1940s, Gerald Dobbins in the 1950s and James and Florence Millington in the 1960s. The Rose and Crown became a Tetley pub and it closed in 1971 for the redevelopment of Broad Street. The last tenants were Michael and Pauline Diggins.

The last of the pre-1830 Pendleton pubs to open was the **Crown and Maypole Inn** on Ford Lane. Robert Bellringer obtained the first licence in 1825 and by the time he left in the 1850s, the name had been shortened to **Maypole Inn**. The next licensees were John and Alfred Openshaw, then James Addison about 1870.

In 1875 a new and bigger Maypole Hotel was built next to the two-storey inn and to celebrate the opening of the billiard room in January 1876, Mr Addison advertised a match between the world professional champion, John Roberts, and his challenger for the title, W Cook.

The original inn was converted into dwelling houses and remained standing for several more years, then it was pulled down when the Lancashire & Yorkshire Railway built their line to Hindley and Wigan through Pendleton New Station (opened 1887). This company may have been responsible for building the new Maypole. They were certainly the owners in the 1880s and their line under Ford Lane also went under the pub.

Ownership passed to the London, Midland & Scottish Railway and then the British Transport Commission in the twentieth century. The hotel was leased by local companies such as the Manchester Brewery in the early 1900s and Wilsons Brewery until 1962. In the 1970s it became a Bass house. Licensees from 1900 included John Bannister until the 1920s, Ferguson Southward in the 1930s and May Tonge from 1939.

Mrs Tonge was the landlady during the pub's heyday in the 1950s. The upstairs concert room was often packed and the local singers included Kenny Worthington and Dee Clarke, with Ray Gerrard on the Hammond organ. Tenants in the 1960s-70s included Douglas and Emily Holt and Donald and Elizabeth Stewart.

Trade at the Maypole declined when the old Pendleton streets were demolished and people moved out of the area. It kept going through the 1980s, then closed for a time in the early 1990s. It was reopened by the Centric company in 1993, then closed the following year. The building is still standing in 2003.

Broad Street

The highway between Cross Lane and Eccles Old Road became known as Broad Street in the 1850s. Before then, it had three names: New Richmond from Cross Lane to Pimlot Street, Paddington from Pimlot Street to Chapel Street and Broad Street from there to Eccles Old Road. In 1830 there were three pubs - the previously mentioned Horse Shoe, Hare and Hounds and Rose and Crown - and these were gradually joined by a variety of beerhouses. Among the first to open were the Thatched House, the Wheatsheaf and the Horse and Jockey.

The **Thatched House** was in a row of shops between Bank Street and Church Street, facing the Church Inn on Ford Lane. Catherine Bohannah was the licensee in 1834, James Balmer a few years later, William Howarth from the 1840s to the 1870s and Richard Cooper in the 1880s.

Tenants in the early twentieth century included Robert Dickson and Edward Creed. When Thomas Kemp took over in 1911, he advertised that the Thatched House had a special room for ladies and he sold Walker &

Thatched House, Broad Street, in 1961

Homfray's ales. The brewery made some improvements and decorated the narrow frontage of the building with coloured tiles. Thomas Kemp ran the beerhouse for over twenty years and he was followed by George Lewis, who was there from the 1930s to the 1950s.

The Thatched House was later owned by Wilsons and the last licensee was Maurice Joseph Roberts, who took over about 1966. In an interview with the Salford City Reporter just before the pub closed early in 1971, Mr Roberts said that many of his old customers were suspicious about the new pubs the brewers were building and the beer they sold. New pubs were equipped to sell keg or tank beer, but Mr Roberts' customers liked to see the 'wickets' on the bar.

The **Wheatsheaf**, part of a row of shops between Chapel Street and John Street, is named on the 1848 map as the **Independent Oddfellows Arms**. Thomas Ellis was the licensee in the 1830s, George Renshaw from about 1840 to the 1870s, George Henshall in the 1880s and Henry Davies in the 1890s.

Wheatsheaf, Broad Street, in 1961

Brewers Watson & Woodhead acquired a lease on the property in 1896 and twenty years later the owners were the Manchester Brewery Company, by then a subsidiary of Walker & Homfray. The brewery altered the ground floor frontage, adding curved windows and coloured tiles. The licensee from 1904 was William Oram, who had been a player with Broughton Rangers for ten years. Mrs Jane Oram took over when he died in 1940 and she continued to run the Wheatsheaf until the 1950s.

The Wheatsheaf became a Wilsons pub and it closed on Monday 21st December 1970. The last licensee was John Shortman and the following day he opened the new Woolpack on the Ellor Street development.

The **Horse and Jockey** was on the end of a row of shops opposite St Thomas's churchyard and it was run by Robert and Alice Hankinson from the 1830s to the 1860s. Other members of this family had businesses in Pendleton and Hankinson Street was named after Edward ('Old Neddy') Hankinson, who lived at New Richmond in the 1820s.

Alexander, Sarah and then Thomas Williams were licensees at the Horse and Jockey from the 1860s to the 1880s. They had a brewhouse and in 1873 Thomas was advertising home-brewed ales in 18, 9 and 6 gallon casks for sale

to private families. A few years later Fulford & Co of the Empress Brewery were leasing the beerhouse from the Hankinson family. In 1885 they took some walls down to open up the interior. The snug and bar area on the left of the lobby were combined to make a new parlour, while the tap room and parlour on the right became a vault and bar. Later tenants included Edward Parry in the 1890s and Edwin Gendall in the early 1900s. The beerhouse was completely rebuilt about 1903.

Joseph Withington was the licensee in the 1920s, when the Horse and Jockey and other Empress houses were acquired by Walkers of Warrington. James Collier was there in the 1930s-40s and Sylvester Billington in the 1950s. It was a Tetley pub when it closed in 1971 and the last licensee was Cyril Plant.

The **Retford Arms** is first listed in the 1836 directory. This beerhouse was next-door-but one to the Wheatsheaf and was run by David Downie until about 1840. Henry and then Mary Pye were licensees from the 1840s to the 1870s and Jane Hall in the 1880s. In the early 1900s it was owned by brewers Walker & Homfray and their tenant in 1908 was a former policeman called George Hurst. At that year's brewster sessions Mr Hurst complained that he was unable to make a living at the house. The brewery had told him they

were going to make alterations, but had done nothing. The Retford closed in 1910 and the licensee for the last year was Walter Topper.

The **Vine Inn** also appears in the 1836 directory. This was on the New Richmond section of Broad Street, about fifty yards along from the corner of Cross Lane. Hannah Wolstencroft had the licence for about twelve years and subsequent tenants included Richard and Ann Barlow in the 1850s, James and Ellen Kay in the 1860s-70s, Naomi Rothwell in the 1880s and William Clough in the early 1900s.

By that time the Vine was owned by the Empress Brewery and in 1903 they rebuilt the beerhouse. The brewery gave the new building a brick and tile frontage and coloured, leaded windows. A third-storey gable rose above the roof line of the original property in the New Richmond row.

A former Broughton Rangers player, John Hardisty, became the licensee in 1916. Ann Hardisty took over from him and she ran the Vine from the 1920s to the 1940s. By then Walkers of Warrington were the owners and their tenants in the 1950s included Frederick Hill and Violet Hart. For its last eight years the Vine was run by Ged and Ellen Yates, who had moved from the Old House at Home on Pimlot Street when that pub closed. The Vine closed in January 1971.

Two years after the Vine made its first appearance in the records, William Mann was listed as a beer retailer at New Richmond. He was also a brewer and his beerhouse, which was on the corner of Pimlot Street and opposite Frederick Road, was called the **Richmond Brewery Inn**. He ran the business for about thirty years and died in 1867. Mrs Mann took over for a short time, then in October 1867 the goodwill, brewing equipment and fixtures were advertised for sale. The brewery was capable of producing seven barrels per brew and there were about fifty barrels of different sizes. The fixtures included fast seating, tables and gas fittings.

James Knight was the licensee for a few years in the 1870s and Martha Cordwell in 1880s. Brewing probably ceased when Mrs Mann left and the beerhouse was given a new name, the **Greyhound Inn**. Edward Casewell took over about 1890 and he was followed some thirty years later by Alfred Casewell. The beerhouse was acquired by Hardy's Crown Brewery and in the 1930s it was rebuilt, so if anything remained of Mr Mann's brewhouse, it probably disappeared at this time. The new Greyhound had a wider frontage to the street and a cladding of cream coloured tiles on the ground floor.

Horse & Jockey, Broad Street, in the 1920s

Later licensees included Horace Pass and Tom Wall in the 1940s, and Thomas Oates and William Wilde in the 1950s. Janet Hinman was listed there from the 1960s until the Greyhound closed in January 1971.

The only beerhouse on the north side of Broad Street, the **Windsor Bridge Tavern**, appeared about the same time as the Richmond Brewery Inn. The 1838 directory lists John Paul Hitchen as a beer retailer and he was also in charge of the public weighing machine which was set into the road outside. The beerhouse was also known as the **Weighing Machine Tavern** and, after the Windsor Bridge Ironworks (later the Crescent Ironworks) was built, the **Windsor Bridge Ironworks Tavern**.

The street next to the beerhouse was called Quay Street and before the Bolton to Manchester railway was built, there was an arm of the canal here. Richard Hitchen was a coal merchant based at the wharf and by 1840 he had taken over from John Paul as the beer retailer. The 1845 directory lists Richard as a coal owner, corn and hay dealer, beer retailer, furniture broker and weighing machine keeper. A busy man.

John Hitchen took over about 1857, followed by John and Elizabeth Ackers. Alfred Stopford of the Imperial Brewery, West Gorton, bought the beerhouse in 1873 and later licensees included Levi Whittaker in the 1880s-90s and George Nutter in the early 1900s.

In 1906 the brewery agreed to give up

The Windsor Bridge in 1951

the licence of the Royal Oak, Oldfield Road, in return for permission to extend the Windsor Bridge into a former saddler's shop next door. The ground floor of the building was decorated with coloured tiles incorporating advertisements for Stopford's ales, wines and Imperial Stout. When James Marshall took over in 1916, he advertised Stopford's mild and bitter, Bass, Worthington and Guinness, and he had a 'handsome club room to let for funeral and other parties'. The public weighing machine was still in use, although there was

now a bigger one outside the Windsor Castle public house on the other side of the road.

The Stopford pubs and beerhouses were taken over by local brewers Walker & Homfray in 1927. Their tenants at the Windsor Bridge included Joseph Parkinson in the 1930s and Edna Parnell in the 1940s-50s, when it became a Wilsons house. The property then included a house next door on Quay Street and an old slaughterhouse and other buildings at the back.

Other licensees in the 1950s included Norman Helsby and John Doughty and during that period Wilsons replaced the tilework and made other alterations. The building was scheduled for demolition in the late 1970s and it eventually closed on 8th September 1980. The last tenants were Frederick and Josephine Sproston.

About twelve years after the Retford Arms first appeared in the directories, a shoemaker's shop next door was converted into a greengrocer's with a beer licence. John Knott Heyes was listed there in 1848, John Hargreaves in the 1850s and Edward Murphy in the 1860s. By the time Mary Kelly was in charge in the 1870s, the grocery side of the business seems to have been given up and the beerhouse was called the **Prince of Wales**.

Thomas McMorrow was the tenant in the 1880s, Catherine Guy about 1890 and Alexander Gillies in the early 1900s. By then the Prince of Wales was owned by Walker & Homfray. It was on the list of beerhouses recommended for closure in 1915, when the police reported that other houses nearby were doing better. Also, the tenant's

The Greyhound, Broad Street, in 1970

living area left a lot to be desired - the bedrooms were reached by a spiral staircase. Darts and other games were played (which could lead to gambling) and there were free and easy concerts on Saturday nights. The brewery wanted to keep the licence and pointed out that their tenant, Thomas Barlow, was selling between three and four barrels of beer a week. They offered to carry out some improvements and the licence was renewed.

There was a new tenant in 1916, when Harry Herbert arrived from the Lower Turks Head on Shudehill, Manchester, and again in 1917, when James Matthews took over. He was also the last licensee, as the Prince of Wales closed in 1919. The building was being used as a chip shop in the 1930s.

The **Cross Keys**, on the corner of Cross Street and opposite Leaf Square (later the site of the Technical College), was opened by Thomas Coulthwaite in 1856. Mr Coulthwaite was the owner as well as the first licensee and he ran the beerhouse for about twenty years. Henry Moss was there in the 1870s-80s and Albert Rogerson took over about 1890.

The beerhouse was acquired by brewers Walker & Homfray and at the beginning of the twentieth century they had plans to rebuild. The plans were withdrawn in 1905, when the company obtained permission to rebuild the Original on Lower Broughton Road instead.

The brewery made some alterations at the Cross Keys, taking down some old buildings on the Cross Street side and

Cross Keys, Broad Street, in 1961

Bay Horse, Broad Street, in 1970

providing a better yard and up-to-date plumbing. Coloured tiles decorated the narrow Broad Street frontage, where there was just enough room for the corner door and the vault window.

Eliza Rogerson took over from Albert and she ran the Cross Keys until about 1920. Later tenants included Clarence Gibson and Margaret McDougall in the 1930s, Catherine Brennan in the 1940s, Bernard Gregory in the 1950s and Raymond Kilby in the 1960s. By then it was a Wilsons pub and the last licensees were Harry and Ada Beamer. It closed in 1971.

In the 1860s there was a confectioner's shop on the corner of Cross Street opposite the Cross Keys, and next door to this was another beerhouse, the **Bay Horse**. The earliest recorded licensee was John Longworth in 1863 and John Proe was there a few years later, when he advertised his 'good ale and porter' in the Salford Reporter. Subsequent tenants included John Harrop in the 1870s and John McIntyre and George Bateson in the 1880s.

Around this time there was a fried fish shop next door, which the authorities described as 'disagreeable to the neighbourhood'. The problem was solved in 1886, when the owners of the Bay Horse were given permission to extend into the shop. At some stage the beerhouse was also extended forwards, when a single-storey vault was built on what had been the front garden. The two properties were originally part of a row of three-storey houses on the New Richmond section of Broad Street.

Brewers Groves and Whitnall took a 21-year lease on the Bay Horse in 1898 and later became the owners. Their tenants in the twentieth century included John Birchwood, Herbert Riley and, from the 1920s to the 1940s, Robert McKinna. The pub's nickname, 'the Monkey', was said to have originated because Bob McKinna kept a monkey as a pet. The brewery rebuilt the Bay Horse in the 1920s, constructing a new three-storey frontage on the site of the old vault extension.

The Bay Horse became a Greenall Whitley pub and the licensee from the 1950s until it closed on 11th January 1971 was Catherine Collier.

Before the Town Hall was built at the top of Broughton Road in the 1860s, the Pendleton Town Offices were on Broad Street, approximately midway between Hankinson Street and Croft Street. When these came empty, James Higham moved from the Borough Tavern on Borough Street and turned the building into a beerhouse called the **New Town Hall Hotel**. It opened in December 1867 and was run by James and then Miss Frances Higham for about five years. The name was shortened to the **Town Hall Hotel** and subsequent licensees included Isaac Bateman in the 1880s and James Farrand in the 1890s.

Brewers Cardwell & Co of Hulme became the owners, then Wilsons

Town Hall, Broad Street, in 1965

Brewery took over in 1899. The following year the company obtained permission to rebuild. The old house was set back from the street and it was described as being in a bad state. The brewery planned to replace it with a three-storey building with a long lobby and to provide a private sitting room for the tenant on the ground floor, where the bar parlour used to be.

Emma Marsden was the tenant at the time of the rebuilding and later licensees included Edmund Lord in the 1920s, then Vincent and Mary Pope in the 1930s and James Hampson in the 1950s. George Penkett took over in the 1960s and he was still there when the Town Hall closed on 10th January 1971.

About the same time as James Higham opened the Town Hall Hotel, another beerhouse opened in a row of shops opposite Pendleton Church. This was the **Hope Cottage Inn**, kept by William and then Jane Ramsbottom for about ten years from 1868. Jonathan Denwood was there in the 1880s and Ann Prestwich in the 1890s. By this time the beerhouse had undergone a change of name to the **Tower Inn**.

It was bought by brewers Walker & Homfray and the licensees from the early 1900s to the 1930s were Alfred and then Mary Barrett. Ann Palin and Vera Dean were there in the 1940s, Elsie Snape in the 1950s and Mark Poole in the 1960s. The Tower closed in 1971 and the last recorded tenants were William and Marian Barlow.

In June 1850 the **British Fleet** was advertised to let. It was on Broad Street, but there is no indication of the exact site and it may have been another name for one of the beerhouses already mentioned.

Hanky Park

One of the earliest maps showing the area which became known as Hanky Park, south of Broad Street and west of Cross Lane, is a field plan of Pendleton, drawn about 1815. The plan shows the lanes which became Seedley Road, Highfield Road and Tanners Lane, and the line of Spring Vale Road and Black Ditch. There were farm buildings and some bigger houses, including Highfield House (later the site of Langworthy Park), Hayfield House (later the site of Hayfield Terrace) and Clay Hall, near what became Lower Seedley Road. There was a little industrial development - Messrs Taylor & Weston's cotton mill is shown (later Pendleton Mills), and between the mill and Broad Street are cottages in what became Croft Street and Gold Street.

By the time the 1831 map was drawn, parts of Hankinson Street, John Street and others off Broad Street had been completed and the line of High Street is shown, but the land between was still open. Twenty years later the building up of Ellor Street was well under way and by the 1890s the last of the open spaces had gone and the whole area was covered with houses and industry.

As rural Pendleton made way for the new streets, older buildings were pulled down and among them was one which was used as a beerhouse. Thomas Gardiner (or Gardner) was listed as a beerseller at **Seedley Gardens** from 1838, then in 1850 he was described as a land and building agent, with a beerhouse at **Clay Hall Gardens**. They seem to have been the same place. Clay Hall, Clay Hall Cottages, Clay Hall Gardens and Seedley Gardens were on the west side of Highfield Lane (later Road).

A few years later James Phelps was the proprietor of the Clay Hall Gardens and in 1859 he applied for a spirits licence, without success. The attractions of his 'pleasure grounds' were advertised in August 1860: they were open daily for the season and a 'first class Quadrille and Brass Band' played every Monday and Saturday. Admission was 4d, with 2d returned in refreshments.

John Jones had taken over by 1863 and the beerhouse is last mentioned in a report of the 1872 brewster sessions, when the renewal of his licence was refused. Alpha Street, Spring Gardens and other streets on the south side of Lower Seedley Road later covered the site of the gardens.

Hankinson Street

The first beerhouse on Hankinson Street was the **Grey Horse Inn**, which probably opened soon after the passing of the 1830 Beerhouse Act. Hankinson Street at that time extended only as far as Primrose Hill and the building was near the top of the street on the west side, on the corner of what later became Newton Street. The earliest recorded licensee was John Dunkerley, who was listed there from 1834 until 1845.

By 1848 Edward Roberts was in charge and he ran the Grey Horse until his death in 1867. In the August the beerhouse fittings - a filling bench, shelving, fast seating and drinking tables - were advertised for sale. There was a brewhouse, and the brewing equipment included a new six-barrel copper pan, a cooler and working rounds. Other items included sixty 36- and 18-gallon barrels, a quantity of old ale, five pockets of Kent and Herefordshire hops and some timber and old iron.

Subsequent tenants at the Grey Horse included George Hulland in the 1870s, William Burns in the 1880s-90s and Mark Crane in the early 1900s. At the brewster sessions in February 1910 the police reported that the beerhouse was no longer needed and the licence was referred for compensation. Brewers Walker & Homfray were then the owners and the last tenant was Thomas Greenhalgh.

The **Lamb Inn** opened on the corner of Hankinson Street and Primrose Hill in the 1860s. Hannah Graham was listed as the licensee in 1869, Isaac Wiltshire in the 1870s and Anna Reddin in the 1880s-90s. In 1895 brewers Groves & Whitnall bought the Lamb, two adjoining shops, two cottages at the back in Turner Street and a slaughterhouse.

Tenants from the early 1900s included William Siddall, Edwin and Ann

The Tower, Broad Street, in 1951

Feeney and James Annette from the 1920s to the 1940s. Mary Street was in charge in the early 1950s and the last licensee was Joseph Hall, who took over about 1956. In 1959, when compulsory purchase orders were being issued in preparation for the redevelopment of Hanky Park, the Lamb was described as well maintained, but it had to go. It closed in January 1962.

The **Royal Oak** ('Brass Handles') on the corner of Rossall Street opened about 1860 and the licensee in the early 1860s was William Bennett. James Heywood was there a few years later, then John Heywood in the 1870s. The Heywoods seem to have been the owners and during this period the beerhouse comprised shop property on the corner and the house next door. The building was given a new frontage in 1875. The 1881 census lists another James Heywood, a coach builder, as the licensee, while his sister Emma looked after the beerhouse.

A few years later James Fletcher was running the Royal Oak and it now belonged to Threlfalls Brewery. The company renovated the building and provided new doors and windows with coloured, leaded glass. Later alterations included the fitting of brass handles on the corner door and these gave the beerhouse its nickname.

Tenants from the early 1900s included John Swarbrick and Thomas Hughes, who was there for about thirty years until the time of the Second World War. Licensees in the 1940s-50s included Andrew Lawler, Lewis Owen and Charles Johnson. Like the Lamb,

The Welcome, Ellor Street, sketched in 1963

the Royal Oak was included in the Ellor Street No.1 compulsory purchase area and it closed in January 1962. The last licensee was William Sloane.

Primrose Hill

In the early stages of development in the Hankinson Street area, a block of back-to-back dwellings and a terraced row were built on the north side of Primrose Hill. More houses and shops were built on the other side of the street and one of these was occupied by a block printer called John Thorpe. By 1869 he had embarked upon a second career as a beer retailer.

The beerhouse was first recorded as the **Museum Tavern** and then as the **Pheasant Inn**. Mary Thorpe took over in the 1870s and Peter Warburton was there in the 1880s. The property was acquired by brewers Walker & Homfray and their tenant in the 1890s and early 1900s was Emma Wain. It was on the list of beerhouses recommended for closure at the 1906 brewster sessions, when the police said that sometimes there were six or seven customers and sometimes none at all. Mrs Wain confirmed that trade was down to about a barrel of beer a week and said that the business had supported her and her daughters until the advent of the electric trams. Her old customers were travelling further afield for their entertainment.

The licence was renewed and the Pheasant survived for a few more years. By 1914 beer sales had increased to about six barrels a week, but at the February brewster sessions the police reported that the popularity of the beerhouse was partly due to the fact that XXX beer, commonly called 'sixpenny', was being sold at twopence a pint. The magistrates were against the practice of selling beer cheaply and decided to refer the licence for compensation. The Pheasant closed the following year and the last licensee was Daniel Sullivan.

Ellor Street

The 1845 directory lists two beer retailers on Ellor Street, George Butterworth and John Howard. There are no clues to the exact sites of their shops, but they were probably at the Cross Lane end and one might have been the Cross Lane Tavern, later the Fusiliers on Cross Lane. Twenty-five years later the number of beerhouses

The Royal Oak, Hankinson Street, about 1960

had increased to about a dozen and there were also two fully-licensed houses. During this period there were 'two' Ellor Streets - Ellor Street (Salford) from Cross Lane to Pimlot Street/Grafton Street and Ellor Street (Pendleton) from there to Fitzwarren Street. The two sections became one in the 1870s, when the houses and shops on the Pendleton section were renumbered.

Starting at the Cross Lane end, the next beerhouse after the Horse and Jockey (see page 6) was the **Welcome Inn**, opened in the 1860s. Among the earliest recorded licensees were Thomas Makin in 1871 and John Braddock, who announced his arrival in 1874 with an advertisement for the 'finest sparkling ales' and London and Dublin stouts. William Thomas was there in the late 1870s and 1880s and Millicent Schofield about 1890.

Licensees in the early twentieth century included Robert Smith, Alfred Blundell and Fanny Wroe in the 1920s-30s. By this time the Welcome was owned by brewers Groves & Whitnall. In post-war years the tenants included William and Lily Brown, James Taylor and Emma Marsden.

When the redevelopment of Ellor Street was being planned in the late 1950s, the City Engineer reported that the Welcome might be left indefinitely. The brewery said it was a good house, but its position was 'a bit cramped' and there was no objection when the compulsory purchase order was served in May 1960.

The last licensee was Sid Harrison and he had a flair for publicity. In January 1961, when the old streets were being pulled down and trade was suffering, he announced that he was taking a penny off the price of a pint. It was a success, and he told a reporter for the Manchester Guardian that within three hours of opening he had to set off in his van to collect three more barrels of mild. For the first time in a month, he said the light was on in his lounge bar on a Monday night. He gained more publicity in February 1962, when he began offering cheaper beer for pensioners at dinnertimes. Bitter was 1/1d (usually 1/3d) and mild 1/- (usually 1/2d).

During this period, many people who had moved from the Ellor Street area to new homes in Little Hulton, Kersal and Silk Street still went back to the old pubs for a Saturday singsong or a Sunday darts match. Then came Black Sunday, 28th April 1963, when ten Hanky Park pubs were due to close. People came from all over to pay their last respects and Ged Yates, landlord of the Old House at Home on Pimlot Street, remembered seeing Sid Harrison being paraded up and down Ellor Street in a coffin.

There was a petition to save the Welcome, but it stayed open for only a few more weeks after Black Sunday.

The **British Queen** was on the north side of Ellor Street, on the corner of Bootle Street. The first licensee was possibly John Frankland, who was listed there from 1855 until 1877. George Walker took over for several years from the 1880s.

The beerhouse was purchased by Chesters Brewery in 1899 and their tenants included William Mundy around 1905, James Foulkes for about twenty years to 1930 and Frank Watson from the 1930s to the 1950s. A compulsory purchase order was served in January 1960, when the property was included in the Ellor Street No.4 clearance area.

The last licensee was Roy Croft, who closed the British Queen after the dinnertime session on Black Sunday. 'The pumps were empty and the bottle shelves were bare,' noted the Salford City Reporter.

About fifty yards along from the British Queen, on the opposite side of Ellor Street, stood the **Crown Inn**. In 1863 William Fothergill was listed as a shopkeeper here, then a few years later he had a licence to sell beer. Subsequent tenants included James Duckworth in the 1870s, Robert Donaghy about 1880 and John Appleton in the 1880s-90s.

Issott's Brewery of Ardwick bought the beerhouse in 1899 and four years later ownership was transferred to Wilsons Brewery. They gave up the licence in 1907 in exchange for permission to make alterations at another of their beerhouses, the Wheatsheaf on Regent Road. The last licensee was Elizabeth Appleton, who had taken over from her husband about 1900.

The **Nelson Inn** opened on the corner of Smethurst Street in the 1860s and the earliest recorded licensee was William Ward, who was listed there from 1869 to the 1880s. Elizabeth Ward took over for a few years, then in the 1890s licensees included Thomas Peover, Joseph Cunningham and James Whitworth.

At that time the Nelson was a small, corner beerhouse, with just two rooms downstairs and two up. It was enlarged in 1899, when two adjoining cottages were taken over. The tenant gained a bigger room in which to sell beer and a kitchen and parlour for himself and his family. The building was given a new ground floor frontage, which now extended from Smethurst Street to Bernard Street.

Licensees in the early 1900s included Peter Garrity and Richard Challinor. By 1911 the Nelson was a Peter Walker house and in that year John Williams became the tenant. His son later recalled the beerhouse in the years

'Like islands in a sea of rubble' - the British Queen in April 1963

before the First World War, when they opened from 6.00am to 11.00pm. He remembered one Saturday when his father took £6.2s.6d. 'It was the best day we had ever had.'

Walkers mild was popular because it was $1^{1}/2$d a pint, when Chesters, Walker & Homfray and other milds were 2d a pint. However, when the war came, the government set the price of mild at $2^{1}/2$d and the Nelson lost a lot of customers, because Walkers had gone up by a penny.

Walkers' lease on the beerhouse ran out about 1920 and Creese's Brewery of Hyde took over. Mr Williams was asked to stay on as a manager, but he declined. His son recalled that he was sorry afterwards, because Tetleys bought the Nelson and turned it into 'one of the best pubs on Ellor Street.' Thomas and then Norman Linney were the licensees from the 1920s to the 1950s.

The property was included in the Ellor Street No.4 clearance area. When the compulsory purchase order was served in 1960, the Nelson was described as being in good condition, having been extensively altered in 1939. It closed on Black Sunday, 28th April 1963, and the last licensees were Frank and Gladys Allanson.

The **Wellington Inn** was across from the Nelson, on the corner of Goodwin Street. The first licensee was John Sawley Whittaker, listed as a poultry and game dealer on Broad Street in 1852 and then as a beerseller at the Wellington on Ellor Street in 1855. He managed to get a full licence and was listed as a publican and a brewer until George Whittaker took over about 1880.

The Nelson, Ellor Street, in 1912

The pub was rebuilt in 1880, probably by Threlfalls Brewery, who were certainly the owners a few years later. Thomas Bulman was their tenant in the early 1900s, then Frank Smith from the time of the First World War until about 1930. The pub had its windows broken during the Lusitania riots in 1915, after Mr Smith was heard to sympathise with a German pork butcher whose shop had been attacked.

Later licensees included Arthur Swift in the 1930s, John Feetham in the 1940s and Thomas Harrison in the 1950s. When the compulsory purchase order was served in May 1960, a survey on behalf of the brewery noted that the building was 'first class in every way,'

but it had to go. The Wellington closed at 9.30pm on Black Sunday, 28th April 1963, and the last licensees, Arthur and Joan Lennon, moved to a pub in Chorlton.

About fifty yards along from the Wellington, the **Etwall House** on the corner of Grafton Street was at the beginning of Ellor Street, Pendleton. It opened in the 1860s, or possibly earlier, and John Holden was listed there from 1865. Mary and Alice Kershaw were licensees in the 1870s, Joseph Ogden in the 1880s and Frederick Rudolph about 1890.

In the twentieth century the beerhouse was owned by Wilsons Brewery and their tenants included John Elwell about 1910, Elizabeth Fleming in the 1920s, Albert and Eva Randall in the 1930s-40s and Mrs Amorel Greatorex in the 1940s-50s.

The Etwall House was included in the Ellor Street No.4 clearance area, a compulsory purchase order was served in May 1960 and it closed in April 1963. A few days before Black Sunday, a reporter for the Manchester Guardian wrote that ten pubs were still standing on the 86-acre Ellor Street/Hankinson Street site. The brewers were claiming nearly £280,000 in compensation for twenty-nine pubs in the slum clearance programme and the 'costly day' had been put off for as long as possible. Now that almost all the 2,500 houses had been demolished, the pubs were like islands in a sea of rubble. Mrs Greatorex at the Etwall House told him that the last winter had been the worst, with the cold 'coming in at every wall' and the wind battering the place from every side.

The Etwall House, Ellor Street, in the 1950s

At the 1857 brewster sessions John Barritt (or Barratt) was refused a spirits licence for a new public house, the **Victoria Hotel**, that had been built on the corner of Ellor Street and John Street. Mr Barritt had to make do with a beerseller's licence, but apparently not for long, since the 1858 directory lists the Victoria as fully licensed. In May 1860 the pub was advertised to let by Messrs Hannay & Dickson, a firm of wine and spirit merchants with stores in Manchester (at the Sun, Deansgate) and Salford (Old Nelson, Chapel Street). The Victoria was advertised with a coach house and stables, which were round the corner in Robert Street.

William Parry was the next listed tenant, then John Vaughan and John Whyatt, who in 1867 was advertising the best wines and spirits from around 1/10d a pint. Around this time Hannay & Dickson took over the Atlas Brewery on Stockport Road and went into the brewing business. They also acquired a few more pubs, but they gave up their interest in the Victoria. From the 1870s to the 1890s the pub was leased by another Manchester wine and spirit merchant, Nathan Sandiford.

By the early 1900s the Manchester Brewery Company owned the Victoria and their tenant was John Ferrey. It became a Walker & Homfray pub and later licensees included Michael McDermott in the 1920s, John W Ferrey and Hannah Morgan in the 1930s and Richard Myerscough in the 1940s-50s. In April 1955 Mr Myerscough applied for a music licence so that he could pay a pianist to entertain his customers, rather than just have 'free and easys,' which didn't need a licence. He told the magistrates he wouldn't be employing singers, 'as they attract coach trippers from Liverpool.'

By then the Victoria belonged to Wilsons Brewery. A compulsory purchase order was served in October 1959 and the pub closed about 1965.

The **Staff of Life** seems to have been the first beerhouse to open on the Pendleton part of Ellor Street. In 1845 Samuel Tate was listed as a shopkeeper on the corner of Congreve Street, then three years later as a beerseller. He was there until about 1880 and subsequent licensees included Henry Tildsley in the 1880s, Edith Boyle in the 1890s and Margaret Chapman in the early 1900s.

There was an objection to the licence in February 1913, following a complaint about prices. The Staff of Life was owned by Swales Brewery and in common with some other Swales houses, it was selling their 'fourpenny' beer at 1½d a pint, instead of the usual 2d. The brewery complained that they had to do this as a nearby house was selling 'sixpenny', or XXX beer, for 2d a pint.

The Staff of Life had a wine licence and a few years later the tenant, James May, was advertising 'May's winery'. Fine old port was 2/6d a quart, 1/10d a pint, 9d a gill or 5d a noggin. Mr May left about 1921 after he was fined for allowing the beerhouse to be used for betting on horses.

The Staff of Life was referred for compensation in February 1932 and it closed about a year later. The last licensee was Michael Harte.

Elizabeth Street was built on the north side of Ellor Street about 1850 and the shop on the corner became a beerhouse called the **Jacobs Well**. James Chambers was listed there in 1855 and when he left two years later the premises were advertised to let by William Groves, who worked for Messrs Bathe & Newbold, owners of the Regent Road Brewery. In 1868 Mr Groves went into partnership with Arthur Whitnall and bought the brewery, but the Jacobs Well remained in private ownership.

James Wright was the licensee in the early 1860s, followed by Joseph and then Elizabeth Bates in the 1870s. Peter Barlow was listed there in the 1880s and Thomas Lambert in the 1890s. Mr Lambert was also the owner and in January 1896 he sold out to Groves & Whitnall. They had probably been the leaseholders and may have had something to do with the change of name from the Jacobs Well to the **Grove House**.

From 1902 until the 1950s the beerhouse was run by members of the Schofield family - John, Elizabeth and then James. A compulsory purchase order was served in 1959 and the Grove House closed the following year. The last licensees were George and Tilly Bramer, who moved to the Park Inn on Tatton Street.

A few years after the Jacobs Well opened, another beerhouse opened next door on the corner of Albion Place. This was the **Vine Tavern** and the earliest recorded licensee was James Duckworth in 1861. William Barlow had taken over by 1863 and William Seddon was there in the early 1870s. The beerhouse almost closed in 1872 and in 1874, when there were objections to Mr Seddon's licence because the rateable value of the building was low.

The next two licensees were Charles and then George Crapper, from the 1870s to the early 1900s. During this period there was a change of name to the **Kings Arms**. Thomas Casewell had taken over by 1910 and he ran the Kings Arms until the 1930s, when Alfred Casewell took over until the 1950s. The beerhouse was known as 'Casewell's' and Thomas was also the owner before it was bought by Tetleys Brewery of Leeds.

The building was included in the Ellor Street No.3 clearance area and a

The Victoria, Ellor Street, in 1961

compulsory purchase order was served in October 1959. It closed about 1964 and the last recorded tenants were Ronald and Sarah Heywood.

The **Four Horseshoes** was across Ellor Street from the Kings Arms, on the corner of Albert Terrace. This beerhouse was first listed in the 1863 directory, when Thomas Clarke was the licensee. Hannah Clarke took over for a year or two in the 1870s and later tenants included James Kenyon in the 1880s-90s and John Broughton in the early 1900s.

In 1916 John Bradbury was running the Four Horseshoes and in that year he gave up his wine licence in return for permission to make some structural alterations. Later licensees included Elizabeth Clare in the 1920s, Mrs Alice Bradbury and then Miss Alice Bradbury in the 1930s-40s. At some stage the beerhouse was acquired by the Cornbrook Brewery and their tenants included John Hampson and Hilda Baguley, who was there from the 1950s until the Four Horseshoes closed in 1965. The building was included in the Ellor Street No.7 clearance area.

A report of the licensing sessions in September 1877 states that Charles Gilbert Jackson was granted the transfer of the licence of the **Derbyshire House** on Ellor Street, Pendleton, to premises on Hayfield Street (the Hayfield Arms). There is no other reference to a beerhouse at this address and the exact site isn't known. It was on the south side, probably

The Joiners Arms, Ellor Street, about 1960

between Hankinson Street and Florin street.

The **Crown Inn** opened on the corner of Ellor Street and Florin Street in the 1860s and the earliest recorded licensee was William Brown in 1865-69. Ten years later Michael Hanlon was in charge and the beerhouse had a new name, the **Masons Arms**. Elizabeth Lambert was there in 1890 and John Mathieson in the early 1900s, when brewers Walker & Homfray were the owners. The beerhouse was a combination of two houses, one

fronting Ellor Street and the other Florin Street, and the brewery also owned two other houses on Florin Street.

At the brewster sessions in March 1907 the police reported that there were never more than five customers in the Masons, when there were thirty in the Joiners Arms across the street. Mr Mathieson said that he was selling about two barrels of beer a week and he couldn't get a living out of the place. It closed the following year and became a greengrocer's shop.

The **Joiners Arms** opened on the corner of Ellor Street and Tanners Lane in the 1850s. The first licensee was probably Edward Fairless, a joiner by trade, who was listed there from 1858 to 1863. Later licensees included James Moorman in the 1870s, James Worthington in the 1880s and Thomas Booth about 1890.

Thomas Lambert, licensee and owner of the Grove House on Ellor Street, also owned the Joiners Arms and he sold both properties to Groves & Whitnall in January 1896. The brewery's tenants at the Joiners in the early 1900s included Ann Seed and James Higginbottom.

John Holmes arrived about the time of the First World War and he was still there in the 1940s, when Edna Holmes took over. The Joiners was included in the first Ellor Street clearance area and Mrs Holmes was still the licensee when it closed in 1963.

Booth Street

Booth Street was the first street off Broad Street from Cross Lane, at the side of the Rose and Crown. The 1831 map shows that this area, between

The Four Horseshoes, Ellor Street, in 1965

Broad Street and Black Ditch, contained a few houses and a variety of gardens and allotments. Two of the houses became beerhouses.

The first to open was the **Highland Laddie**, originally one of four dwellings abutting the west side of Booth Street and with front gardens down to Black Ditch. By 1845 the garden of the end house had been built over and the house had become a shop, occupied by Henry Nicholson. Three years later Mr Nicholson was listed as a beer retailer.

Alice Nicholson took over the running of the business in the 1860s and subsequent licensees included Alexander Fairclough in the 1870s-90s, Mark Colley about 1900 and finally Joseph Bell. The Highland Laddie closed in 1902 and the building became a shop.

The 1848 map shows three houses on the east side of Booth Street, with what appears to be a large garden down to the Black Ditch. The houses are named as Richmond Place and are on the corner of Richmond Street (formerly Short Street, later Peel Street). In the 1860s the house on the corner became the **Foresters Arms**. It was advertised to let in July 1867 - eight rooms, a wash house and a garden for £40 a year.

The earliest recorded licensee was Stephen Emery in 1869. Two years later Richmond Place - the beerhouse, two dwellings fronting Peel Street and the land at the back - was advertised for sale. The former garden was now building land, suitable for cattle sheds,

The Foresters, Booth Street, in 1962

stables or a joiner's shop. The adjoining streets had been paved and sewered and the property was being sold on a long leasehold from 1840. The purchaser isn't recorded, but it may have been Boddingtons Brewery, who were certainly the owners at the beginning of the twentieth century.

Stephen Emery left about 1874 and among later licensees were William Connell in the 1870s-80s, William Booth from the 1890s to the early 1900s and John Bond in the 1920s. The last licensee was Hilda Salt, who took over in 1936.

The Foresters was included in the Ellor Street No.4 clearance area and a compulsory purchase order was served in January 1960. A survey showed that Boddingtons hadn't been looking after the property. The condition of the building was 'not too good'; it was damp, there was no proper food store and no proper cooking facilities. Mrs Salt and her mother, 85-year-old Claire Woodhead, closed the Foresters when the beer ran out on the afternoon of Black Sunday, 28th April 1963.

Cross Street

This was the next street off Broad Street after Booth Street, at the side of the Cross Keys. A report of the 1870 brewster sessions mentions a beerhouse here called the **Yorkshire Grey**, which had been 'licensed for a long time'. The first recorded beerseller on the street was William Fisher in 1838. He left in the 1850s and John Withington took over about 1860.

The Yorkshire Grey was mentioned at the 1870 sessions, when the magistrates refused to grant a beerseller's certificate to a new tenant, Thomas Campbell, because John Withington had kept a rat pit for the entertainment of his customers. The situation was resolved somehow (no doubt the rat pit was filled in) and John and Ann Withington continued to be listed as licensees until the 1880s. By then the beerhouse had a new name, the **Albion Inn** and it was owned by Messrs Wheater & Swales of the Victoria Brewery, Ravald Street.

Licensees around 1890 included John Newsome and George Barlow. The Albion closed about 1905 and the last occupant was Thomas John.

The Old House at Home and Red Lion, Pimlot Street, in the 1960s

Pimlot Street

Pimlot Street went from Broad Street, opposite Frederick Road, to Ellor Street. The 1848 map shows the street when it was partly built up. At the lower end there was a block of houses between Black Ditch (later Spring Vale Road) and Ellor Street. The block was built about 1836 and it seems to have been the location of the first beerhouse on Pimlot Street, the **Prince of Wales**. Directories give various addresses for what was probably the same place: Jelly's Buildings, Wilkinson Place, Spring Vale Road and finally Pimlot Street.

William Jelly appears in directories as the licensee between 1840 and 1852. Mr Jelly was also in business as a plasterer and painter, with premises on Broad Street. Another member of the Jelly family, Frederick, was listed at the beerhouse from the 1860s to the 1880s. Harriet Jelly succeeded her husband and by 1890 Joseph Jones had the licence.

Catherine Price took over a few years later and she almost lost the licence in 1897 after being fined for having a disorderly house and being drunk on the premises. The owners, brewers Watson & Woodhead, put in a new tenant and by the early 1900s the Prince of Wales was being run by Harry Ralphs.

In 1912 the beerhouse and two adjoining cottages were acquired by Walker & Homfray. The following year the Prince of Wales was on the closure list, but the licence was renewed after the brewery said that annual sales had increased from 296 barrels of beer in 1910 to 394 in 1912. They had dropped the price of a pint from 2½d to 2d, which no doubt helped.

The Prince of Wales eventually closed in 1924 and the last recorded licensee was Michael McDermott.

Two Pimlot Street beerhouses - the Red Lion and the Old House at Home - were next door to each other and both were first listed in the 1858 directory. The **Red Lion** was on the corner of Raven Street and the licensee in that year was Jabez Sykes. Sarah Jelly was there in the 1870s, Thomas Burton in the 1880s and John Cordwell about 1890, when Chesters Brewery acquired the Red Lion from Messrs Richardson & Goodall of the Altrincham Brewery. Ten years later Chesters spent something like £900 on rebuilding the property.

Tenants in the early twentieth century included John Blackburn and Thomas Knight, who was there for over twenty years from about 1907. There was a move to close the Red Lion at the 1913 brewster sessions, when the police stated that it wasn't needed, as there were 43 other licensed houses within 300 yards. Chesters argued that it was a modern house, having been rebuilt, and trade was good, so they managed to get the licence renewed.

Later licensees included Nora Griffin, who was there from the 1930s to the 1950s, and Harold Gillingham in the late 1950s. The Red Lion was in the Ellor Street No.3 clearance area and a compulsory purchase order was served in September 1959. An inquiry in January 1960 found that the building was well maintained, but like all the others it had to be demolished. It closed in 1963, when it was being run by Kenneth and Audrey Marland.

The earliest recorded licensee of the **Old House at Home**, next door to the Red Lion, was James Buckley. William Johnson was there in the 1860s, Henry Tomlinson in the 1870s and Edwin Dugmore in the 1880s. Brewers Groves & Whitnall were the owners by the 1890s and their tenant in the early 1900s was Charles Parker.

Like the Red Lion, the Old House at Home was on the list of beerhouses being considered for closure at the 1913 brewster sessions. The police reported that other houses nearby were doing better, but all were doing over six barrels a week in this area because it was so densely populated. Mr Parker continued to run the beerhouse for a few more years, then Esther Parker had the licence until about 1930.

In 1937 John Yates moved to the Old House at Home from the Manor Inn on Church Street. His son Ged took over about 1950 and he was the last licensee. The building was included in the Ellor Street No.3 clearance area and Ged pulled the last pints on Black Sunday, 28th April 1963. At the farewell party, two of the pub's entertainers, Billy Melia (accordion) and H Johnson (banjo) were presented with silver cigarette lighters.

The **Druids Rest** was on the other side of Pimlot Street, on the corner of Peel Street. Robert Kirkman was the earliest recorded licensee in 1858. Subsequent tenants included Ralph Grundy and Arthur Davies in the 1860s, George Bell in the 1870s, Edward Casewell in the 1880s and Robert North about 1890.

The beerhouse was acquired by Threlfalls Brewery and their tenants in the early 1900s included Fred Stoddard and Alfred Rimmer. In 1907 there was an objection to the licence after Mr Rimmer was fined for serving over-measure. He told the magistrates that the Red Lion and the Old House at Home were also doing the 'long pull', so what could he do? He was selling nine or ten barrels of beer a week, but if he didn't do the long pull, sales would be down to about six barrels. To prove his point, he showed the court some bottles of beer that had been bought from the other two beerhouses. There was more than a pint in each bottle. Mr Rimmer's licence was renewed and the police were told to have a look at the Red Lion and the Old House at Home.

Like the other two, the Druids Rest was on the closure list in 1913. The premises were too small, so Threlfalls

Druids Rest, Pimlot Street, in the 1920s

were given permission to demolish a cottage at the back to make room for a private yard, and rearrange the bedrooms so that a bathroom could be installed. The frontage was rebuilt and the ground floor was decorated with coloured tiles.

Harry Ralphs moved to the Druids Rest from another Pimlot Street beerhouse, the Prince of Wales, about 1913. Mary Jane Ralphs took over after five years and she was still in charge in the late 1930s. Later tenants included Ellen Roberts in the 1940s and Clyde Witham in the 1950s. The property was included in the Ellor Street No.4 clearance area and a compulsory purchase order was served in January 1960. The Druids Rest closed on Black Sunday, 28th April 1963 and the last licensee was Walter Jack Mills.

In April 1853 the **Highland Laddie** on Pimlot Street, with its own brewhouse, was advertised to let. This may have been a fifth, short-lived beerhouse, or maybe it was an earlier name for the Prince of Wales.

Chapel Street

The next street off Broad Street after Pimlot Street was Chapel Street. The 1848 map shows the street going from the side of the Bethesda Chapel to Chaney Street. The lower part, from Chaney Street to Ellor Street, was at that time called Picton Street. Off the east side of Picton Street, about halfway down, was Goddard Street, and on the corner was the **Nottingham Arms**.

Directories list William Batty as a smallware dealer on Goddard Street in 1843 and then as a beer retailer in 1845, so his shop may have been the one which became the Nottingham Arms. Ten years later Edward Stanley was

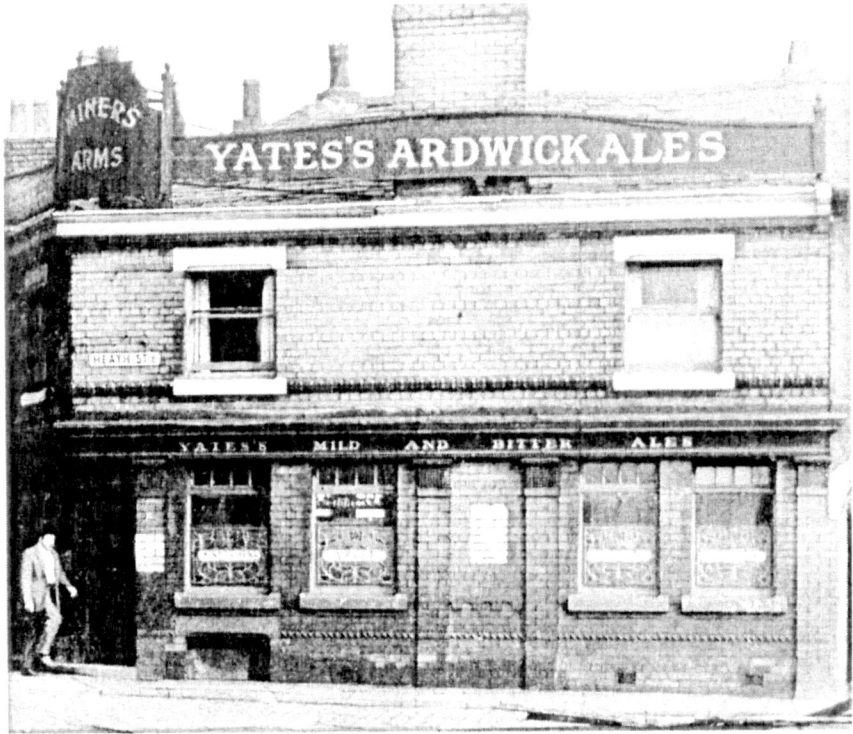

Miners Arms, Chapel Street, in 1961

there, followed by Henry and then Margaret Stanley in the 1860s. Later licensees included Edward Beech Jones in the 1870s and Moses Hall from the 1870s to the 1890s.

For its final years the Nottingham Arms was owned by Boddingtons Brewery. It closed in 1906 after the police reported that 'it was doing practically nothing'. The last licensee was Joseph Tomlinson and the building was later used as a greengrocer's shop.

The **Alexandra Inn** was on the west side of Chapel Street, in the middle of a row of houses about halfway down. The earliest recorded licensee, John Gregory, was there for about ten years

from 1848. Thomas and then Joseph Blakeley were in charge from the 1860s to the 1880s, George Fisher about 1890 and Isaac Ogden from 1892.

The beerhouse was acquired by Hardy's Crown Brewery and in 1902 they rebuilt it 'from cellar to roof' at a cost of £1,100. A few years later Isaac Ogden died and his widow, Ann, took over. She became Ann Simpson and was the Alexandra's last licensee. At the 1913 brewster sessions the beer sales, draught and bottled, were estimated at four-and-a-half barrels a week. The magistrates decided that the Alexandra was no longer needed and it closed the following year, with the brewery receiving £2,544 in compensation.

The **Miners Arms** on the corner of Chapel Street and Heath Street survived until more recent times. This had a first licence date of 1853, but the earliest identifiable beerseller was John Royle in 1865. George Mitcham was there in the 1870s, George Jones about 1880, William Smith about 1890 and Thomas Tildesley in the early 1900s.

By then the Miners was owned by Yates's Castle Brewery of Ardwick and their tenant from 1905 was Samuel Spivey. There was an objection to the licence at the 1914 brewster sessions, when Mr Spivey sold beer in an unsealed bottle to a child under 14. The lad told the policeman that he was 14, but the policeman went home with him and asked to see his birth certificate and he was only nine.

Emma Spivey took over from her husband about 1915 and in 1923 she was in trouble for giving the 'long pull'. She told the magistrates she was

The Alexandra, Chapel Street, in the early 1900s

selling six barrels a week and had a respectable class of customers. Her licence was renewed after she promised to stop giving generous measures of beer.

The last licensee of the Miners Arms was Elsie Walters, Sam and Emma Spivey's daughter. She took over in 1949 and was 72 years old when the pub closed in 1963. The building was in the Ellor Street No.3 clearance area and a compulsory purchase order was served in September 1959. In an interview with the Salford City Reporter a few days before Black Sunday, 28th April 1963, Mrs Walters said, 'I'm lucky if I can fill a table on weekdays, but they're very loyal on Saturday nights; some of them come a fivepenny bus ride to drink here again. But the ladies don't like coming down from Broad Street, with no street lights and all the bricks.'

John Street

John Street went from Broad Street to Ellor Street, opposite St Paul's Church. Near the top of the street, on the east side, there was a beerhouse called the **Just Another**. Anthony Brocklehurst was listed as the licensee from 1861 until the 1880s and Stephen Beswick in 1890. The premises were extended in 1880, when a former broker's shop next door was converted into a drinking vault.

The last licensee was Albert Prince in the early 1900s, and by then the beerhouse had a new name, the **Footballers Arms**. The property was owned by Thomas Kay, who had a butcher's shop on Broad Street and

who was leasing it to Issott's Brewery of Ardwick for £50 a year. Wilsons Brewery took over the lease in 1903, then Elliott's Brewery of Cheetham Hill the following year.

In 1905 Mr Prince was selling less than two barrels of beer a week. Elliott's had plans for alterations, but at the 1906 brewster sessions it was decided that the Footballers should close. Mr Kay received £420 in compensation.

Chaney Street

Three beerhouses were listed on Chaney Street, which went from Gold Street to Pimlot Street. The first to open seems to have been the **Black Horse** on the corner of John Street. It was advertised to let in September 1854 and the first recorded licensee was John Thomason in 1858. A second advertisement in July 1863 mentioned a coal yard attached.

George Grimshaw became the licensee in the 1860s and he ran the Black Horse for about twenty years. After her husband died, Jane Grimshaw stayed on as landlady until the 1890s. Later tenants included Isaac Gartside in 1905 and Ernest Barlow in 1910. By then the beerhouse was owned by Wilsons Brewery.

James Hetherington Wilson, who took over in December 1916, was the last licensee. Sales in previous years had averaged seven barrels of beer a week, but it was now wartime, there were fewer customers and there were six other licensed houses within 130 yards. The Black Horse closed in 1919.

The **Crown Inn** on the corner of

Chaney Street and Chapel Street first appears in the 1863 directory, when George Booth was running it. John Walker was listed there from 1869 to 1886 and subsequent licensees included James Kilgour in the 1890s and William Wildman around 1910.

The Crown was acquired by Taylor's Eagle Brewery and their tenant from the time of the First World War until the 1940s was Mary Rimmer. Thomas and Ellen Roberts took over in the 1950s and were there when the property was included in the Ellor Street No.3 clearance area. A compulsory purchase order was served in September 1959 and the Crown closed in 1962.

The **Turf Tavern** was on the south side of Chaney Street, not far from the Crown. It opened in the 1860s and George Dickinson was listed there in 1869, then William Turner in the 1870s. Licensees in the 1880s included Alfred Walker and Mary Bohanna and during this period there was a change of name to the **Moulders Arms**.

Later licensees included Amelia Hall in the 1890s and William Stansfield in the early 1900s, when the Moulders was owned by Walkers of Warrington. The brewery extended the beerhouse into the cottage next door. By 1910 Samuel Rainey was the tenant and after he died Mrs Mary Rainey took over. She was still there in 1927, when the Moulders was on the list of beerhouses being considered for closure. The police reported that the building was structurally unsuitable and the licence was no longer needed; there was an average of only six customers and there were twenty-two other licences within three hundred yards. In the previous year, Mrs Rainey had sold 155 barrels and 411 dozen bottles of beer. The Moulders closed in 1927.

Gold Street

There were three beerhouses on Gold Street, which went from Broad Street, opposite Strawberry Road, to Pendleton Mills. The two oldest, the Star Inn and the Plumbers Arms, were opposite each other at the Broad Street end. Both were first listed in the 1841 directory.

The **Star Inn** was on the corner of Hills Croft and in 1841 the licensee was James Atkinson. William Dickinson had taken over by 1848 and another William Dickinson, probably his son, was running the beerhouse in the 1880s. William Pheasey was there in 1890 and Edward Barnes in the early 1900s.

By then the Star, along with three adjoining houses and some stables, was owned by brewers Watson, Woodhead & Wagstaffe. In 1906 the

Samuel Rainey at the door of the Moulders Arms, Chaney Street, in 1912

police reported that the building was in need of repair and it lacked separate lavatories. There were only about eight customers, even on a Saturday night, and closure was recommended. Instead of closing, the brewery was given permission to rebuild.

The Star lasted only a few more years. At the 1912 brewster sessions the police reported that there had been seven changes of licensee since 1904. On weekdays there were no more than seven customers; on Saturdays there were fourteen. Beer sales averaged three barrels a week and other beerhouses nearby were busier. The Star closed the following year and the last licensee was Charles Bradford.

The earliest recorded licensee of the **Plumbers Arms** was James Pearce in 1841. Elizabeth Pearce had taken over by 1845 and Elizabeth Travis was there in the 1850s. Subsequent tenants included John Hackett and William Davies in the 1860s, Edward and Ann Williams in the 1870s-80s and Albert Ellis about 1890.

Holts Brewery bought the Plumbers in 1897, but they didn't have it for long. Along with the Star, it was on the list of beerhouses being considered for closure at the 1906 brewster sessions. Beer sales were about two barrels a week and there were usually no more than six people in the place. It closed the following year and the last licensee was John Grundy.

Gold Street's third beerhouse was halfway down the street on the east side, on the corner of Chaney Street. James Wilcock was listed as a shopkeeper here in 1863 and then as a beerseller a few years later. It was called the **Turtle Inn** and there were just two drinking rooms, a corner vault and parlour behind. The owner in the 1870s was Margaret Westbrook of Swinton and she leased the property to J H Twigg of the Manor Brewery on Church Street, near Salford Town Hall. In the 1880s, when the licence was transferred from William Benson to Samuel Garside, the Turtle Inn had been renamed the **Lamplighters Arms**.

Frederick Lyons took over in 1900 and by then there had been another change of name to the **Bee Hive Inn**. Mr Lyons, who moved here from the Just Another on John Street, was also a draper and clothier and at one time he had kept a shop on Broad Street. He continued his clothing business at the Bee Hive, but he didn't stay long. In about 1903 Jack Rhapps, a well known local rugby player, was the tenant, but he couldn't make it pay either. The Bee Hive closed in 1907 and the last licensee was Martin Corcoran.

In March 1908 the former Bee Hive was advertised to let for ten shillings a

week. It was a draper's shop in the 1930s and was condemned as a dangerous building in 1936.

Bury Street

Most of the beerhouses on the streets south of Ellor Street are first recorded in the directories printed in the 1860s. The **Albert Inn** on the corner of Bury Street and Albert Street appears in the 1869 directory, with Samuel Topper the licensee. Later tenants included William Hulland in the 1880s and James Royle about 1905.

The Albert was on the closure list in 1912 and at the brewster sessions the police reported that there were fewer customers here than in nearby beerhouses. The sanitary arrangements were below Corporation standard and since the scullery was built on the yard, this and the kitchen had poor lighting and ventilation.

James Walker, the licensee, said the trade was satisfactory and it was enough to keep him and his family. Holts Brewery, the owners, said the house was open seventeen hours a day and if it only had six different customers per hour, that meant 102 customers per day. If they consumed about 105 quarts of beer between them, it would mean three barrels a week. The magistrates were not persuaded and the Albert closed.

The **Bee Hive** was at the other end of

the same row as the Albert, on the corner of Paul Street. It was first licensed in 1866 and John Yates was there in 1869. Later licensees included Robert Brierley in the 1870s, John Booth in the 1880s-90s and Thomas Wilkinson in the early 1900s.

Brewers J W Lees purchased the Bee Hive in 1905 and their tenant from then until it shut was Samuel Anderson. It almost closed in 1906 after Mr Anderson was fined for allowing gambling. The police reported that 'a good deal of domino playing and gambling went on,' but the magistrates decided to renew the licence. Seven years later a police survey found that there were usually only about five customers and Mr Anderson was selling less than three barrels of beer a week, plus a gallon and a half of wine and some bottled beer and minerals. The brewery agreed that it was a small house, but trade was increasing now that the Albert Inn had closed. The magistrates decided that the neighbourhood could manage without the Bee Hive as well; it closed in 1914.

The **Printers Arms** on the corner of Bury Street and Harrison Street was first listed in the 1869 directory, with Thomas Ginder the licensee. Walter Turton was there in the 1880s-90s and John Walton by 1905. The beerhouse was acquired by the Cornbrook Brewery and the licensee when it closed in 1920 was Thomas Berry.

John Mawdsley at the door of the Church, Albert Street, in 1912

Albert Street

Of all the old beerhouses in this part of Pendleton, the **Church Inn** on Albert Street survived the longest. It opened in 1861 and the earliest recorded licensee was James Bates, who applied for a spirits licence in 1864, without success. John Pratt was there in the 1870s, Christopher Cranshaw in the 1880s and William Roberts about 1890.

Walkers Brewery were the owners by the beginning of the twentieth century and their tenants included Edgar Briggs in 1905, John Mawdsley for about twenty years from 1910, Mary Archibald in the 1930s, Andrew Cahill in the 1940s, and Arthur Wright in the 1950s.

The Church became a Tetley pub in the 1960s and it was still standing after the area around Pendleton Precinct had been redeveloped. Albert Street disappeared and for the last few years before it was pulled down in 1976, the Church was on Mulberry Road. The last licensee was Edward Dalton.

Harrison Street

This was one of the first streets to be built on the south side of Ellor Street and a beerseller called John Aldred was recorded here from 1848 to 1855. The beerhouse was the **Oddfellows Arms**, and later tenants included Hannah and William Banham in the 1850s-60s, Samuel and Sarah Scholes in the 1860s-70s, William Wilding in the 1880s and George Newsome in the 1890s.

The beerhouse and adjoining shop, stables and outbuildings were owned by Thomas Lambert, who also owned the Grove House on Ellor Street. In 1896 he sold the Grove House and the Harrison Street property to brewers Groves & Whitnall.

The Oddfellows was on the closure list in 1908, when the police reported there were fewer customers here than in the four beerhouses nearby. However the tenant, Thomas Higson, was able to show that he was selling between six and seven barrels of beer a week and Groves & Whitnall were allowed to keep the licence, providing they made improvements to the building.

Licensees after Mr Higson included Florence and James Raymond until the 1920s, Joseph Haigh in the 1930s, William Eaton in the 1940s and Ethel Evans from the 1950s until it closed in 1965. The Oddfellows was included in the Ellor Street clearance area.

The **Dog and Partridge** was on the corner of Harrison Street and Bury Street, diagonally across from the Printers Arms. The earliest recorded licensee of this beerhouse was James Gibbon in 1861. Mary Kershaw was there in 1865, George Banham in the 1870s and John Lyons in the 1880s.

The Empress Brewery of Old Trafford acquired the Dog and Partridge in the 1890s and their tenants included Charles Williamson in the early 1900s and George Crookell in the 1920s. While Mr Crookell was in charge, Walkers of Warrington took over the

Empress Brewery and its pubs and beerhouses. Later licensees included Susan Buckley in the 1940s and Joseph Grimshaw in the 1950s.

The Dog & Partridge became a Tetley house in the 1960s, and by then it had been included in the Ellor Street No.4 clearance area. It closed in 1962 and the last licensee, Edward Dalton, moved to the Church on Mulberry Road.

Grafton Street

Grafton Street was off Ellor Street and crossed the eastern end of Bury Street. On the corner of Alma Street and facing Bury Street was a beerhouse called the **Vulcan Inn**. The earliest identifiable licensee was Edward Thornton, who was mentioned in a newspaper report in January 1880 after being acquitted of being drunk on the premises.

John Barr was listed at the Vulcan in 1881 and a few years later Richard Huntbatch took over and stayed for about twenty-five years. The Cornbrook Brewery were the owners by the early twentieth century and later licensees included Edwin Barrett about 1918 and Jonathan Shaw in the 1920s-30s.

At the 1939 brewster sessions the Corporation building inspector reported that the side wall was bulging and the lavatories were in need of improvement. The police said the licence was not needed, as there were only three customers when they called and there were seven other licensed houses within a hundred yards. The Vulcan closed later that year and the last licensee was John Marsh.

Allen Street

Allen Street went from Harrison Street to Astley Street and on the north side there was a row of twelve houses. The two at the Astley Street end were combined to form a beerhouse called the Havelock Inn. The first licence was taken out in 1868, probably by Thomas Foster, who was there in the 1870s. Margaret Foster took over after her husband died and their daughter, Annie, was running the business by 1890.

The Havelock was bought by Swales Brewery and their tenants in the first half of the twentieth century included Herbert Dean in 1910, Henry Dorning in the 1920s and Thomas Sheard in the 1930s. In 1939 the police reported that there were usually only about four people in the beerhouse and the sanitary arrangements were unsuitable. Swales said they had spent £300 on the building over the past fifteen years and promised to make some more improvements, so the licence was renewed.

The Dog & Partridge, Harrison Street, about 1930

Florence Johnson took over at the Havelock in the 1940s and she was still there in July 1965 when a compulsory purchase order was confirmed and the beerhouse closed.

High Street

At the brewster sessions in August 1885 James Walwyn applied to transfer the licence of his beerhouse on the corner of Gardner Street and Gloucester Street to a new building on High Street. The beerhouse, the Priory Hotel, was about to be pulled down to make way for Pendleton New Station. He also applied for a spirits licence for the new building, but the magistrates refused both. Mr Walwyn took his case to the Quarter Sessions and managed to get the beer licence transferred.

The new **Priory Hotel** opened on the corner of High Street and Ruthin Street in 1886. Mr Walwyn continued to apply for a spirits licence, but was always turned down. In 1891 the magistrates noted that the house had been built by a firm of brewers in the face of their refusal to grant a licence. The brewers were probably Threlfalls, who were listed as the owners a few years later.

By 1897 Anthony Hepper had taken over and he too applied for the full licence, without success. Mr Hepper ran the Priory for over twenty years and for most of that time he was chairman of the Salford Licensed Victuallers' Association. After the beerhouse had its windows broken during the Lusitania riots of 1915 because he had a German-sounding name, he had posters printed offering £10 to anyone who could prove he was not born English.

George White was running the Priory in the 1920s-30s and Gertrude Hargreaves in 1937-38. The house became fully licensed in 1937, when Threlfalls obtained a transfer of the licence of the Raven Hotel on Chapel Street, which was due to be pulled down to make way for Victoria Bus Station.

Later tenants included Harry Smith in the 1940s and Bernard Cooken in the 1950s. A compulsory purchase order was confirmed in July 1965 and the pub closed later that year. The last occupants were Charles and Georgina Inman.

Tanners Lane and Florin Street

Tanners Lane is shown on early nineteenth century maps running southwards from Church Street, through Spring Vale to Hayfield. As house building progressed, the lane was extended across High Street and in the 1870s the lower section was renamed Florin Street.

Two Tanners Lane beerhouses are listed in the 1843 directory - the Spring Vale Tavern and the Queens Arms. The **Spring Vale Tavern** was on the end of a row of houses called Victoria Terrace (later Victoria Place) and was run for about ten years by Samuel Watson. John Mather was there in the 1860s-70s and Thomas Eades in the 1880s. Around this time the beerhouse and two adjoining cottages were owned by brewers Watson & Woodhead.

By the early 1900s another local brewery, Groves & Whitnall, had taken over, but the Spring Vale didn't have long to go. In February 1907 an application to transfer the licence to an off licence between Hereford and Monmouth Streets, Ordsall Lane, was refused. The tenant, Henry Gregory, had paid the brewery £100 ingoing two years earlier, but the Spring Vale wasn't doing much trade. When the magistrates announced that they were not renewing the licence, they asked Mr Gregory if he would get his money back. 'I hope so,' was the reply.

According to licensing records, the **Queens Arms** opened in 1837. John Turner was running the beerhouse in 1843 and he was the owner until his death thirty years later. William Turner had the licence in 1850, when the Queens was listed as a beerhouse with pleasure gardens. These were probably Victoria Gardens, on the other side of Tanners Lane, an area eventually covered by Meldrum and Melrose Streets. Two other members of the family are listed as licensees - Mary in the 1850s and George in the 1870s.

In July 1873 the leasehold of the Queens Arms, two adjoining cottages, brewhouse and outbuildings, was auctioned at the Horse Shoe on Broad Street. The purchasers may have been Messrs Wheater & Swales of the Victoria Brewery, Ravald Street, since the Queens was a Swales house in later years.

In 1875 Thomas Valentine was the licensee and he applied for a spirits licence, saying that £2,000 had been spent on improvements. The application was turned down and the Queens remained a beerhouse. George Bowring took over a year or so later and he was in charge when the address of the Queens changed from Tanners Lane to Florin Street.

Licensees in the twentieth century included Donald Fraser in 1905, Henry Groves in 1910 and Margaret McRitchie from the time of the First World War to the 1950s. The property was included in the Ellor Street No.7 clearance area and a compulsory purchase order was served in 1963. The Queens - known as the 'Stumps' - closed in 1965 and the last licensee was Elsie Heald.

In September 1874 James McLoughlin obtained permission to transfer the beer licence of the former Cross Keys on Broughton Road to a shop on the corner of Florin Street and Coomassie Street. The shop became the **Coomassie Hotel**. The following year the owner, Charles Mottram of the Sun Brewery, Ford Lane, wanted to replace the building with a new, fully licensed

The Priory, High Street, in the 1920s

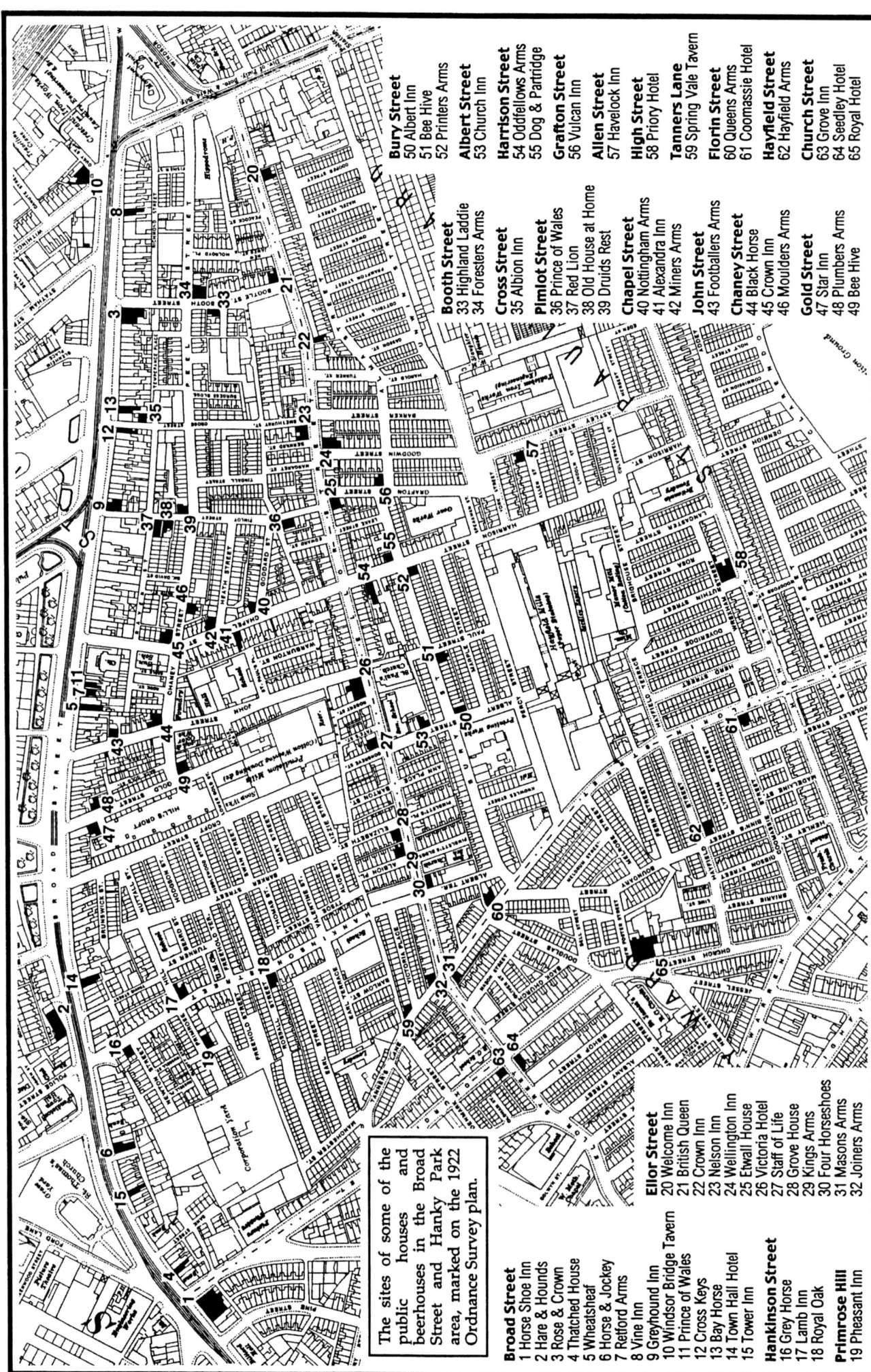

The sites of some of the public houses and beerhouses in the Broad Street and Hanky Park area, marked on the 1922 Ordnance Survey plan.

Broad Street
1 Horse Shoe Inn
2 Hare & Hounds
3 Rose & Crown
4 Thatched House
5 Wheatsheaf
6 Horse & Jockey
7 Retford Arms
8 Vine Inn
9 Greyhound Inn
10 Windsor Bridge Tavern
11 Prince of Wales
12 Cross Keys
13 Bay Horse
14 Town Hall Hotel
15 Tower Inn

Hankinson Street
16 Grey Horse
17 Lamb Inn
18 Royal Oak

Primrose Hill
19 Pheasant Inn

Ellor Street
20 Welcome Inn
21 British Queen
22 Crown Inn
23 Nelson Inn
24 Wellington Inn
25 Etwall House
26 Victoria Hotel
27 Staff of Life
28 Grove House
29 Kings Arms
30 Four Horseshoes
31 Masons Arms
32 Joiners Arms

Booth Street
33 Highland Laddie
34 Foresters Arms

Cross Street
35 Albion Inn

Pimlot Street
36 Prince of Wales
37 Red Lion
38 Old House at Home
39 Druids Rest

Chapel Street
40 Nottingham Arms
41 Alexandra Inn
42 Miners Arms

John Street
43 Footballers Arms

Chaney Street
44 Black Horse
45 Crown Inn
46 Moulders Arms

Gold Street
47 Star Inn
48 Plumbers Arms
49 Bee Hive

Bury Street
50 Albert Inn
51 Bee Hive
52 Printers Arms

Albert Street
53 Church Inn

Harrison Street
54 Oddfellows Arms
55 Dog & Partridge

Grafton Street
56 Vulcan Inn

Allen Street
57 Havelock Inn

High Street
58 Priory Hotel

Tanners Lane
59 Spring Vale Tavern

Florin Street
60 Queens Arms
61 Coomassie Hotel

Hayfield Street
62 Hayfield Arms

Church Street
63 Grove Inn
64 Seedley Hotel
65 Royal Hotel

hotel and convert two nearby cottages into stables. The magistrates were not in favour. An application for a spirits licence in 1883 was also rejected.

Charles and then Frances Westbrook had the licence from the 1880s to the early 1900s. The Coomassie became a Threlfalls house and later tenants included Harold Kelsey in the 1920s, Joseph Malpas and Thomas Buckley in the 1930s, James Brownhill in the 1940s and Percy Middleton and Joseph Livesey in the 1950s. Walter Jack Mills took over in 1963 after his old pub, the Druids Rest on Pimlot Street, closed on Black Sunday. The Coomassie closed under a compulsory purchase order in 1968.

Hayfield Street

In 1877 the Derbyshire House on Ellor Street closed and the licence was transferred to a shop on the corner of Hayfield Street and Binns Street, which became the **Hayfield Arms**. Allan Macadam was listed there in 1877 and James Sinclair the following year. The beerhouse belonged to the Cornbrook Brewery and later licensees included Thomas Wilding in the 1880s, George Allen about 1890 and George Lever in the early 1900s. James Holden had taken over by 1910 and he was the last licensee. The Hayfield Arms closed in 1924.

Church Street

Two beerhouses and a fully licensed hotel opened on Church Street. The beerhouses were on the corners of Ellor Street and opened in the 1860s; the hotel opened in 1881 and is still standing.

The Coomassie in the 1950s

The earliest recorded licensee of the **Grove Inn** was John Andrews in 1871. John Mulroy was there a few years later, when the owner, Colonel Deakin of the Britannia Brewery (later the Manchester Brewery Company), was given permission to give the building a new frontage, put a vault door on the corner and a sign advertising 'Celebrated Ardwick Ales' over the windows on the Church Street side. James Valentine was the licensee in the 1870s-80s and Thomas Howard in the early 1900s. The property passed to local brewers Walker & Homfray in 1912.

Later tenants included Thomas Jackson in the 1920s, Alice Black in the 1930s,

Emily McCarthy in the 1940s and Edna Parnell from the 1950s until the Grove closed in 1966. It was a Wilsons house and the brewery retained the licence and then gave it up, along with some others, when the Woodman opened on the Ellor Street development.

Across Ellor Street from the Grove, the **Seedley Hotel** was first licensed in 1868. Thomas Griffiths, Richard Parker and James Mulroy were listed there in the 1870s, Thomas Whittaker in the 1880s and Benjamin Dunkerley about 1890.

The Seedley was a Boddingtons house and James Luty was their tenant in the early 1900s. James Jones took over in 1916 and he was still pulling the pints in 1963, when he was in his 90th year. The Seedley - well known as 'Jimmy Joneses' - was included in the Ellor Street No.7 clearance area and closed in 1967.

In 1880 Mark Baxter had his plans for a new hotel on Church Street accepted by the Corporation. Two semi-detached houses on the corner of Foster Street were demolished and building began. The plans show thirteen bedrooms on the top floor and eleven on the first floor, plus a breakfast room overlooking Church Street. There was a dining room on the ground floor, along with the usual parlour, smoke room and commercial room, and stables were built at the back in Foster Street. At the 1881 brewster sessions Mr Baxter was given permission to transfer the licence of his old pub, the Ring o'Bells on Bury Street, to the new building. The **Royal Hotel** was intended to be a leading residential hotel for the growing Pendleton district, but it was in the wrong place. At the brewster sessions five years later, the magistrates were

The Grove, Church Street, in 1961

told that the Royal was in an area with a low-class population and only three beds had been occupied in the last six months.

Mark Baxter died in 1894 and the pub was then owned by Threlfalls Brewery. John Mills was the licensee in the early 1900s and James Swann about 1910. Harry Dean took over a few years later and ran the Royal until the 1930s, when he moved to a hotel in Blackpool. Joseph Neary was there in the 1940s, William Murdon in the 1950s and Wilfred and Hilda Broadbent in the early 1960s.

At the beginning of 1969, with the redevelopment of Hanky Park well under way, work began on alterations at the Royal. Most of the old ceilings were removed and the original bar counters were replaced with veneered wood. When the work was completed in December, the pub had a new name and address, the **Flat Iron** on Market Way. The refurbishment was on the theme of Salford's markets and there was a showcase containing decorated flat irons in the lounge. The licensee during the alterations was Lena Wheeler.

There have been a few changes at the Flat Iron since then and the pub is still there, one of the surviving landmarks of old Pendleton.

New Pubs

Nine new pubs opened in the Ellor Street redevelopment and around Pendleton Precinct:

First off the mark was the **Pied Piper** on Broadwalk, built for Tetleys Brewery and opened in early 1970. It was leased to Burtonwood Brewery in 1992, closed in 1999 and was demolished in 2003.

At the Cross Lane end of Broadwalk, work on the **Flemish Weaver** began in September 1969 and the pub opened on 3rd September 1970. The name was chosen by Frank Cowen of Whitbreads Brewery after he read about Sir John Radclyffe bringing Flemish weavers to the area in the book 'Salford Through the Ages'. The two lounges were named the Radclyffe Room and the Flanders Room.

The first licensee was Joe Wagner, an ex-boxer who had been with Threlfalls Brewery for over twenty years. In the 1960s he ran the London and North Western on Cross Lane, the Horse Shoe on Broad Street and the Worsley on West Worsley Street.

The Flemish Weaver was bought by a pub company in 1997 and it is still going in 2003.

On Monday 21st December 1970 John

Shortman closed the Wheatsheaf on Broad Street and the following day opened the **Woolpack** on Meyrick Road. The pub was built for Wilsons Brewery and it had taken 24 weeks to complete, using prefabricated sections made in a factory in St Helens and then erected on site. The interior was decorated on the theme of ships which carried wool across the world. There were paintings of ships on the walls and the main bar was constructed in the form of stacks of bales of wool.

The Woolpack saw a change of ownership in the 1990s and it is still going in 2003.

The provisional licence for the **Woodman** was granted in February 1970. The pub was built on Belvedere Road, between the Woolpack and the Flemish Weaver, and opened the following year. In return for the new licence, Wilsons Brewery gave up some licences the company had been holding in suspension, including those of the Grapes on Cross Lane, the Grove on Church Street and the Prince of Wales Feathers at Windsor Bridge.

The Woodman was converted into **Sports** theme pub in 1985 and closed in 1990. The building was demolished at the end of 1993.

On the south side of Broadwalk, the **Champion** was opened next to the Unwin Street flats by Greenall Whitley in 1970. It closed early in 1993 and was pulled down later in the year for redevelopment.

In December 1970 the Salford City

Reporter announced that a new lock-up pub called 'The Dollies' was under construction on Market Way. When the octagonal-shaped pub opened in July 1971 the owners, Tetley, had changed their minds about the name and it was now called the **Keystone**. The ground floor was decorated in 'Roaring Twenties' style and Keystone Cops films were to be shown to the accompaniment of silent film chase music. A spiral staircase connected with the first floor, which was fitted out as a discotheque. The first licensee was Albert West, who had previously run the Albert on West Dixon Street and the Kings Arms on Whit Lane.

The Keystone was refurbished in 1984 with a 1940s decor and more alterations were made in 1988. It was bought by Burtonwood Brewery in 1992, but closed two years later and was demolished in September 1998.

The **Kettledrum** was opened by Bass North West on Heywood Way in December 1974. The pub was shaped like a drum, with bars on the first floor and the cellar and living accommodation on the ground floor. The first licensee was Fred Cullen, who had previously had the Buck on Cross Lane. The building was demolished in 1999.

The **Brass Handles**, Edgehill Close, was built by Whitbread and opened in 1975. The pub is still there in 2003.

The **Winston** was opened by Holts Brewery on Churchill Way in 1977. There was a change of ownership in 1998 and the pub is still going in 2003.

The Woodman, Belvedere Road, in 1972

Ford Lane to Whit Lane

Today's Ford Lane is a short stretch of road from Broad Street to Broughton Road, one side of the triangle enclosing the grounds around Pendleton Church. Two hundred years ago the lane went all the way down to the Irwell, where there was a ford across the river to Lower Broughton Road. The line of the lane today is approximately along Broughton Road from the Maypole, turning right towards Frederick Road, then left in the area of Seaford Road and right to the ford, which was about 75 yards south of Cromwell Bridge.

Just beyond where Ford Lane/Broughton Road turned to the right, Whit Lane went off to the left, through Charlestown and along the Irwell valley towards Agecroft.

The 1848 map shows this area when it was beginning to be built up. The canal and the Manchester to Bolton railway are shown passing under Ford Lane and some rows of houses had been built between the churchyard and the railway. On the north side of the line are Elkanah Armitage's New Pendleton Mills, a dyeworks and the first streets of Charlestown. There was little development along Ford Lane beyond that, but Whit Lane led to bleach works, chemical works, mills at Douglas Green and Pendleton Colliery.

Tracing the origins of some of the beerhouses in this part of Pendleton can be difficult. The people who

The Church, Ford Lane, in 1965

compiled the street lists for the Manchester and Salford directories seem to have had a struggle to keep up with the developers in defining the new thoroughfares. A beershop with an address on Ford Lane one year could be listed on Broughton Road or Whit Lane the next.

Starting from Broad Street, the first pub on Ford Lane was, and still is, the **Church Inn**. The earliest directory listing for the pub comes from 1838, when the address was given as Broad Street. The Church opened as a fully licensed house and the first licensee, James Cooper, was also recorded as a commercial brewer. A wine and spirit merchant called Grayson Wroe took over about 1864 and Mrs Elizabeth Wroe was running the pub in the early part of the twentieth century.

The Church was acquired by Wilsons Brewery in 1893, becoming one of the company's first tied houses in Pendleton. Elizabeth Wroe was followed by James Cooper Wroe in the 1920s and 1930s, and later tenants included Elsie and Harry Taylor in the 1940s and 1950s. Today the Church is a busy pub selling Holts beers.

Broughton Road

The 1848 map shows that the top of Ford Lane near the Church Inn was narrow compared with the road on the other side of St Thomas's churchyard. Only a few buildings are shown on this part of the lane, whilst at the top of what became Broughton Road there was Rose Villa, the residence of Elkanah Armitage, some gardens and other property. A bit further along, opposite St Thomas's Church School at the northern end of the churchyard, was the site of the Unicorn Inn.

The first lease on the site was taken out in 1836, but the beerhouse was not licensed until the 1860s. Joseph Embley was the earliest recorded tenant and he was there for about ten years from 1869. Like the Church Inn, the Unicorn had some long-serving licensees. James Broughton was there for thirty years from about 1904 and Chris Broughton, who took over at the time of the Second World War, was still in charge in the 1960s.

The Unicorn, Broughton Road, in the 1970s

The Unicorn was owned by Groves & Whitnall by the 1890s and it became a Greenall Whitley house in the 1960s. The brewery sold the pub in the early 1990s and, like the Church Inn, it is still in business today.

On the corner across Albion Street (renamed Aden Street in the 1960s and now called Agnew Place) from the Unicorn there was another beerhouse which also seems to have opened in the 1860s. This was the **Cross Keys**, with John Pilling the licensee for about ten years from 1865. Next came Caroline Tomlinson, then in January 1881 the licence was transferred to William Barlow.

The Cross Keys closed a few years later, when the site was acquired by the Lancashire & Yorkshire Railway and Pendleton New Station was built between Albion Street and Gloucester Street.

An account of the Maypole Hotel appears in the section about Pendleton's pre-1830 pubs (see page 19). The next licensed house was just past the Maypole, on a site covered by the former Pendleton Co-op building. The 1848 map shows a row of houses with front gardens between the Maypole and Mill Lane. The building at the Mill Lane corner became the **Lin Mill Tavern**, a beerhouse first recorded in the 1850 directory, when James Chadwick was the tenant. Thomas Sanders, a cattle dealer as well as a beerseller, was there in the 1860s, then James Baker in the 1870s.

In September 1876 Mr Baker applied for a licence for a new public house on what was called the Strawberry New Road and Camp Street extension (later Frederick Road). The owners of the Lin Mill Tavern, Threlfalls Brewery, had arranged to purchase a plot of land from Sir Robert Gore Booth and the company wanted to built a £4,000 hotel there. The application was turned down and the Lin Mill Tavern survived for another ten years.

The last licensee was probably Isaac Worthington, who was listed at the beerhouse in the early 1880s. The Pendleton Co-op building opened on the site in 1887.

The **Railway Inn**, on the other side of Broughton Road/Ford Lane, is first mentioned in a report of a licence application in August 1859. The beer retailer was John Scott and he was applying for a licence to sell spirits to cater for people using Pendleton Station. Every day fifty-four trains stopped at the station and Mr Scott estimated that 3,000 passengers came and went. As proof of his good character, he said he had been employed by Elkanah Armitage as a

book-keeper for twelve years. His application was turned down and the Railway had to make do with a beer licence until the 1960s. Licensees after Mr Scott included William Hulland in the 1870s, James Parkinson in the 1880s and Thomas Walker in the 1890s.

The Railway became a Boddingtons house and the brewery's longest-serving tenant was Sam Moores, who had the licence from about 1904 until the 1930s. Sam had been a champion wrestler and he fitted out a gym at the Railway. Later tenants included Joseph Lynch in the 1940s-50s and Albert and Edith Wilson in the 1960s-70s. The pub was closed in the summer of 2003.

Further along from the Railway Inn and just past Lissadel Street, Broughton Road turned to the right, along the line of what is now Cumbria Walk. About two hundred yards from the turning was the **Wellington Inn**, on the right hand side and on the corner of Trentham Street. It opened in the 1850s and the 1858 directory lists Thomas Stanton as the beerseller. John Fish had taken over by 1859 and he turned up at the same brewster sessions as John Scott of the Railway Inn to apply for a licence to sell spirits. His application was also turned down and Mr Fish left.

William Whitby ran the Wellington until about 1870, then Ann Prestwich in the 1870s-80s. John Howell was in charge in the 1890s and he got into trouble with the licensing authority in 1892 when he turned a stable next to the house into a concert room without permission. He was told to rebuild the wall he had knocked down and then apply through the proper channels. By the August 1893 brewster sessions he had rebuilt the wall, so he was permitted to knock it down again.

The Wellington was acquired by Swales Brewery and they made some alterations for the comfort of their customers in 1911. The bar counter was turned round so that it wasn't between the fire and the people sitting in the room, and some screens were put up to keep the draught out of the room which opened on to the street. Licensees in the 1920s-30s included Joseph Baxter, Thomas Walmsley and Hannah Haslam. In the post-war years, Jane Bolland was there in the 1940s and Alice Lewis from the 1950s until Wellington closed about 1971.

Whit Lane

At the beginning of the twentieth century Pendleton New Mills covered an extensive area of land on the west side of Broughton Road/Whit Lane between Pendleton (Old) Station and Orchard Street. Fifty years earlier, only about a third of the site was taken up by mills and there were shops and houses next to the road. This was the likely location of three beerhouses which are listed at a variety of addresses in the directories. The names of the beerhouses are not recorded.

The first to be listed was tenanted by John Hardy, a beerseller on Whit Lane according to the 1834 directory. Later directories give his address as Charlestown, Ford Lane and Bank Buildings. He had the licence until about 1848, then subsequent directories list Martha, Mary, Margaret and Maria Hardy at Ford Lane and Whit Lane until 1865.

John Aldcroft is listed at Bank Buildings and Ford Lane in 1840-43. Two years earlier he was described as a 'navigator', so maybe he was employed on the canal which ran

Elephant & Castle, Whit Lane, in 1965

alongside the mills. The last tenant of this beerhouse seems to have been Dennis Hall in 1845.

The third beerhouse was tenanted by John Hulme, who is listed at Bank Buildings and then Ford Lane between 1841 and 1851.

The next Whit Lane beerhouse had a much longer history. The **Elephant and Castle** was on the left hand side, past Borough Street and just before the lane curved round to the left. (This section of Whit Lane is now part of Cromwell Road.) It opened in the 1840s and Samuel Heathcote is listed there as both a brewer and beer retailer from 1850 until 1871. An earlier tenant may have been John Green, who was a beerseller on this part of Whit Lane in 1843-45.

James Howarth was the licensee in the 1880s and 1890s and by then the beerhouse was owned by brewers Cardwell & Company. Wilsons Brewery took over in 1899, when the property was described as a beerhouse with brewery, stable and other outbuildings. The brewery was still in use in the 1880s, when it was being rented by a John Venables.

Wilsons later decorated the two-storey frontage with cream-coloured tiles, complete with their 1920s draughtboard trademark above the vault door. Their tenant from 1918 to the 1930s was Alice Trafford and she was followed by Herbert Smeeton until about 1950. One of the tenants in the 1950s, William Durrant, tried to get a music licence but his application was turned down. He said he wanted to

The Jubilee, Whit Lane, in 1973

employ a piano player and artistes, rather than have 'free and easys' with the customers, 'some of whom think they can play the piano but can't.'

The Elephant and Castle was run by Edward and Frances Tatler from the 1960s until the pub closed about 1973.

The next beerhouse was just beyond the Elephant and Castle, near where Whit Lane turned to the left. The **Cloggers Arms** seems to have opened in the 1850s and Thomas Evans was the licensee in 1858. The 1861 census lists Abraham Earnshaw, who as well as being a beerseller was an overlooker in a cotton factory. The last recorded

licensee of the Cloggers was George Roscoe and by 1873 the premises had become a cabinet maker's shop.

The **Jubilee Inn** was just round the corner from the Cloggers, on the end of a row of shops between Chapel Place and Chapel Street (later New Chapel Street). The beerhouse was originally called the **Druids Harp** and was first recorded in the 1860s. Thomas and Eliza Foster are listed there from 1865 until the 1880s. The name was changed to the Jubilee by a later licensee, probably at the time of Queen Victoria's Jubilee.

The beerhouse was acquired by Groves & Whitnall in the early twentieth century and for a time the company leased it to another brewer, J W Lees. The tenants until about 1930 were Samuel and Elizabeth Hindley and while they were there the Jubilee was extended into the shop next door and the ground floor frontage was given a covering of coloured tiles, with a cement rendered, black-and-white effect on the upper floor.

John and then Malcolm McFarland ran the Jubilee from the 1930s until the 1950s. Later tenants included Harold and Muriel Lever in the 1950s-60s and Sid Harrison in the 1970s. The building was demolished about the same time as the Elephant and Castle in the early 1970s. The site is now where Langley Road South runs off Cromwell Road.

Across Chapel Street from the shops next to the Jubilee was a short-lived beerhouse called the **New Kings Arms**. (The Kings Arms public house was just across Whit Lane - see page 18). Nathan Barnes was the beerseller according to the 1852 directory, then William Barnes from 1855 until it closed in 1863. In the October the

The Royal Oak, Whit Lane, in 1973

contents of the beerhouse, including tables, fast and loose seating and beer taps, were auctioned. There was also some brewing equipment - a seven-barrel capacity wrought iron boiler, cooler, mash tuns and 36, 18 and 9-gallon barrels. The premises were later used as a grocer's shop.

The **Royal Oak** on the corner of Williams Street, almost next door to the New Kings Arms, seems to have opened when Mr Barnes's beerhouse shut. The 1863 directory lists the building as a shop belonging to a smallware dealer called Abraham Collier. Two years later Mr Collier had embarked on a new career as a beerseller and he was still there in the 1870s. Noah Stringfellow was in charge around 1880, Joseph Pearson by 1890 and James Withington in the early 1900s.

The Royal Oak was later owned by the Rochdale & Manor Brewery and their tenant in the 1920s and 1930s was Ellen Morris. Richard Sheen was in charge in the 1940s, when Yorkshire brewers Sam Smiths took over the Royal Oak and other Rochdale & Manor houses in Salford. Tenants in the 1960s-70s included John and Clara Costello and Thomas and Eunice Capper. The pub, nicknamed 'Mad Mullers', was demolished along with others in the Charlestown area in the early 1970s.

The **Turf Tavern** had only a brief existence. It was on the east side, just past St George's Church and near Gerald Road. Robert and then Margaret Bentley were there in the late 1850s and John Booth, a dyer and beerseller, had the licence at the time of the 1861 census. The Turf Tavern seems to have closed soon after that.

The Clarence, Whit Lane, in 1973

Further down Whit Lane was the **Clarence Hotel** on the corner of Enys Street, opposite Gerald Road. This had its origins in a beerhouse which opened when there were still fields alongside the lane. The 1848 map shows a few streets in the Charlestown area, then the next buildings were about 200 yards along the lane: Whit Lane House, Whit Lane Cottage, Holland Cottage (where Holland Street was built) and a brewery opposite Suspension Road (later Gerald Road). Between 1834 and 1848 this brewery was run by Thomas Marriott. He had a retail beer licence and the beerhouse was called the **Whit Lane Tavern**.

The next beerseller was Stephen Roose, who was also a farmer with eight acres of land. He had the licence for over twenty years and during that time areas of farmland around Whit Lane were sold off for house building. St George's Church opened in the 1850s and the beerhouse was given a new name, the **Church Inn**. By the 1870s there were plans to pull down some of the old Whit Lane buildings so that Holland, Enys, Withycombe and other new streets could be laid out. Mr Roose's farm was still there - in September 1872 a boy was charged with stealing milk after being caught milking one of the cows into his mouth.

Four years later Thomas Lees was running the Church Inn and he applied to transfer the licence to another building. The application was turned down, but in July 1883 the transfer was allowed and a new beerhouse, the Clarence Hotel, opened on the corner of Enys Street. At the brewster sessions the following month there was another application, this time for a full licence for a hotel to be built on the site at a cost of between £3,000 and £4,000. The owner was John Davies, who also owned the Big Derby on Derby Street, and the licensee was John Pennington. It was refused, and so was a later application to transfer Benjamin Mawdsley's licence to the Clarence from the George the Fourth at Windsor Bridge, which was being pulled down for railway extensions.

At the brewster sessions in March 1886 it was stated that Mr Davies had so far spent £3,000 on the new building and proper stabling had been erected since the last application. The beer licence

The Britannia, Whit Lane, in 1973

was confirmed, then five months later a full licence was granted to Henry Raynor.

The Clarence became a Threlfalls house and their tenant from the 1890s until after the First World War was John Godbert. Later licensees included George White in the 1930s and 1940s, Leonard Brooks in the 1950s and Thomas and Barbara Harrison in the 1960s. The pub was demolished in the 1970s.

On the corner of Clegg Street and Whit Lane was the **Britannia**. This opened in the 1850s and Thomas Edwards was listed there from 1858 until the 1870s. A plan drawn at this time shows a four-room layout - tap room and sitting room on the left of the central lobby, parlour and kitchen on the right. The building was owned by Edmund Clegg.

Holts Brewery acquired the beerhouse in 1893 and their tenant for about twenty years was Abraham Roscoe, better known as 'Yeb'. Arthur Potts, who lived nearby in Britannia Street, recalled that Mr Roscoe was always well dressed, with fancy silk scarves, an overcoat with velvet lapels and brass studded clogs. He used to attend race meetings and was also a bowler, carrying his bowls in a distinctive velvet bag.

Frank Roscoe took over from 'Yeb' in the 1920s, then Agnes Roscoe from the 1940s. Mrs Roscoe's brother, Squire Scott, succeeded her about 1956 and the last landlady was Ellen Scott, whose husband was Squire Scott's nephew. The Britannia, still known as 'Yeb's', closed on 4th July 1974.

Irwell Castle, Whit Lane, in 1971

Fifty yards along from the Britannia stood the **Wellington Inn**, opened by James Hargreaves, who obtained a licence to sell beer at his corner shop in the 1860s. James and then Mary Billings were there in the 1880s-90s, then Joseph Greenhalgh in the early 1900s. The Wellington was on the end of a row of houses between Wellington Street and Franklin Street and the whole row was owned by brewers Walker & Homfray. By the 1920s the brewery had extended the beerhouse into the house next door.

Later licensees were Mary Getliffe in the 1920s, John Brownhill in the 1930s,

Arthur Blundell in the 1940s and Fred and Audrey Gould in the 1950s-60s, by which time the Wellington was a Wilsons house. John and Ada Phillips were there in the late 1960s and the pub closed when the area was being redeveloped in the early 1970s.

The **Irwell Castle** on the corner of Franklin Street was a plain, double-fronted brick building, first recorded as a beerhouse in the 1861 directory, when Thomas Foulkes was the tenant. It was advertised to let in December 1863, when prospective tenants were asked to apply to James Cooper at the Church Inn, Ford Lane. William and then John Blakeley were beersellers at the Irwell Castle in the 1870s and 1880s, then George and John Pope until the early twentieth century. By then the Irwell Castle belonged to the Worsley Brewery Company of Swinton. Enoch Pee was the tenant in 1910 and Arthur Potts recalled that when he was a boy he played the piano to accompany Mr Pee's son on the violin: 'Our classic was "For All Eternity"; we used to start together and finish together, although I couldn't say that of every piece. We used to get a round of applause from the customers.'

The Irwell Castle passed to Walkers Brewery in the 1920s and one of the longest serving licensees in this period was Albert Lewis, who was in charge from the 1930s to the 1950s. It became a Tetleys house in 1960 and their tenants in the mid-1960s were Frank and Nellie Marland. The pub closed in the early 1970s.

The 1861 census records George Hardman at a beerhouse called the **Live and Let Live** on the next corner, Indigo Street. A few years later Mr

The Wellington, Whit Lane, in 1961

Hardman began applying for a public house licence and by then it was known as the **Friendship Tavern**. He owned the building, which he claimed was one of the largest houses in the borough and at that time it contained a shop as well as the beerhouse. The licence was granted at the brewster sessions in September 1874 and the Friendship Tavern was renamed the **Albert Hotel**.

George Hardman was still there at the beginning of the twentieth century. Arthur Potts recalled that the Albert 'was the posh tavern because it had a full licence... It was the local pub for the Agecroft Rowing Club; I don't know whether you had to be baptised in their beer to become a member, but I know men who stuck to the one pub for forty years.'

In 1909 the Albert was bought by Holts and their first tenant was Arthur Darlington. The brewery refitted the interior and rendered the outside walls, complete with an advertisement for their ales, wines and spirits on the Indigo Street side. John Burns was the licensee in the 1920s-30s, Sydney Thornton in the 1930s-40s, and Ernest Hudson and Robert Riley in the 1950s. Tenants in the 1960s included William and Mary Sneyd and Thomas and Ruth Hignett.

The Albert, known as 'Tush's', was included in the Whit Lane compulsory purchase area and closed in 1973.

Holts' other pub on Whit Lane, the

Old House at Home, Whit Lane, about 1970

Old House at Home, is still there. It stands across from the site of the Albert and was opened as a beerhouse about 1854 by William Bond. Like George Hardman across the road, Mr Bond owned his beerhouse and he also wanted a licence to sell spirits. He made several applications at the brewster sessions, but none was successful. In August 1867 he said that his house was in the midst of dyeing and bleaching works, collieries and other industries employing a large number of workers. Many of these, owing to the damp and dangerous nature of their jobs, were frequently in need of brandy for inward or outward application. The magistrates evidently decided that George Hardman's house was the better place for poorly workers to have brandy applied and the Old House at Home remained a beerhouse until the 1960s.

Martha Bond and then Matthew Bond had the licence in the 1870s and tenants over the next twenty years included James Bamford and Samuel Shepherd in the 1880s and Henry Marshall in the 1890s. Holts Brewery bought the Old House at Home in 1899 and their tenant at the beginning of the twentieth century was Robert Williams. Enoch Williams was there until about 1930, then Elijah Hope took over. While he was there, in 1938, Holts obtained permission to build a new Old House at Home. The next licensee was Sydney Thornton, who took over in the 1940s after running the Albert across the road.

Jack and Irene Collier were at the Old House at Home in the 1960s, then Ged and Ellen Yates in the 1970s. Their first pub was another Old House at Home on Pimlot Street and after that closed for the Ellor Street redevelopment, they ran the Vine on Broad Street. They retired in 1984.

Langley Road South

When the new houses were being built, Whit Lane was replaced by Langley Road South and in 1977 Whitbread opened a new pub there called the **Lowry**. It was remodelled and decorated with Lowry prints by the Delamere Inns division of the company in 1986, but closed in 1991. The building is now St George's Church.

The Albert Hotel, Whit Lane, in 1973

Brindleheath and Charlestown

The 1848 map shows Brindleheath before the area became built up. Brindleheath Road winds down from where Ford Lane meets Broad Street, past the old St Thomas's Chapel, and ends at Duchy Farm. From the farm, there are paths through the fields up to Bolton Road and along the valley towards Pendleton Colliery. Some houses had been built at the top of the road near Broad Street, and Pendleton Mills, Sovereign Street and Wharf Street are shown behind the Maypole Inn on Ford Lane.

Lower down Brindleheath Road, there are buildings around Brierley Street and what became Laundry Street. Cock Robin Bridge crosses the Bolton & Bury Canal and the Bolton railway line, giving access to Whit Lane and the collieries, dyeworks and other works in the valley. The map also shows a dyeworks, a rope works and a brewery near Brindleheath Road. Most of the land was still open, with some areas marked off as gardens, nurseries and orchards.

The 1834 directory names three beer retailers in Brindleheath: Ralph Hobson, Robert Daniels and William Blinkhorn. Mr Hobson was listed as a gardener in the 1820s, then as a gardener and beer retailer, and in the 1840s he seems to have moved to a farm on Kersal Moor. Robert Daniels was a plumber by trade and the address of his beerhouse was given as Pollitts Buildings or Pollitts Row. A Mr Pollitt owned land near Cock Robin Bridge, so the beerhouse may have been on what became Laundry Street.

William Blinkhorn's beerhouse was on Brierley Street, on the corner of what later became Railway Street, and it acquired a name reflecting the occupation of many of the ladies in the locality - the **Washerwomans Arms**. George and Jane Hargreaves took over in the 1850s and at the 1859 brewster sessions George applied for a full licence. The house had been 'considerably enlarged to meet the growing requirements of the district.'

The magistrates pointed out that there was sometimes a little noise and quarrelling among the washerwomen of Brindleheath. One asked, 'Would their combative propensities be ameliorated by the facility to get gin?' And, 'If there is all this noise with beer, what would there be with gin?' Mr Hargreaves' attorney argued that it was dangerous for the women to drink too much beer in hot weather as it was 'apt to cause diarrhoea. A little brandy would act as as a preventative.' The application was turned down and so was an 1875 proposal to transfer the full licence of the Royal Veteran on Stanley Street, which was about to be pulled down, to the Washerwomans Arms.

Thomas Bumby and James Deller were licensees in the 1870s, followed by Samuel Ogden about 1880. During this period the beerhouse was owned by Hardy & Sons of the Ellesmere Brewery, Hulme, later Hardy's Crown Brewery.

The Washerwomans Arms closed in 1900 and the building was used as a shop until 1938. In that year the shop and adjoining houses were declared unfit for habitation and were pulled down under the Goodiers Buildings clearance order.

Directories for the 1840s list more beersellers in the Brindleheath area. A brewer called John Wood had a retail licence for premises in Woods Yard, which was next to Goodiers Buildings, and from 1843 William Brierley was listed at the **Blue Bell** on Sovereign Street. Mr Brierley seems to have been the only licensee. He was still there in the 1870s and the building was pulled down about 1879, along with other property in and around Sovereign Street. The site, near Pendleton Old Station, became a small recreation ground and from 1885 home to the Pendleton Pole.

Laundry Street

The name Laundry Street first appears in directories for the mid-1850s. Before then, Pollitts Row and Elizabeth Street are given as locations of beerhouses which seem to have been in the Laundry Street area. Robert and Sarah Daniels were listed at Pollitts Row, and James Brookes at Pollitts Row, Elizabeth Street and then Laundry Street.

The earliest a beerseller can be identified with a particular location on Laundry Street is 1855. Sarah Walker was listed at what became the **Rolling Mill Inn** from then until 1871. Later licensees included Joseph Atkin in the 1870s and Thomas Fowler and Peter Asprey in the 1880s.

Around this time, a considerable amount of property in the area was pulled down to make room for the Lancashire & Yorkshire company's new railway from Manchester to Hindley. The line was carried on a viaduct across Brindleheath and it went over Laundry Street next to the Rolling Mill. Railway building continued in the 1890s, when sidings were laid out on land behind Laundry Street and the remaining part of Duchy Farm disappeared. During this period and into the early 1900s, the beerhouse was run by Mary Ellen Cooper.

In 1914 the police reported that the Rolling Mill didn't have much trade and the licence was no longer needed. It closed the following year and the last licensee was John Walton; the owners were Walkers Brewery.

There were two beerhouses on the other side of the railway viaduct from the Rolling Mill, the Feathers and the Dyers Arms. Both can be traced back to 1858, but they may have been older. The **Feathers Inn**, on the corner of Radley Street, was kept by Richard Faulkner until about 1865. Edward Lowndes was there a few years later and in 1876 he tried, unsuccessfully, to

The Feathers, Laundry Street, in 1961

get a full licence for a public house to be built on a plot of land nearby, on the corner of Cobden Street and Villiers Street. He argued that a new pub was needed since Brindleheath's population was increasing and the railway company was considering extending its goods yard.

Margaret Lowndes took over from Edward in the 1880s and Richard Lowndes was there in the 1890s. Brewers Walker & Homfray became the owners and in 1904 the company made some alterations, extending the beerhouse into the adjoining house on Laundry Street. The original plan shows five small rooms: a corner vault and a parlour, and behind them a smoke room, sitting room and kitchen. The vault was enlarged by knocking through into the parlour and a new bar parlour was fitted out in the house next door. The tenant, George Mellor, got a new kitchen and improved plumbing.

Mr Mellor continued to run the Feathers until about 1920 and later licensees included Dorothy Mawdsley and Michael Fleming in the 1930s, Annie Hughes in the 1940s, Kathleen Exley in the 1950s and Walter and Olive Smith in the 1960s.

By 1960 the adjoining houses had been pulled down, but the Feathers survived for several more years. It was advertised for sale by the Grand Metropolitan group in 1987 (offers around £35,000) and closed a year or so after that.

The **Dyers Arms** was on the same side as the Feathers, near Cock Robin Bridge, and James Valentine was the licensee in 1858. A plan drawn about 1810 shows this area was 'Pollitt's Land', so the Dyers may have been one of the beerhouses listed earlier at Pollitts Row. John Valentine took over from James about 1870 and Thomas Howard was there from the 1880s.

Brewers Groves & Whitnall acquired the Dyers and the cottage next door in 1891 and Mr Howard continued as their tenant for another twenty years. At the brewster sessions in March 1916 the building was described as unsuitable and the sanitary arrangements were 'bad'. The Dyers closed the following year and the last licensee was Jessie Barnfield.

The **Perseverance Inn** was on the corner of Laundry Street and Brierley Street and was first listed in 1869, with Elizabeth Edwards the licensee. James Aldred was there in the 1870s, Hannah Trow in the 1880s and Patrick Casey about 1890.

The Perseverance became a Boddingtons house and the brewery's tenants in the early 1900s included

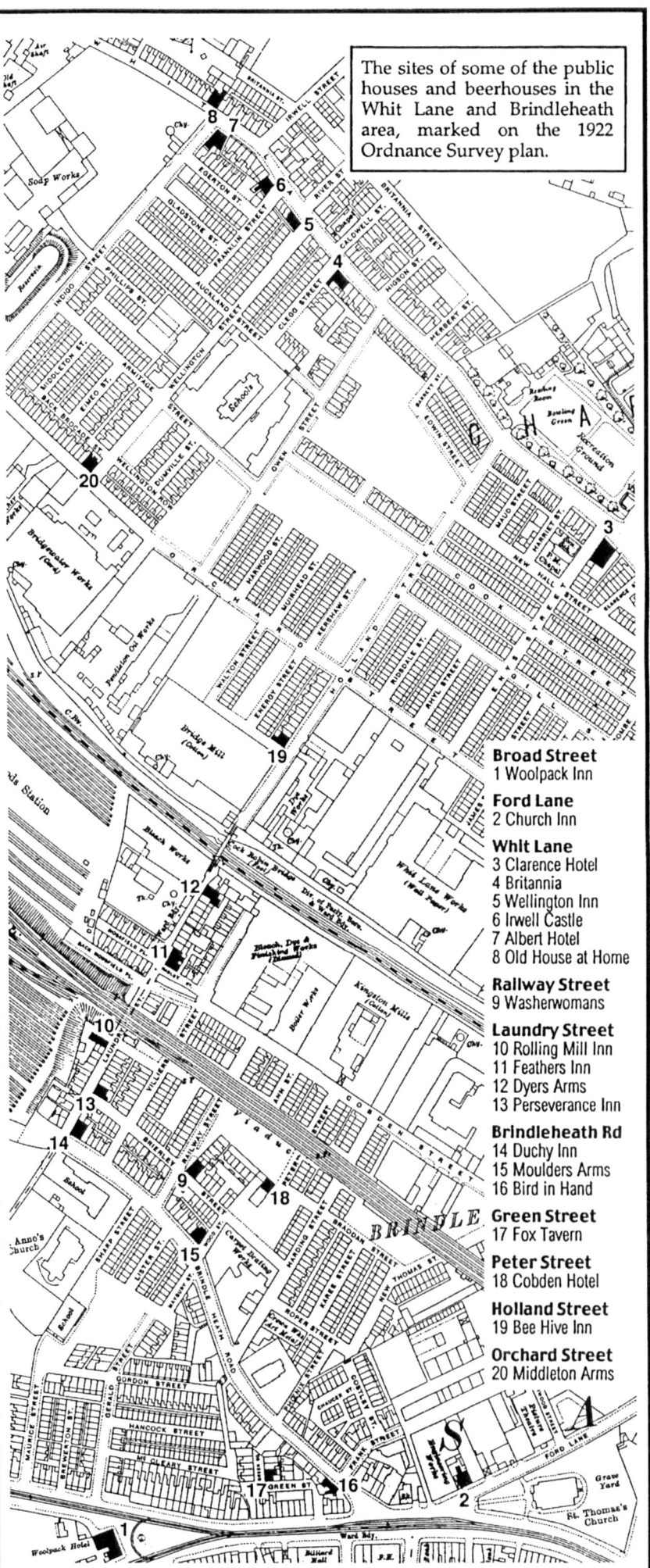

The sites of some of the public houses and beerhouses in the Whit Lane and Brindleheath area, marked on the 1922 Ordnance Survey plan.

Broad Street
1 Woolpack Inn

Ford Lane
2 Church Inn

Whit Lane
3 Clarence Hotel
4 Britannia
5 Wellington Inn
6 Irwell Castle
7 Albert Hotel
8 Old House at Home

Railway Street
9 Washerwomans

Laundry Street
10 Rolling Mill Inn
11 Feathers Inn
12 Dyers Arms
13 Perseverance Inn

Brindleheath Rd
14 Duchy Inn
15 Moulders Arms
16 Bird in Hand

Green Street
17 Fox Tavern

Peter Street
18 Cobden Hotel

Holland Street
19 Bee Hive Inn

Orchard Street
20 Middleton Arms

William Sheridan and William Blood. There was a move to close the beerhouse in 1912, but the magistrates decided to renew the licence, partly out of sympathy for the tenant. He was an old cab driver and there wasn't as much demand for that line of work as there once had been.

In 1915 the Perseverance was again on the closure list. The licensee, Frederick Arkwright, was in training with the army at Morecambe and Mrs Arkwright was running the business, selling about two barrels of beer a week. The magistrates were told that it would not be a particularly cheery message to send to the husband on active service that his living had gone, but they decided the Perseverance should close.

Brindleheath Road

The **Duchy Inn** on the corner of Laundry Street can be traced back to 1863, when Margaret Mercer had the licence. Before that, directories list a Samuel Mercer in Brindleheath, described variously as a laundryman, a carter, a coal dealer and as a beer retailer (in 1852), who might have been at the same premises.

Mrs Mercer was still running the Duchy in the 1870s, then about 1880 John Valentine took over. Robert Valentine lived with his family at the grocery shop next door and his son Jim was a well known Swinton rugby player. Jim became the licensee of the Duchy about 1890 and his younger brother Edward took over a few years later.

Brewers Groves & Whitnall owned the Duchy, the shop next door and two houses round the corner in Laundry Street and in 1904 they rebuilt the beerhouse and shop. Another Jim Valentine took over from Edward about 1930 and a few years after that the shop, latterly used as a hairdresser's, became part of the licensed premises. Later licensees included Daniel Crockett from the 1930s to the 1950s, Sid Harrison in the 1960s and Ronald and Ruth Plaister in the 1970s.

In 1971 the Duchy was excluded from the Brindleheath compulsory purchase area. It was later a free house and the building is still standing in 2003.

About a hundred yards up Brindleheath Road from the Duchy, the **Moulders Arms** was on the corner of Wood Street. Robert Atherton was the licensee for a few years from 1865, Charles Smith in the 1870s, Thomas Brundreth in the 1880s and Samuel Rudge in the 1890s.

In the early 1900s the Moulders was owned by the Manchester Brewery Company and their tenant was George

Booth. A plan of the building at this time shows the beerhouse had three rooms - a corner vault, a parlour and a kitchen on the Wood Street side. Improvements were made in 1906, when a separate lavatory was built for the customers. Two years later more changes were allowed after the brewery gave up the licence of the Cricketers on Fenney Street.

Local footballer Dai Davies took over at the Moulders after Mr Booth left, then when war began in 1914 Dai enlisted in the Salford Pals and the licence was transferred to John Hayes. Subsequent tenants included Albert Hestford in the 1920s and Frederick Stephens in the early 1930s.

At the brewster sessions in February 1937 the police reported that the Moulders had an average of only two customers, compared to seventeen or so in nearby pubs. Annual sales amounted to around 82 barrels and 670 dozen bottles of beer. The property was in sound condition, but the magistrates decided that the Moulders should close. The last licensee was Mary Getliffe. The building was still there in the 1960s, when it was being used as a carpenter's shop.

Near the top of Brindleheath Road, the **Ring o'Bells** was first licensed in 1862 and the tenant in 1870 was William Roberts. James Green was there in 1873 and two years later the beerhouse had a new name, the **Bird in Hand**. It was owned by a Mr George McWilliams of Cheetham.

Licensees over the next twenty years included Thomas Trow, William Dunn and James Bamford. By the early 1900s the Bird in Hand was owned by Kay's Atlas Brewery and the last tenant was

Joseph O'Brien. At the 1907 brewster sessions it was stated that Mr O'Brien usually had fewer than four customers and beer sales were about 100 barrels a year. The beerhouse was closed and demolished and in 1951 the Corporation bought the land from Kay's for the construction of an amenity garden.

Green Street

The 1848 map shows the land between the upper part of Brindleheath Road and Broad Street was called Pendleton Higher Green. There were two rows of houses called Cheshire View on the Broad Street side and behind them were some houses in what became Gordon Street. Within a few years these had been joined by houses in Gerald, McCleary, Green and other streets, completely covering Pendleton Higher Green.

The **Fox Tavern** opened on the corner of Green Street and Green Place and was kept by Isaac Matthews from about 1863 to the 1870s. Abraham Matthews had taken over by 1880 and another Isaac had the licence in 1890.

In 1905 the Fox and two cottages in Green Square were owned by the Empress Brewery and their tenant was William Richardson. The beerhouse closed in 1912, when draught beer sales were down to about a barrel and a half a week, and the brewery received £761 in compensation.

Peter Street

The earliest reference to the **Cobden Hotel** on Peter Street comes from a report of the brewster sessions in August 1868, when beerseller Squire Brierley had his application for a full

The Duchy, Brindleheath Road, in the 1970s

licence rejected. William Roscoe was there in the 1870s-80s and John Doyle in the 1890s.

In the early 1900s the Cobden was owned by Walkers Brewery and their tenant until about 1930 was Malachi Ryan. Christopher Garnett was there in the 1930s, George Walker in the 1940s and Peter Burden in the early 1950s. Wilf Nuttall took over about 1956 and ran the pub until it closed on 18th June 1972. For many months before it was pulled down, the double-fronted building was a prominent landmark in the Brindleheath demolition area.

Holland Street and Orchard Street

There were two beerhouses in the streets between the Bolton railway line and Whit Lane and one of them, the **Bee Hive Inn**, is still there. It probably opened in the 1870s, on the end of a row of houses on Holland Street, on the other side of Cock Robin Bridge from Laundry Street. Henry Chapman had the licence in 1881, Alice Chapman in the early 1900s and their son Albert was in charge about 1910. Brewers Groves & Whitnall became the owners in 1891.

Later tenants included George Hutchinson in the 1920s, Edward Valentine in the 1930s, Harriet Acton in the 1940s and Albert Coleridge in the 1950s. The Bee Hive became a Greenall Whitley pub and their tenants in the 1960s-70s were George and Doris Hinds.

Orchard Street crossed Holland Street at the other end of the Bee Hive row

The Cobden, Peter Street, in 1912

and the beerhouse here was the **Middleton Arms**, on the corner of Wellington Street. It was first recorded in 1869, when this part of Orchard Street was called Brocade Street and the licensee was Joseph Macarty. Emma Macarty took over about 1880 and Emma Baxter was listed as the licensee in the early 1900s.

The Middleton Arms was acquired by the Manor Brewery and later licensees included John Crook and finally Samuel Brown. It closed following the 1934 brewster sessions, when the building was described as structurally unsuitable and beer sales averaged 130 barrels a year. At the hearing, it was stated that the beerhouse had been in Mr Brown's family for forty-six years.

Charlestown

A plan of Pendleton in 1815 shows Charlestown after the first streets - Union Street and Back Union Street - had been laid out. Only five buildings are marked on the plan and one of these was the Kings Arms public house (see page 18), although it may not have been licensed at that time. The 1831 map shows more houses and another street, Pendleton Street.

The **Gardeners Arms** on the corner of Pendleton Street and Pump Street can be traced back to 1838, when James Markland was the licensee. Ann Markland was in charge by the 1860s, followed by their son, another James, and then James Dawson in the 1880s. The Marklands owned the lease on the property and in 1894 James sold it to Issott's Brewery of Ardwick.

The Charlestown area had been built up by then and part of Pendleton Street disappeared to make way for the construction of Cromwell Road. Hannah Hardman was the licensee in the early 1900s, when Wilsons Brewery acquired the leasehold. The company had a problem at the brewster sessions in 1908, when there was a complaint that the Gardeners was badly run. The licensee was John Fleming, who had been an electrician at Mather & Platt's for twenty years. The magistrates were sympathetic, but said he wasn't up to the job of looking after a beerhouse and had to go.

Later tenants included Horatio Nelson in 1910 and William Hampson in the

Gardeners Arms, Pendleton Street, in the 1950s

1920s. Wilsons bought the Gardeners in 1926 and the building was given a cement rendering, complete with the pub and brewery names and draughtboard 'Sign of Quality' trademark in relief. These features disappeared during another renovation about 1960.

William Soar, Harold Tucker and Albert Collins were licensees in the 1950s. John and Dorothy Shortman were there in the late 1960s and the last recorded tenants were Gordon and Margaret Watson. The Gardeners closed about 1973, when it was part of the Whit Lane compulsory purchase area.

The **Three Terriers** on Union Street probably opened in the 1860s and it was kept by Thomas Hutchinson in the 1870s and 1880s. Philip Stones was there in 1890 and Hannah Seddon in the early 1900s. By then the three-storey beerhouse was owned by Boddingtons Brewery.

Later licensees included Joseph Tomlinson from about 1910, John Hardman about 1930, William and Edith Ratcliffe in the 1940s, Thomas Langford in the 1950s and Wilfred and Veronica Roberts in the 1960s. The Three Terriers remained standing after most of the Union Street area was cleared and eventually closed about 1973.

There were three other beerhouses in this part of Pendleton. On the other side of Whit Lane from Pendleton Street and Union Street were New

Bird in Hand, Back Borough Street, in 1963

Chapel Street and Borough Street. The **Rose, Shamrock and Thistle** was on the end of a short row of houses in New Chapel Street and opened in the 1860s. Martha Fearnhead was the licensee until about 1875, when Richard Asten took over. Mr Asten was also the owner and the short street at the side of the beerhouse was called Asten Street.

James Bromlow had the licence in the 1880s-90s and James Roscoe in the early 1900s. By then the Rose, Shamrock and Thistle was owned by brewers Walker & Homfray, but it didn't have long to go and Mr Roscoe was the last tenant. In 1907 the licensing magistrates were told that there were two very small rooms and if there were ten people in there, it would be crowded. The beerhouse was in a back street off Whit Lane and on Saturday nights there tended to be only about six customers. It closed in 1908 and the brewery received £436 in compensation for the licence.

The **Bird in Hand** was in a nearby back street - Back Borough Street - but this beerhouse survived until more recent times. Sarah Travis may have been the first licensee and she was in charge for about twenty years from 1843. Richard Travis took over in the 1860s and he was still there in the 1890s.

The beerhouse was acquired by Cardwells Brewery and it passed to Wilsons with other Cardwells property in 1899. James Booth was their tenant in the early 1900s and George Lewis from the 1920s to the 1940s. Since the Bird in Hand was hidden away behind the houses and shops of Whit Lane, Wilsons provided a variation on their usual style of flat, against-the-wall signboard. A sign advertising 'Wilson's Ales & Stouts' was fitted above the door at an angle, so passers-by on Borough Street could see it was there.

Mary Kathleen Redford was the licensee after the Second World War

Three Terriers, Union Street, in 1973

and she was still there in the 1960s. The Bird in Hand closed about 1973 and the last recorded tenants were Ernest and Lilian Bedforth.

The **Borough Tavern** was on Borough Street, just a few yards from the Bird in Hand. It could easily be seen from the main thoroughfare of Broughton Road/Whit Lane, but it didn't last very long. James Higham was the licensee from about 1862 until 1867. In the December he opened a new beerhouse on Broad Street called the New Town Hall Hotel and the Borough Tavern seems to have closed. The building was a fried fish shop by 1880.

Littleton Road and Lower Kersal

From the early 1900s to the 1920s, brewers Groves & Whitnall tried to get permission to transfer the licence of the Bulls Head on Greengate to a new hotel near the football ground at the corner of Weaste Lane and Willows Road. In 1926-28 they turned their attention to another sporting venue, Castle Irwell racecourse. They had two sites on Littleton Road in mind, one not far from Littleton Bridge and the other at the corner of Mesnesfield Road, near Oaklands Road. The magistrates finally gave the go ahead for the new pub in February 1929, after the local brewery companies had got together to co-ordinate applications for new licences in the developing districts. Groves & Whitnall built the Racecourse Hotel and Threlfalls built the Weaste Hotel.

The **Racecourse Hotel** was built on the site near Littleton Bridge and the Bulls Head licence was transferred on 29th December 1930. The new hotel was 'one of the most palatial in Salford,' according to the Salford City Reporter. It was built in Tudor style, with oak beamed ceilings and panelled walls. There were guest rooms with hot and cold water laid on, and a bathroom for every three bedrooms. The licensee for about ten years was Nora Walker, who had previously been at the Salisbury on Trafford Road. Later licensees included Benjamin Casey in the 1940s-50s and Nigel Warren in the 1950s-60s.

Brewers Greenall Whitley became the owners and in 1984 they gave the pub a refit in 'country manor style'. It closed in the 1990s, then reopened under new ownership in 2002.

Further along Littleton Road, the **Kersal Cell** was operating as a pub in the 1980s. In 1989 it was acquired by the company which owned the Adelphi Riverside and reopened as **Byroms**. This closed in 1993.

The **Castle** on Cheadle Avenue, Lower Kersal, was opened by Greenall Whitley in the 1970s. It closed in 1994.

Brunswick and Lissadel Street

The 1848 map shows the area on the north side of Broad Street before most of the streets had been laid out. The Brunswick Chapel, Brunswick Place, Brunswick Terrace, Chester Place and other large houses faced Broad Street. Rose Villa, later the site of Pendleton Town Hall, was opposite Pendleton Church and down Ford Lane was the Priory, another large house in its own grounds. Bedlam Lane (later Strawberry Road) wound its way past Brunswick House and across the Bolton railway line and canal to Wallness. Most of the land on the north side of the canal - the site of Lissadel Street and its mills - was still open.

Gardner Street

Twenty years after the map was printed, rows of houses were being built on the land between Broad Street and Broughton Road, with factories alongside the railway and canal. Gardner Street ran northwards from Broad Street to connect with another new street, Gloucester Street, which covered part of the site of the Priory. In 1867 the **Priory Hotel** opened on the corner of the two streets.

The beerhouse and shop were advertised to let in January 1868 and in the August the licensee, Joseph Waterhouse, applied for a spirits licence. He told the magistrates that the area could do with a fully licensed house. The streets were now paved and

sewered and vacant land was rapidly being taken up for building. The application was turned down.

James Walwyn took over in 1869 and he ran the Priory until it closed. In the 1880s the Lancashire & Yorkshire Railway Company was building a new line through Pendleton and a station - Pendleton New - was planned for the east side of Broughton Road. To make room for this, property on Gardner Street had to be pulled down and the line of Gloucester Street altered. In August 1885 Mr Walwyn was refused permission to transfer his licence to a building on High Street. The Priory Hotel was pulled down, but he appealed against the decision at Quarter Sessions and got his transfer in 1886. The new station opened the following year.

Another Gardner Street beerhouse, the **Priory Arms**, opened on the corner of Higham View several years before the Priory Hotel. This was first listed in the directory for 1861, with John Buckley the licensee. Samuel Southern was there in the 1880s and the Robinson family - Elizabeth, Alfred and then Alice Jane - from the 1890s to the 1920s. Martha Finney ran the Priory from the 1930s to the 1950s and Arthur and Joan Seed were there in the 1960s.

In June 1979 the Priory was excluded from the Brunswick clearance area and a few months later the owners, Boddingtons, began work on modernising the pub and extending it into the house next door. The Priory is still there in 2003.

The Priory Arms, Gardner Street, in 1975

Strawberry Road

The **Bridge Inn** on the corner of Strawberry Road and Strawberry Bank opened in the 1860s and the earliest recorded licensee was Jane Miles in 1869. Thomas Makin was there in the 1870s, when the premises were enlarged by taking over the house next door to make a new taproom and living room. The property was then owned by a Mr John Rhodes of Oldham. Thomas Lambert, licensee of the Grove House on Ellor Street, was the owner in the 1890s and in 1898 he sold the Bridge Inn to John Henry Davies. Tenants in the 1880s-90s period included a builder called John Wilkinson and Frederick Burnett.

John Henry Davies was associated with Walker & Homfrays and the Manchester Brewery Company, but at some stage the Bridge Inn was acquired by Wilsons Brewery. In the first quarter of the twentieth century the licensees were James and then Hannah Bell. Harriet Jeffs was there in the 1930s and later licensees included Harry Boardman in the 1940s, Annie Grainger in the 1950s-60s and William and Henrietta Lundy in the 1960s-70s.

The Bridge was sold to a pub company in 1989 and it closed in 1996.

Lissadel Street

Five beerhouses were recorded on Lissadel Street in the 1850s, four of them on the north side and one, the **Dog Inn**, on the south. John Seal, a brickmaker and beerseller, was listed there in 1858-63, and John Williams in 1865. The Dog was pulled down to make way for one of the mills that were built between Lissadel Street and the canal.

On the north side, the **Farmers Arms** was on the corner of Bird Street. Richard Hardy was the beerseller in

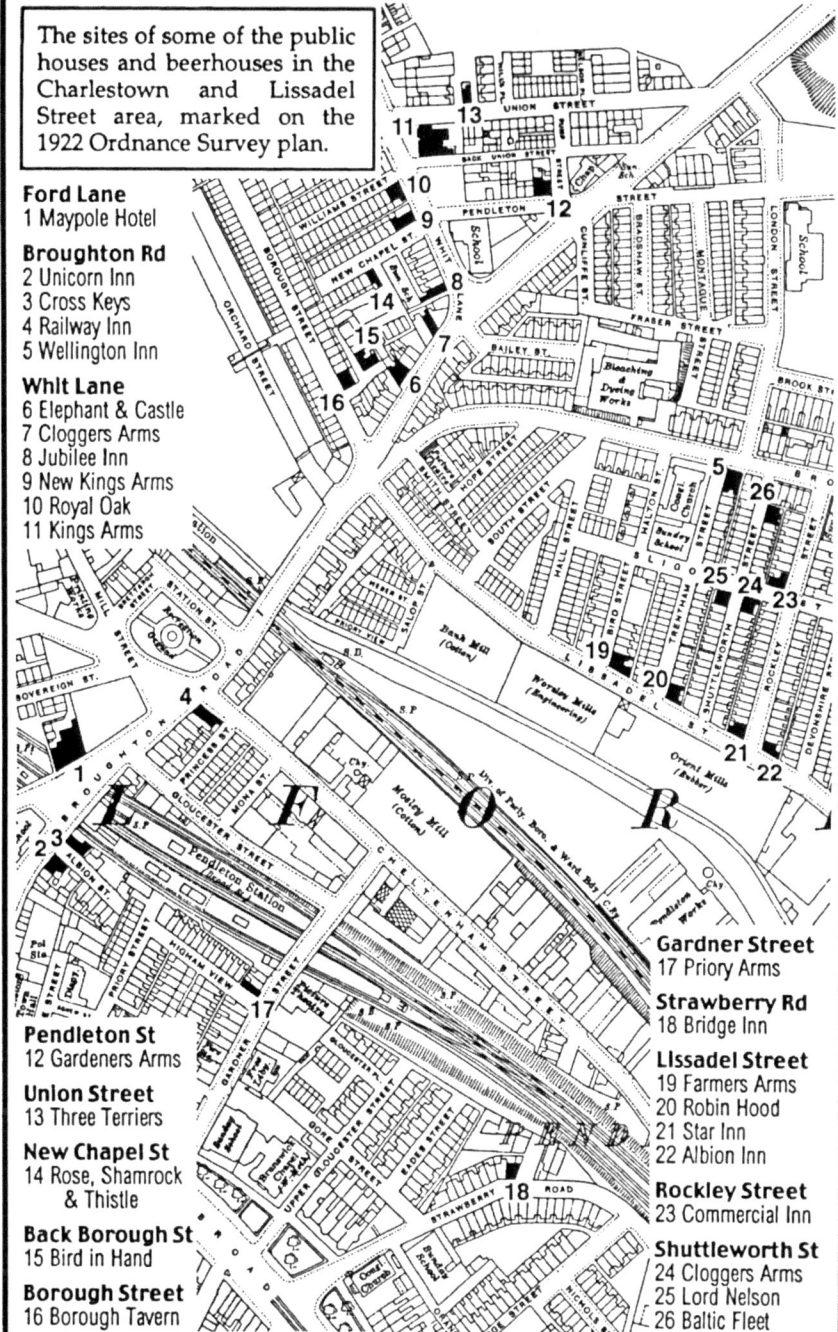

The sites of some of the public houses and beerhouses in the Charlestown and Lissadel Street area, marked on the 1922 Ordnance Survey plan.

Ford Lane
1 Maypole Hotel

Broughton Rd
2 Unicorn Inn
3 Cross Keys
4 Railway Inn
5 Wellington Inn

Whit Lane
6 Elephant & Castle
7 Cloggers Arms
8 Jubilee Inn
9 New Kings Arms
10 Royal Oak
11 Kings Arms

Pendleton St
12 Gardeners Arms

Union Street
13 Three Terriers

New Chapel St
14 Rose, Shamrock & Thistle

Back Borough St
15 Bird in Hand

Borough Street
16 Borough Tavern

Gardner Street
17 Priory Arms

Strawberry Rd
18 Bridge Inn

Lissadel Street
19 Farmers Arms
20 Robin Hood
21 Star Inn
22 Albion Inn

Rockley Street
23 Commercial Inn

Shuttleworth St
24 Cloggers Arms
25 Lord Nelson
26 Baltic Fleet

Lord Nelson, Shuttleworth Street, about 1915

1855, Thomas and Mary Ann Charlton in the 1860s, James Harris in the 1870s and John Armitt in the 1880s.

By the time Sarah Armitt took over from her husband about 1890, the Farmers was owned by the Swinton Brewery Company. It passed to the Worsley Brewery Company in 1897 and their tenant in the early 1900s was John Lewis. The last licensee was James Stott and the beerhouse closed in 1910, following a police report which stated that it was no longer needed as there were usually only about four customers in the place.

The next beerhouse along Lissadel Street was the **Railway Tavern** on the corner of Trentham Street. Joseph Hadfield was listed there from 1858 to 1865 and Thomas and Mary Bromley until about 1870. Robert Boardman was in charge in 1873 and by then the beerhouse had a new name, the **Robin Hood**. Henry Caton had the licence in the 1880s and William Hope about 1890.

Brewers Walker & Homfray had acquired the beerhouse and the house next door on Trentham Street by the early 1900s, when Charles Schneider was the licensee. A few years later Martin Gatley took over. He was a former Salford policeman who had held a licence in South Africa for a time. At the 1909 brewster sessions the magistrates were told that the Robin Hood, like the nearby Farmers Arms, didn't have many customers, but they decided to renew Mr Gatley's licence.

Mary Jane Pearson ran the Robin Hood from the time of the First World War until the beerhouse closed in 1929. At that year's brewster sessions the Corporation buildings inspector said the lavatories were inadequate and customers had to go through the kitchen and scullery to get to the yard. Mrs Pearson was selling three or four barrels of beer a week, which wasn't bad for a small house, but it had the poorest trade for the area and there were sixteen other licences within 300 yards.

The 1855 directory lists Thomas Lord and Samuel Martinscroft as beer retailers on Lissadel Street, but doesn't

The Star, Lissadel Street, in the 1960s

give precise addresses. However, one of them was probably at the **Star Inn** on the corner of Rockley Street, which was advertised to let in July 1855.

John Edwards, a shoemaker, had taken over by 1858 and he was there for about six years. Subsequent licensees included Thomas Cordwell in the 1870s, Cornthwaite Barlow in the 1880s and Joseph Parkinson in the 1890s. The Star was purchased by Chesters Brewery in 1903 and their tenant until about 1920 was Samuel Knight. James Clarkson and Joseph Allen were there in the 1930s, Robert Butler in the 1940s, Clarence Townsend in the 1950s and Alfred and Joan Smith in the 1960s. The Star closed about 1965.

Across from the Star, on the other corner of Rockley Street, there was a beerhouse called the **Puddlers Arms**. Joseph Johnson was listed there in 1858 and Christopher McConnell in the 1860s, when it was known as the **Foresters Arms**. When Richard Horrocks was in charge, from the 1870s to the 1890s, there was a final change of name to the **Albion Inn**.

Wilsons Brewery were the owners at the beginning of the twentieth century and their tenant in 1905 was Frank Walsh. At the 1910 brewster sessions the brewery reported annual sales of 177 barrels of beer, plus another ten barrels in bottle trade, but the police complained that the licensee, Annie Howard, had a reputation for doing the 'long pull'. They wanted the Albion closed as it was no longer needed in the neighbourhood. They got their way and the beerhouse shut the following year.

Rockley Street

The **Commercial Inn** was about eighty yards along Rockley Street from the Star and the Albion, on the corner of Sligo Street. It opened in the 1850s and the earliest licensee who can be

Baltic Fleet, Shuttleworth Street, about 1930

identified with the beerhouse was Horatio Nelson, who was listed there from 1861 to 1877. Robert Walker was there in the 1880s, Elizabeth Wills about 1890 and Thomas Jones in 1905.

In 1911 John Henry Lees of the Moss Side Brewery had a three-year lease on the Commercial and the tenant was Bridget Wickman. At the brewster sessions, the police reported that trade was declining and weekly beer sales amounted to only a barrel and a half. Mrs Wickman agreed, saying that the Commercial used to be a free house and now that it was tied to a brewer, the beer was 'all legs and no body!'

Mrs Wickman moved out at the end of February, leaving the house unoccupied. It reopened in June and four months later J H Lees reported an increase in sales, but this didn't convince the magistrates and the Commercial closed in 1912. The last licensee was William Walton.

Shuttleworth Street

The houses on Shuttleworth Street were completed in the early 1850s and three beerhouses opened. John Smith was listed at the **Cloggers Arms** on the corner of Sligo Street in 1858. Duncan McIntyre had taken over by 1861 and David Ditchfield was there from 1863 to 1869. The licence was given up about 1870 and the premises became a shop.

The **Lord Nelson** was across from the Cloggers on another corner of Sligo Street. Thomas Cookson, beer retailer and provision dealer, was there from 1858 to about 1870 and Richard Lees from the 1870s to the 1890s.

There was a move to close the Lord Nelson in 1908, when it was being run by Mr Lees' son-in-law, Edwin Peat. The beerhouse was owned by Kay's Atlas Brewery and selling about three barrels of beer a week, which was more than several other beerhouses on the closure list that year, so the licence was renewed.

Later licensees included James Acton in the 1920s and Mary Rushton in the 1930s, by which time the Lord Nelson was owned by Robinsons Brewery of Stockport. Elizabeth Brittain was their tenant in the 1940s-50s. Wilfred and Vera Marrs took over in the early 1960s and Frederick and Alice Thomas were there for a few years until the beerhouse closed in 1969.

The **Baltic Fleet** was near the Broughton Road end of Shuttleworth Street and opened in 1852. The earliest recorded licensee was Henry Brookes, who ran the beerhouse from the 1850s to about 1863. James Dunn and then James Ryan were there in the 1860s-80s and Timothy McDonald about 1890.

The beerhouse and two adjoining cottages were acquired by the Empress Brewery and licensees in the first quarter of the twentieth century included Charlotte Kirkwood, John Hardisty and Elizabeth Dutton. Walkers Brewery took over the Empress pubs and beerhouses in 1929 and their tenants at the Baltic Fleet included John and Louie Pollitt in the 1930s, Bessie Willetts in the 1940s and Violet Brunt in the 1950s. The licensee from the 1960s until it closed in 1971 was Richard Foster.

The Height

The oldest pubs at Irlams o'th'Height, the Pack Horse and the Waggon and Horses, are included in the account of Pendleton's first licensed houses on pages 14-15. By the second half of the nineteenth century these two had been joined by five beerhouses.

Going up the road from Pendleton Church, the first licensed house is the **Red Lion**. The original beerhouse was one of three old cottages and the tenant about 1860 was Elijah Kay. It may well have opened much earlier than this, but there are problems with identifying licensees of some of the Height beerhouses, because directory compilers in the 1850s-60s tended go out only as far as Acresfield Road.

Mary Kay became the licensee after her husband died, then in the 1880s her son, Joseph Proctor, took over. The property was acquired by Holts Brewery, who no doubt wanted eventually to replace the old beerhouse with a modern pub. In August 1900 the licensing magistrates expressed concern about the possibility of illegal trading. Twenty cottages shared a yard at the back, and since the Red Lion's kitchen and wash-house windows opened to the yard, the local residents could get their beer without being seen from the road.

This situation was resolved in a dramatic way a few months later. On 26th December there was a fire at the Red Lion. It was put out by the Pendleton Fire Brigade, who rescued Mr Proctor and his family from a bedroom window. Two downstairs and one upstairs room were affected by the blaze and the damage to furniture and the building was estimated at £200.

A few days later Edward Holt was given permission to demolish the beerhouse and the two adjoining cottages, which by then were in a dilapidated condition, and build a new Red Lion. One of the magistrates commented, jokingly, that the fire was a rather convenient one for Mr Holt.

Alice Proctor took over for a few years after her husband's death, then in the 1920s Charles Broadhurst was in charge. The Red Lion became fully licensed in 1926, when the brewery was allowed to transfer the spirits licence from the Boat House on Oldfield Road.

Later licensees included William Smith from the 1930s to the 1950s, and Herbert and Irene Jackson in the 1960s-70s. The Red Lion is still a Holts pub and still going strong in 2003.

The **Three Pigeons** was about twenty yards from the Red Lion, on the corner

The Red Lion, Bolton Road, in 1994

of Irlam Square. Moses Yates was the beerseller from the 1860s to the 1880s and Peter Brookes about 1890. The beerhouse was leased by brewer Edward Issott in the 1890s and the lease was taken over by Wilsons Brewery in 1903.

Two years later Wilsons obtained a new ten-year lease on the property. They paid the owners £65 a year and were responsible for the rates and doing any repairs. Plans to make some improvements were drawn up but not carried out, since the Three Pigeons was on the list of beerhouses being considered for closure in 1907. The licensee, James Greenwood, admitted that he wasn't selling much beer and said that his predecessor had got trade by drawing teeth free. The beerhouse closed in 1908 and Wilsons received about £1,500 compensation for the licence.

The next Bolton Road beerhouse was in a row of cottages next to Irlams Square. The 1838 directory lists James Williamson as a shopkeeper at the Height, then five years later he was at the **Swan Inn**. This was probably the beerhouse later known as the **White Swan**.

Thomas Kennedy, beer retailer and shopkeeper, was at the White Swan from about 1845. Elizabeth Kennedy took over after her husband's death, then in 1866 she married John Singleton and he had the licence for a time. Elizabeth was widowed again about 1870 and continued to run the White Swan for several more years. Subsequent licensees included William

White Swan, Bolton Road, in 1956

Greenhalgh in 1880 and George Hindley in 1890.

The White Swan was acquired by Boddingtons and licensees in the first half of the twentieth century were Matilda, John, David and then Florence Barlow. The beerhouse was made up of two cottages combined and at some stage the brewery rebuilt the frontage and added a gable facing Bolton Road. This was decorated with a relief picture of a swan and the rest of the frontage was given a black-and-white 'Tudor' effect.

Walter Beswick became the tenant about 1950 and the last licensees, Louis and Nellie Bateman, took over about 1956. The White Swan closed in June 1970 and the building was pulled down to make way for new shops.

Further along Bolton Road is the **Wellington Inn**. The pub has its origins in a beerhouse that was part of a row dating from the beginning of the nineteenth century. In 1828 this property, described as cottages, loomshops and a schoolroom, was bought by Richard Dawson, the innkeeper at the nearby Waggon and Horses. The next owner was James Cooper in the 1860s and at that time the property was described as five cottages and a shop.

Within a few years the six properties had been altered to become two shops and a beerhouse. John Rothwell was the licensee in the 1860s and Richard Robinson in the early 1870s. The beerhouse and shops, plus three houses round the corner in King Street, were bought by Holts Brewery in 1874. Their tenant until the 1890s was Edward Probert.

Later licensees included James Sharples in the early 1900s, John Bradley in the 1920s, Charlotte Roscoe in the 1930s, William Barnes in the 1940s, Joe and Marjorie Booth in the 1950s-60s and Clifford and Bessie Brown in the 1970s. The Wellington was included in the Height Extension clearance area in 1966, but it survived a few more years. The beerhouse, the carpet shop next door, the confectioner's on the corner and the King Street property were pulled down and the new Wellington opened in 1973.

Three Pigeons, Bolton Road, in 1904

The **Dog and Partridge** on the other corner of King Street has its origins in a beerhouse which was kept by Isaac Aldcroft from the 1830s to the 1870s. Thomas Hampson was there from the 1870s to the 1890s. Like most of the other shops and beerhouses on Bolton Road, the Dog and Partridge was in old cottage property and in 1899 licensee Thomas Blackburn obtained permission to have the place rebuilt, probably on behalf of the Openshaw Brewery, who were certainly the owners a few years later.

George Probert was the licensee in the early 1900s and Edwin Dugmore in the 1920s-30s. Arthur McGhie took over in the 1940s and in February 1946 the brewery was given permission to make some alterations. The licensed room upstairs would be done away with and the downstairs rooms altered. The work, costing £6,000, would begin when building materials became available and the brewery promised that this would not conflict with post-war house building.

From the 1960s to the 1980s the Dog and Partridge was run by Alan and Doris Jolly. By then it was a Bass pub and in 1982 the company enlarged the premises by taking over the site of the shop next door.

Bank Lane

The Britannia Inn at the junction of Manchester Road and Bolton Road, Pendlebury, was demolished to make room for the Height roundabout in 1975. Two years later, on 7th December

The Osborne, Eccles New Road, in 1951

1977, Wilsons Brewery opened a new **Britannia** on Bank Lane. The first licensee was Alan Parsons. The hexagonal-shaped building was reached by a footbridge from Bank Lane, so the lounge and games room were on the upper floor and the living accommodation was downstairs. The pub closed in 1994.

In 1989 a building which used to belong to Langworthy Rugby Club became a private members' club called **Summervilles**. It operated as a Bass pub for a time and then closed about 1993.

Eccles New Road and Weaste

In 1868, the year after race meetings were first held at New Barns, Samuel Young opened a beerhouse on the corner of Eccles New Road and Cross Lane called the **Turf Tavern**. He applied for a full licence, but this was refused.

He tried again in the 1870s, when he had plans to take down the beerhouse and the butcher's shop next door and build a new hotel with several bedrooms, a six-horse stable and coach house. The nearest public house was the Railway Inn on Cross Lane, only 150 yards away, but the railway company was planning to pull this down and Mr Young suggested that his hotel would make a good replacement. The application was rejected and when eventually the Railway Inn was pulled down, it was replaced with the London & North Western Hotel.

Samuel Young finally got the go-ahead for his new hotel in August 1888, twenty years after he first started applying for the licence. By now the Ship Canal was under construction and the imposing three storey building on the corner of Cross Lane opened as the **Ship Hotel**. Mr Young may not have seen the completion of the work; by 1890 he was dead and his widow, Lydia, was running the business.

The property was now owned by Walker & Homfray, whose Woodside Brewery was nearby in Wilmslow Street. Harry Richardson, who had started with the company in the early 1900s and became the brewery foreman, recalled that sometimes when it was quiet in the yard, men would be

Ship Hotel, Eccles New Road, in 1951

given the job of rolling a hogshead of beer along Wilmslow Street and along Eccles New Road to the Ship.

The licensee from about 1906 was William Moreton and he advertised the Ship as 'the theatricals' house of call', because the Regent Theatre was next door on Cross Lane. At that time, entertainment at the pub was of the 'free and easy' variety, whereby customers got up and sang what they liked. Mr Moreton wasn't keen on this and wanted it better organised. He put in for a music licence so that he could pay a singer, but this was refused at first and for several years he had to put up with the musical selections of his clientele.

William Moreton was still there in 1930, when he advertised select concerts every night: 'Everything in good taste. Nothing offensive. Nothing vulgar or rowdy.' The Ship was 'The Winter Garden of Salford,' with 'Congenial company, pleasant surroundings.' Later licensees at the Ship included Tom Eatock and Bernard Fitzpatrick in the 1930s, William Johnston in the 1940s, George Hannay in the 1950s and Ronald and Marjorie Parkes in the 1960s. By then the Ship was a Wilsons pub. It closed in 1973 and the last licensee was Robert Twamley.

The Ship was next to a row of shops and at the other end of the row, on the corner of Adderley Street (formerly Strasburg Street and before that, Prospect Place) there was the Grove Inn beerhouse. This was first licensed in 1857 and was run by Richard and then Hannah Cassidy in the 1860s-70s.

The Grove, Eccles New Road, in the 1950s

Later licensees included William Johnstone in the 1880s and Thomas Hebblethwaite in the 1890s. By then the property was owned by Stopford's Brewery of West Gorton and in 1899 they extended into the adjoining cottage to make more living room for the licensee.

Edward Hallows ran the Grove from the early 1900s to about 1930 and while he was there the beerhouse was acquired by Walker & Homfray. William O'Donoghue had the licence in the 1930s and Elsie O'Donoghue in the 1940s, when there was another change of ownership. The next beerhouse along Eccles New Road was the Osborne Inn, next to Walker & Homfray's Brewery. The company thought it would be a good idea to acquire this property, as they could use part of the upper floor as an extension to their canteen. They approached the owners, Wilsons Brewery, and as a result Walker & Homfray got the Osborne and Wilsons took over the Grove. Since the Osborne was selling nineteen barrels of beer a week and the Grove only nine, Walker & Homfray handed over a £2,500 'cash adjustment'. Just two years later the two companies agreed on a merger and so Wilsons got the Osborne back.

Later tenants at the Grove included Thomas Smeeton in the 1950s, and James and Gladys Swift in the 1960s-70s. The building was scheduled for demolition in 1979 and closed about 1980.

The Osborne Inn opened on the corner of Wilmslow Street in the 1860s and Jane and Teresa Birkby were listed as the licensees in the early 1870s. In 1874 there was an attempt to turn the beerhouse into a fully licensed hotel. The Dog Inn on Chapel Street was about to be pulled down and the owners wanted to transfer the licence to the Osborne. The magistrates turned down the application, saying that three hotels had been licensed in the area (probably meaning the Waverley, Clowes and Regent) and that was enough.

The Waverley, Eccles New Road, in 1996

Frederick Jones was the beerseller at the Osborne in the 1880s and William Peake in the 1890s. By then the property was being leased by William Kay of the Britannia Brewery, Hulme, and Mr Peake advertised Kay's best milds and bitter, Bass and Guinness bottled ales and stouts.

In 1904 Wilsons Brewery acquired the Osborne and adjoining property and in 1910 applied to extend the beerhouse into the plumber's shop next door and take over the next house on Wilmslow Street. They said the living space for their tenant was cramped and customers had to go through the kitchen to get to the lavatory in the yard. The magistrates ruled out the extension into the shop, but allowed improvements to the private accommodation and the back yard.

Tenants in the first half of the twentieth century included Walter Nash, Charles Bradley, William and Josephine Cavanagh and Sidney Smeeton, who was there when Walker & Homfray acquired the Osborne in the deal which transferred the Grove Inn to Wilsons Brewery.

The Osborne was back in Wilsons ownership at the beginning of the 1950s, when the licensee was John Hobson. Clifford and Ella Stanley took over a few years later and were there until the 1960s. The brewery finally got permission to extend into the shop next door in 1961. The shop entrance became the main entrance to the pub

and the old corner door was bricked up.

In 1980 the Osborne and two derelict shops next door were the only buildings left standing near the corner of Eccles New Road and Cross Lane. The pub closed early in 1983 and the last licensee was Leslie McGowan.

In September 1874 Thomas Shepherd was granted a provisional full licence for premises under construction on the corner of Eccles New Road and Thurlow Street. The **Waverley Hotel** was completed and opened the following year. Mr Shepherd ran the hotel until about 1892, when he was advertising Threlfall's celebrated ales, Bass and Allsopp bitter, and Truman, Hanbury & Buxton stout on draught. There was 'every accommodation for travellers', good stabling and cyclists were welcome.

Threlfall's owned the pub and their tenants in the first half of the twentieth century included John Bradbury in the early 1900s, John Shorthouse in the 1920s, Herbert Henson in the 1930s, William Barlow in the 1940s and Frederick Webbon in the 1950s. The Waverley became a Whitbread pub and their tenants included Daniel Hanvey in the 1960s and Clifford & Myra Sheldon in the 1970s-80s. It eventually closed in 1995.

In the late 1860s Henry Bowden obtained a beerseller's licence for a house at the end of Nottingham Terrace, near the corner of Cemetery

Road. He called his beerhouse the **Royal Hotel** and began applying for a full licence. In August 1871 his solicitor explained to the magistrates that since the Royal was the nearest public house to Weaste Cemetery, it ought to be able to provide funeral parties with strong drink. As things were at present, ladies who fainted whilst attending funerals had to be carried 430 yards to the Swan Hotel on the corner of Weaste Lane in order to get a glass of brandy to revive them. The magistrates turned that application down, but Mr Bowden got his licence the following year and the reviving of widows with brandy at the Royal could begin.

In 1892 Thomas Nelson applied to build a bigger public house on the adjacent plot of land at the corner of Cemetery Road. Mr Nelson had owned the Royal for about ten years and his tenant, Sarah Jane Gaskell, was doing good business. The new hotel would have eleven bedrooms to accommodate commercial gentlemen and the old pub would be converted into shops. The plans were turned down and the land at the corner of Cemetery Road was put to use as a bowling green.

Applications to build a new Royal Hotel were made regularly in the early 1900s, when the pub was owned by Hardy's Crown Brewery. All were rejected, so in 1913 there was a less ambitious plan to alter the existing pub and make a smoke room in the adjoining house. Hardys wanted to

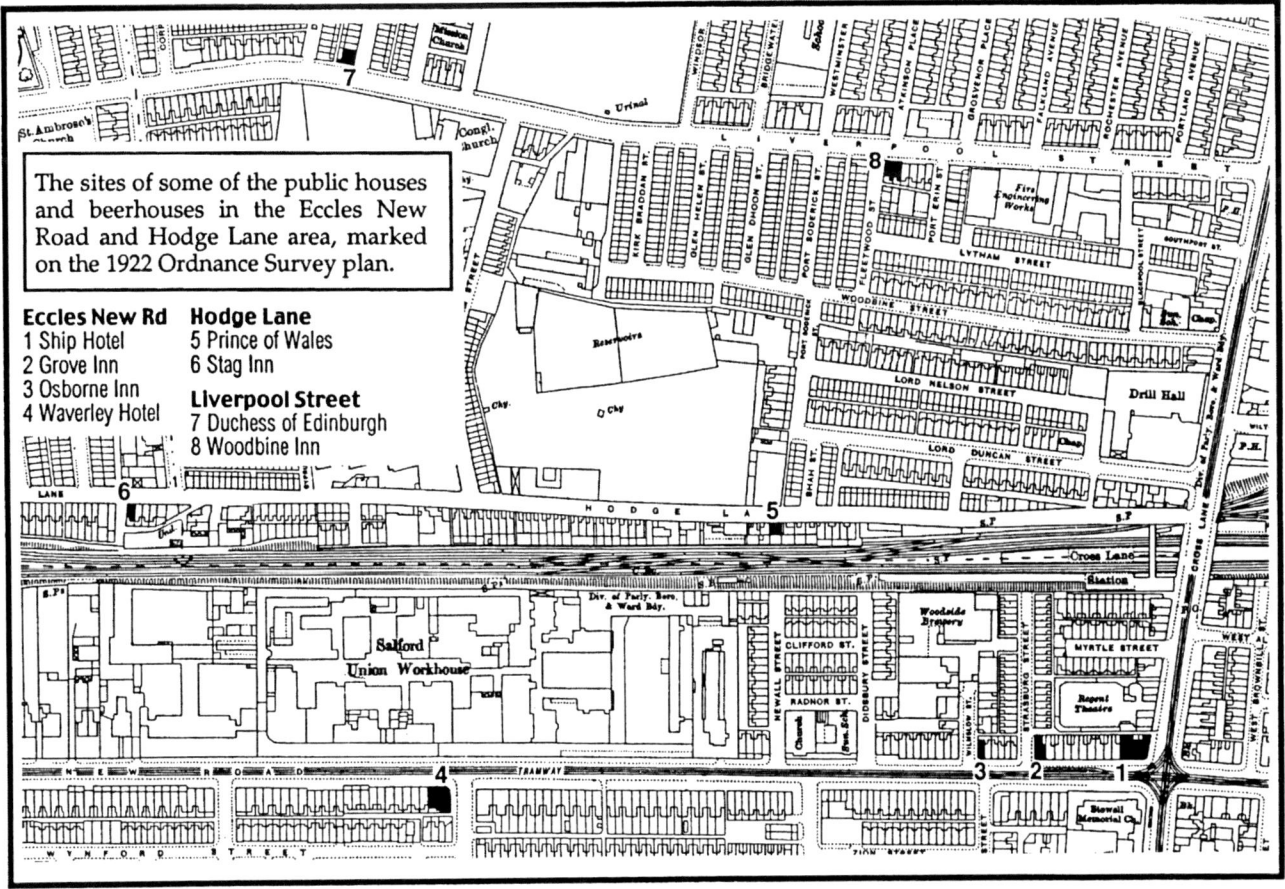

The sites of some of the public houses and beerhouses in the Eccles New Road and Hodge Lane area, marked on the 1922 Ordnance Survey plan.

Eccles New Rd
1 Ship Hotel
2 Grove Inn
3 Osborne Inn
4 Waverley Hotel

Hodge Lane
5 Prince of Wales
6 Stag Inn

Liverpool Street
7 Duchess of Edinburgh
8 Woodbine Inn

improve the accommodation for the licensee and his family and give their customers more elbow room. This plan, too, was rejected. They tried again in 1915, explaining that the Royal was a very busy pub, selling 24 barrels of beer a week, but they were up against the Vicar of Weaste, who was definitely against licensed premises near the cemetery.

Plans to relieve congestion in the vault and lobby were eventually passed in 1925. At the brewster sessions, the police stated that the lobby tended to get so packed that it was impossible to get through and there were only a few small private rooms for the tenant. The magistrates were against drinking in lobbies, so something had to be done. Licensees of the Royal since 1900 included James Yates, Thomas Baldwin, William Denson, Ernest Barnes and Arthur Bowden.

Hardy's Brewery finally got permission for a new pub in the late l930s. This was built on the site of the original building and part of the land at the corner of Cemetery Road. Tenants of the new Royal Hotel included Thomas Oates in the 1940s and Frank Fryer in the 1950s-60s. Gerald Johnson was the licensee in the 1980s, when Bass North West refurbished the building and enlarged the lounge area.

In the mid-1990s the pub was renamed the **Widows Rest**, a nickname since

The Grapes, Eccles New Road, in 1951

Victorian times. It closed in 1999 and the building was derelict in 2003.

The 1863 directory lists James Maychell as a householder at Beech Villas, a row of three houses on the north side of Eccles New Road. Two years later he had a beer licence and his house had become the **Cemetery Inn**. John Owen took over about 1876 and John Wainhouse about 1880. Mr Wainhouse was described as a retail wine and beer merchant, so he may have been responsible for the change of name to the **Grapes Inn**.

William Furniss had the licence in the mid-1880s and Ellen Holland about 1890. Five years later the Grapes, the two adjoining shops and houses in Weaste Avenue and Leopold Street at the back were bought by brewers Walker & Homfray. Herbert Buckler was the tenant in 1905, when the brewery was given permission to make alterations, on the condition that there would be no drinking allowed in the kitchen. The ground floor frontage was decorated in coloured tiles which were still in place, although painted over, seventy years later.

Hector Lithgow was the licensee at the time of the First World War, William Moreton in the 1920s and Jane Moreton in the 1930s-40s. The Grapes was acquired by Wilsons Brewery and their tenants included Patrick Brennan and Clifford Blay in the 1950s and David Ricketts in the 1960s. The last licensee was James Doughton ('Honest Jim'), who ran the Grapes until his death in 1979.

Beech Villas and most of the other houses and shops which lined Eccles New Road were built in the 1850s-70s. One exception was Gorton's Buildings, a development near the corner of Weaste Lane which is shown on the 1848 map. Beerseller James Birch was listed here from 1843 to 1871 and James Thorley a few years later. The beerhouse was at first called the **Oddfellows Arms**, then when Joseph and Sarah Willcock were there in the 1880s-90s it was the **Coach and Horses**.

The beerhouse was selling Wagstaffe's ales and stouts in the 1890s, then in the early 1900s it was owned by the

Coach & Horses, Eccles New Road, in 1974

Rochdale & Manor Brewery. Alice Butler was the licensee until about 1911, when Robert Mason took over.

In 1913 the brewery drew up plans to take down the Coach and Horses, the house next door and two cottages in Robinsons Buildings at the back, and build a new pub. The old house was said to be in a good state of repair and sales were good, averaging ten barrels of beer a week, but the building was too small. The domestic arrangements were so bad that Mr Mason had to go through the servants' sleeping quarters to get to his bedroom.

William Wilday was the first tenant of the new Coach and Horses and he was still there in 1962. There was a change of ownership in 1948, when Sam Smiths took over and the pub is still going today.

The **Grey Mare Inn** was the oldest of the Eccles New Road beerhouses. It was probably opened by Thomas Gorton, who was listed as a beerseller at Weaste Lane in 1838. From 1840 his address was given as Gorton's Buildings, Eccles New Road. James Gorton took over in the 1850s and he had the licence for about twenty years. Later licensees included Samuel and Sarah Allcock in the 1870s-80s and George Gerrard in the 1890s.

In 1898 brewers Groves & Whitnall bought the beerhouse, together with two shops and thirteen cottages. James Allen became their tenant in 1900, then John Thomas Allen took over in 1905. In 1912 Mr Allen was selling seventeen barrels of beer a week and the old beerhouse was described as a bit

Grey Mare, Eccles New Road, in the 1920s

cramped. The downstairs rooms consisted of a bar parlour and kitchen, which was used for drinking, a scullery and an outdoor department. The brewery drew up plans for alterations, which involved converting the shop next door into a parlour and the kitchen into a smoke room. They also wanted to enlarge the upstairs clubroom, improve the tenant's accommodation and provide better lavatories. To create more room, two of the cottages at the rear, which were practically condemned, would be demolished.

The licensing magistrates allowed the

brewery to go ahead with most of the improvements, apart from the extension into the shop. The beerhouse and the shop (a tobacconist's) were given a new frontage, decorated with columns of cream-coloured tiles and pediments above the first floor windows. The shop was eventually taken over and made part of the beerhouse in the 1930s and the pediments were removed during alterations at a later date.

When John Thomas Allen died in 1933 his daughter, Jessie Hampson, took over and she ran the Grey Mare until she retired in 1960. Later licensees included Alfred and May Rigby in the 1960s and George and Catherine Dunbavin in the 1970s. The Grey Mare became the subject of a compulsory purchase order, but this was withdrawn in 1977 after a campaign to save the pub. It is still going in 2003, now a free house.

Eccles New Road was completed in 1806 and its earliest public house, licensed in 1823, was the **Swan Inn**, also recorded as the **White Swan** and the **Swan with Two Necks**. It appears in licensing records under 'Pendlebury', as the land hereabouts was part of an estate called Pendlebury Detatched. This first Swan Inn was recalled as a small, whitewashed building, standing back from the road in Weaste Lane. The lane was a much older thoroughfare, which went from Eccles Old Road to a mill next to the Irwell at Mode Wheel.

The first alehousekeeper at the Swan was John Dixon. William Clay took over in 1828, James Andrews was there from the 1830s to the 1850s, Peter Jump in the 1860s and Walter Dowie in the

The Swan, Eccles New Road, in 1974

1870s. In 1872 the pub and two cottages in Weaste Lane were bought by Thomas Chesters, the founder of the Ardwick Brewery. Mr Chesters died a few months later and the running of the brewery passed to younger members of his family. They were responsible for rebuilding the Swan at the corner of Eccles New Road and Weaste Lane in the early 1880s.

John William Hicks, who had been employed in the brewery offices, became the licensee of the new pub and he ran it until his death in 1906. He was a well known local character and one of the more unusual attractions of the Swan was his collection of birds - canaries, bullfinches, linnets, lovebirds and a parrot - mentioned in a Salford Reporter article in 1891. There were over sixty of them and they were free to fly around the vault, perching on door and window frames, pictures and chandeliers. The birdsong was described as welcome and splendid music, which 'poured forth quite as loudly and sweetly as any feathered songsters of the forest.'

The brewery made some alterations at the Swan in 1908, when Robert Hall was the licensee. The layout of the ground floor rooms was altered and lavatories for customers were built in the yard. The gentlemen's urinal, reached by going out of the front door and along Eccles New Road, was demolished.

The Stag Inn, Hodge Lane

Later licensees included James Glover in the 1920s-30s, Albert Todd in the 1940s, Fred and Esther Hudson in the 1950s-60s, Stanley and Eileen Robinson in the 1960s and Dilys Dixon in the 1970s. The Swan became a Whitbread pub in the 1960s and by 1993 it was owned by Vaux Breweries. It closed three years later and was demolished to make way for the Metrolink line to Eccles.

In 1988 Banks's Brewery gave up the site of the Druids Home on Silk Street and, in exchange, the brewery obtained some land at the corner of Howard Street and Eccles New Road for a new pub. The **Stowell Spire** opened here in August 1988. It was closed at the end of 2001, then was reopened by a pub company in April 2002.

Duxbury Street

In August 1880 Henry Hargreaves, after serving in the Salford Borough Police for twenty-four years, obtained a licence for his house on the corner of Duxbury Street and Stowell Street. The following month his plans for converting the house into a beerhouse were accepted by the magistrates. These show a 'refreshment room' (vault) to the left of the front door, a parlour on the corner and next to that, on the Stowell Street side, a newsroom. He called the beerhouse the **Old Veteran Tavern** and he was still there in 1891, when brewers Groves & Whitnall were the owners. Licensees in the twentieth century included Charles Parkinson about 1910, Percy Telford in the 1920s-30s, Herbert Henson in the 1940s-50s and Robert and Lilian Gregory in the 1960s-70s.

By then the Old Veteran was a Greenall Whitley pub and it was included in the Bridson Street compulsory purchase area. However, with help from the Campaign for Real Ale, the brewery managed to save the building from demolition. The licensee at the time was Danny Grayson. It closed in 1984, then reopened in February 1986 after the brewery had rebuilt it, incorporating the two adjoining houses. The opening ceremony was performed by Manchester City manager Billy McNeill and the licensees were Mike and Pauline Morton.

Busy Pubs Ltd became the owners in 1997 and there was a change of name to the **Ugly Duckling**.

The Old Veteran, Duxbury Street, in 1977

Hodge Lane

Hodge Lane went from Cross Lane Station to Langworthy Road. Most of the houses between the lane and the railway were built in the 1840s-50s and someone who may have had a hand in the building work was William Brookes (or Brooks). He was listed as a bricklayer living on Hodge Lane in the 1830s, then also as a beerseller and shopkeeper in the 1840s.

The 1863 directory lists Edward Wilson as the licensee of the **Prince of Wales**, with Mr Brookes the bricklayer living next door. James Kemp was running the beerhouse in the 1870s and Elizabeth Rohan in the mid-1880s.

In October 1892 brewer Edward Issott acquired the leasehold from William Brookes (the former bricklayer or one of his relatives), then in 1903 it was taken over by Wilsons Brewery, along with Issott's other licensed houses.

The Prince of Wales closed in 1909, after the police objected to the renewal of the licence. The tenant, Thomas Casserley, had been holding whist drives for unemployed men. It was a form of gambling and so not allowed on licensed premises.

Further along Hodge Lane, the **Stag Inn** probably opened in the 1850s and the licensee in the 1860s was James Robinson. Sarah Stafford was there in 1870 and later tenants included John Grindrod in the 1880s and Thomas Wood in the 1890s-1900s. The beerhouse and the cottage next door were owned by brewers Groves & Whitnall.

Duchess of Edinburgh, Liverpool Street, in 1961

The tenant at the time of the First World War was Evan Thomas and he was followed by Martha Thomas, who had the licence in the 1920s-30s. James Stephenson was there in the 1940s-50s. The last recorded occupants were Alexander and Edith Davidson and the Stag closed in 1968.

Liverpool Street (west)

Two beerhouses opened on Liverpool Street between Cross Lane and Langworthy Road. The first was the **Duchess of Edinburgh** on the corner of Siever Street (renamed Birley Street). It probably opened in the late 1860s and Robert Handley was the licensee in the early 1870s. He transferred the licence to William Eaves in 1874 and three years later Mr Eaves tried and failed to get a full licence. Around this time the property was owned by Charles Mottram of the Sun Brewery on Ford Lane. Andrew Fisher was the tenant in the 1880s and John Clegg for about twenty years from 1890.

Brewers Walker & Homfray acquired the beerhouse, together with eleven houses in Birley Street. Later tenants included Edward McIntyre in the 1920s, James Farrar in the 1930s-40s and then Margaret Farrar until the 1960s. The Duchess of Edinburgh became a Wilsons house and their tenants until the pub closed about 1970 were George and Ellen Rawlinson.

At the brewster sessions in August 1887 magistrates sanctioned the transfer of the beer licence from the Strugglers Rest on Toft Street, Ordsall Lane, to the corner of Liverpool Street and Fleetwood Street. A house and an off-licence on the corner were rebuilt as the **Woodbine Inn**, which opened the following year. Joseph Hind was the licensee about 1890 and Frank Osborne in the early 1900s.

The Woodbine was owned by brewers Groves & Whitnall and subsequent tenants included Benjamin Whalley in the 1920s, Joseph Fell in the 1930s, Harold Kemp in the 1940s, Rachel Hyde in the 1950s and Albert and Jane Bramer in the 1960s. It closed about 1971.

The Woodbine, Liverpool Street, about 1970

Three new pubs have opened on this

part of Liverpool Street. The first was the **Mariner**, built for Wilsons Brewery (then part of the Watneys group) and opened in December 1976 by Harry and Jean Cole.

The brewery said they had a choice of three names (the Lowry and the Liner were the other two) and they chose the Mariner to go with the theme of the pub, which 'sets out to preserve the warmth and tradition long associated with Salford's seaport taverns of old. A colourful portrait of a pipe-smoking sea dog hangs over the door.'

The Mariner stayed in business until 2000 and the following year the building was acquired by the Corporation.

The name of Greenall Whitley's new pub on Liverpool Street, the **Brass Tally**, was selected from a shortlist which included Lala's Laughing Fox, Mark Addy, Ensign Ewart and November Handicap. The pub opened on the corner of Westerham Avenue in August 1978 and it closed in 1993.

Among the names considered for Joseph Holt's new pub on the corner of Ashley Street were the Chimney Pot Tavern, the Land o'Nod and the Alistair Cooke. The brewery settled for the **Ashley Brook** and it was opened in December 1990 by Gwen and Eric Whitworth.

Holts first applied to build on this site in 1924, when they had plans for a hotel costing between £6,000 and £7,000. They wanted to transfer the

licence from the Boat House on Oldfield Road, but after the plan was rejected they settled for a transfer of the Boat House licence to the Red Lion beerhouse on the Height.

Langworthy Road

At the brewster sessions in August 1897, Thomas Pike asked the magistrates to transfer the licence of the Barley Sheaf on Chapel Street to a new hotel that Threlfalls Brewery was intending to build on Langworthy Road and which he was going to run. Mr Pike was told the application was premature. The houses were still being built and anyway, people moved to Seedley to get away from areas overrun by public houses.

The following year the magistrates had a change of heart and agreed to the transfer. Threlfalls got on with the building and the **Langworthy Hotel** was completed and opened in 1900. Mr Pike left after a year or so and in 1908 William Moores came from the Veevers Arms Hotel in Blackpool to take over. Mr Moores advertised the Langworthy as the 'Finest house in the district, beautifully decorated, well ventilated' and with the best billiard room in the borough. There was a public telephone as well.

William Moores was at the Langworthy until the 1930s, Harold and Lily Bromley were there for a few years after that, then Arthur Bethell in the 1940s and Arthur Chesters in the 1950s. John Lamb took over in the 1960s and he was still there in 1985

when the owners, Whitbread, modernised the pub. It was fitted with plush upholstery and catering facilities were provided. The Langworthy lasted only a few more years and closed in October 1993.

Edward Avenue

In the early part of the twentieth century, five brewery companies tried to get the agreement of Salford's magistrates for a new public house in Weaste. Holts Brewery had two sites: one on Eccles New Road between Ariel Street and Falcon Street (for the proposed Falcon Hotel) and the other at the corner of Liverpool Street and Ashley Street (Dolphin Hotel). Groves & Whitnall had a site on the corner of Weaste Lane and Willows Road, Threlfalls on the corner of Weaste Lane and Liverpool Street (Weaste Hotel), Walker & Homfray on the corner of Eccles New Road and Langworthy Road (Central Hotel) and Kay's Atlas Brewery on Vere Street (De Vere Hotel).

For thirty years the planning applications for Weaste were opposed and rejected, then in the late 1920s the brewers agreed to co-ordinate their efforts to get licences in developing districts. As a result, Threlfalls made the only application for a site in Weaste in 1929 and this was accepted by the magistrates, despite strong opposition from local church leaders and the Salford Band of Hope and Temperance Union.

The brewery stated that 1,615 houses had been built within half a mile of their new site on Edward Avenue and that the **Weaste Hotel** would be a credit to the developing neighbourhood. It would cost between £11,000 and £12,000 to build and would have a club room for dinners, suppers and concerts on the first floor. On the floor above there would be seven bedrooms for visitors. To get the new licence, the brewery agreed to give up the licence of the Bulls Head on Hampson Street and seven off-licences in congested areas of the city.

The pub was completed the following year and the licensee until about 1938 was Arthur Robey. Later tenants included George Haslam in the 1940s, Lawrence Hartley in the 1950s, Arthur and Alice James in the 1950s-60s and Fred and Nellie Webbon in the 1960s-70s.

The building was renovated by Whitbread in 1984, when Alan Roberts was the licensee. It was done out in Victorian style with oak panels, dark wood fittings, leafy plants and coal-effect gas fires. The old club room upstairs was extended to cater for wedding receptions and parties. The Weaste Hotel is still going in 2003.

The Langworthy Hotel in 1973

Eccles Old Road

Salford's most westerly beerhouse was the **Thatched House** on Eccles Old Road. This old thatched cottage was at the corner of St Georges Crescent, near the Gilda Brook, the boundary between Pendleton and Eccles. It opened in the early 1830s, with Thomas Bradburn the licensee. Thomas Drinkwater was listed at a beerhouse at Gilda Brook in 1852, which was probably the same place, and Thomas Bradburn was listed there again three years later.

A drawing of the beerhouse which was made at a later date shows the name Alice Bradburn over the door and a note states that it was known as the 'Tate Hole'.

A later licensee was John Grundy Birchwood and when he died in 1871, Elizabeth Birchwood took over. The Thatched House closed three years later, when it was ruled that the building did not have a high enough rateable value to qualify for a licence.

In the mid-nineteenth century there was another beerhouse on Eccles Old Road. Between 1845 and 1855 Robert Chorley, beer retailer and shopkeeper, was listed on Broomhouse Lane, which was the old name for Eccles Old Road between Buile Hill and the Gilda Brook. The building was probably near Stott Lane but its name, if it had one, isn't known.

In 1973 Robinsons Brewery opened a new **White Horse** on the Pendleton side of the Gilda Brook. This was a replacement for the White Horse on the Eccles side of the border,

The Thatched House at Gilda Brook, sketched in the 1890s

demolished in 1969 for the building of the M602 motorway.

In 1978 Wilsons Brewery, then part of the Grand Metropolitan group, obtained planning consent to turn the Heath Mount Hotel at the corner of Eccles Old Road and Lancaster Road into a public house. The alterations were carried out by the Tudor Taverns subsidiary and the **Inn of Good Hope** opened in 1981. More recent changes resulted in a change of name to the **Hope**.

Lancaster Road

In 1935 Threlfalls Brewery offered Salford Corporation £1,000 for a plot of building land on Lancaster Road, on condition that they would be allowed to build a hotel there. The offer was accepted and the following January magistrates sanctioned the provisional removal of the licence of the Factory Tavern, George Street, to the new hotel.

The **Oakwood Hotel**, a Tudor-style building with oak framing and herringbone brickwork, was designed by Manchester architect Benjamin Waterhouse and opened in February 1938. The transfer of the Factory Tavern licence was confirmed and Threlfalls also gave up the licence of the Old House at Home, Regent Road, and off licences in Lord Byron Street and Holroyd Place.

As well as the vault, lounge, two smoke rooms and assembly room, the Oakwood featured a 'palm court'. This extended almost the entire length of the building, with a bay overlooking the garden. There was a licensed dining room upstairs and a bowling green. The first manager was Herbert Henson, who moved here from the Waverley on Eccles New Road.

Later licensees included Ernest Lee in the 1940s-50s and Joe and Peggy Dalton from the 1960s until they retired in 1981. Whitbreads Brewery became the owners in the 1960s and in 1969 they turned the bowling green into a car park.

In August 1981 the Oakwood reopened as a Beefeater Steakhouse. The interior was transformed: the vault disappeared and meals were served in the Yeoman Room. The pub lasted another twenty years and was demolished in July 2002.

The Heath Mount Hotel, later the Inn of Good Hope, in 1966

Street Index

This index includes streets, roads, lanes, courts, etc, associated with the licensed houses described in the three volumes of Salford Pubs. In most cases, the first page reference to a street is the main one.

Page numbers with the letter A refer to Salford Pubs Part One, B to Part Two and C to Part Three.

Adderley Street	C56		Bird Street	C51		Canal Street	B29
Adelphi Street	A78		Birley Street	C61		Canning Street	A57
Adelphi Terrace	A78		Birtles Square	A21		Cannon St	A70-A72,A26,A68
Aden Street	C40		Black Ditch	C29,C30		Canon Green Drive	A52
Agnew Place	C40		Blackburn Street	A72		Carter Street	A77,A76
Albert Street	C34,C33		Blackfriars Rd	A6,A7,A8,		Castle Street	B47
Albert Terrace	C28			A18,A25,A26,A47,A48,		Cathedral Approach	A2,A3
Albert Terrace, Hall St	C13			A50,A52,A53,A74		Catlow Street	B65
Albion Place	C27		Blackfriars St	A36,A7,A8,A9		Catteralls Buildings	B41
Albion Street	C13,C11		Bloom St	A59,A60,A14,A58		Cemetery Road	C57,C58
Albion St, Broughton Rd	C40		Blossom Street	A54,A55		Chadwick Street	B11,B44
Albion Way	B27,C11,C13		Bolton Rd	C53-C55,C15,C16		Chaney Street	C32,C33
Alexandra Street	B64		Bolton Street	A46,A16		Chapel Street	A2-A17,A64
Allen Street	C34		Bombay Street	A56,A57		Chapel Street, Broughton
Allendale Street	A69		Boond Street	A50,A22,A49			B74,B75
Allwood Street	B29,B30		Booth Street	A37,A9		Chapel Street, Pendleton
Alma Street	C34		Booth Street, Pendleton				C31,C32
Anderson Street	B32,B33			C28,C29,C18		Chapel Street, Whit La	C41
Andrew Street	B59		Bootle Street	C25		Charles Street	B15,B16
Ann Street	A73		Borough Street	C50		Charlotte Street	B74
Arlington Place	A71		Boundary Street	B15,B16		Cheadle Avenue	C50
Arlington Street			Bowling Green Pl	B29,B30		Church Place	A34
	A67-A69,A66,A71		Bramley Street	B68		Church Street	A64,A65
Armitage Street	B60		Brewer Court	B6		Church Street, Pendleton
Ashworth Street	B13		Brewery Street	A66,A65			C37,C16
Asten Street	C49		Bridgewater Street			Churchill Way	C38
Astley Street	C34			A29,A30,A24,A27,A33		Clare Street	B37
Back Arlington Street	A77		Brierley Street	C45,C46		Clarence Street	B67
Back Borough Street	C49		Briggs Street	A70		Clay Hall Gardens	C23
Back Cranbourne St	B40		Brighton Place	B40		Clegg Street	C43
Back Cross Street	A36		Brighton Street	B53		Cleggs Court	A6
Back Davies Street	A25		Brindleheath Road	C47		Cleminson St	A63,A64,A78
Back Frederick Street	A58		Broad Street			Cliburn Street	A74
Back Garden Street	A12			C19-C23,C16,C17,C18		Clifden Place	B73
Back Hampson Street	A51		Broadwalk	C38		Clifton Street	B45
Back Hope Street	B70		Broadway	B56		Clowes Street	A37,A10
Back Lane	B6,B18		Brocade Street	C48		Cobourg Street	A26
Back Park Street	B2		Broken Bank	A17,B34		Cockpit	A29
Back Richmond Row	A71		Brooks Street	A77		Coke Street	B75
Back Roman Road	B73		Broomhouse Lane	C63		Collier Street	A49,A50
Back Union Street	C18		Broster Street	A30		Comus Street	B25
Back Water Street	A7		Broughton Road			Congreve Street	C27
Bank Buildings	C40,C41			A23-A27,A18		Cook Street	A58,A11,A13
Bank Lane	C55		Broughton Rd, Pendleton			Coomassie Street	C35
Bank Parade	A16,A17			C39,C40		Cooper Street	B72
Bank Street	B75		Broughton Spout	B57		Cornet Street	B70
Barlows Buildings	B41		Broughton St	A52,A26,A47		Corporation Street	A75
Barlows Croft	A9,A10		Brown Street	A37,A38		Cottage Street	A57
Barlows Road	B41,B40		Brownbill Street	A76		Cottenham Lane	B64
Barnett Drive	A70		Browncross Street	A42,A43		Cow Lane	B33
Barrow Street	B3,B4,B2,B29		Browning Street	A62,A63		Cranbourne Street	B40,B41
Bedford Street	A30,A27		Browns Place	A49		Crescent	B34,B35
Bedlam La	C18		Brunswick St	A65,A63,A64		Crescent Parade	B34
Beech Villas	C58		Bull Street	A19		Cromwell Road	C41,C48
Bell Gates	A18,A19		Burgess Buildings	A52		Crookell Street	B43,B6,B24
Belvedere Road	C38		Bury New Road	B57,B73		Cross Court	A20
Bernard Street	C25		Bury Street	A53-A56		Cross Lane	C3-C10,C55
Bexley Square	A62,A63		Bury St, Pendleton	C33,C34		Cross Lane South	B54
Bexley Street	A62		Cable Street	A34,A35		Cross Street	A53,A58
Bigland Street	B42		Calder Street	B24		Cross St, Pendleton	C29,C22
Binns Street	C37		Camp Street	B69,B61		Crown Street	A55

Crowther St	B43,B44,B21		Ford Street	A63,A64
Cumbria Walk	C40		Ford View	B58
Dale Street	B63		Foster Street	B43
Dalton Terrace	B60		Foster St, Pendleton	C37
David Street	B43		Franklin St, Ordsall	B45
Davies Street	A30		Franklin St, Whit La	C43
Dawson Street	A20		Frederick St	A55,A56,A58
Deal Street	A57,A58,A11		Frederick St, Pendleton	C18
Dean Rd	A27,A28,A29,A30		Front Salford	A18
Dearmans Place	A37		Gallemore Street	B63
Derby Street	B44,B45,B51		Garden Lane
Derwent Street	B42			A50,A51,A24,A47,A54
Doddington St	B48,B25,B52		Garden Street	B63
Dorset Street	A26		Gardner Street	C50
Ducie Place	B40		Garnett St, Broughton	B74
Duke Street	B67		Garnett Street, Ordsall	B12
Duncan Street	B69		George Street	B2,B3
Durham Street	A30		Gilda Brook	C63
Duxbury Street	C60		Gills Court	A7
East Street	B37		Gladstone Terrace	B53
East Church Street	A34		Gloucester St	B45,B51,B53
East Market Street	A63		Gloucester St, Pendleton	C50
East Ordsall Lane	B7,B8		Goddard Street	C31
East Philip Street	A28		Gold Street	C32,C33
East Robert Street	A30,A29		Goodiers Lane	B50
East Stanley St	A30,A31,A25		Goodwin Street	C26
Eccles New Rd	C55-C60		Gore St	A44,A45,A14,A15
Eccles Old Rd	C63,C16		Gortons Buildings	C58,C59
Edge Place	A52,A53		Grafton Street	C34,C26
Edgehill Close	C38		Gravel Lane
Edward Avenue	C62			A34,A35,A20,A22
Edward Street	B65,B63,B64		Great Cheetham St East	B73
Eliza Street	B63		Great Cheetham St West	B58
Elizabeth St, Brindleheath			Great Clowes Street
	C45			B65-B67,B69
Elizabeth St, Ellor St	C27		Grecian Street	B69
Ellen Street	B42		Green Bank	A52,A18,A25
Ellesmere St	B48,B49,B53		Greenbank Terrace	A51
Ellor Street			Green Lane	A50
	C24-C28,C3,C6,C7,C37		Green Place	C47
Elton Court	A50		Green Square	C47
Elton Street	B64		Green Street	C47
Encombe Place	A77		Green Vale	A24
Enys Street	C42		Green Vale Street	A27
Errington View	B59		Greengate	A18-A27,A34
Essex Street	B17		Griffin Court	A15
Everard Street	B43,B12		Grove Place	B4
Every Street	A66,A67		Guy Fawkes Street	B54
Eveson Street	A60		Hall Street	C13
Factory Lane	B30		Halls Street	A74
Fairbrother Street	B13		Halstead Street	B75
Farrands Buildings	A22		Halton Bank	C16
Farrell Street	B65		Hampson Street
Fenney St	B70,B71,B72			B14,B15,B7,B29
Fleet Street	B30		Hankinson St	C23,C24,C20
Fleetwood Street	C61		Hardings Buildings	A35
Florin Street	C35,C28		Harrison St, Broughton
Ford La	A73,A74,A72			B59,B67
Ford La, Pendleton			Harrison St, Pendleton
	C39,C40,C41,C19			C34,C33
			Harrogate Street	C13
			Hattons Court	A4
			Hayfield Street	C37
			Heath Street	C31
			Henrietta Street	B46
			Heywood Way	C38
			High Holborn Terrace	A74
			High Street	C35
			Higham View	C50
			Highclere Avenue	B74
			Highfield Lane	C23
			Highfield Road	C23
			Hill Street	A70
			Hills Croft	C32
			Hilton Street	B72

Hodge Lane C61,C8
Hodson Street A53,A50
Holland Street C48
Hope Place B3
Hope Street B35-B37
Hopefield A74
Hopwood Street A47,A49
Hothersall Street B65
Hough Lane B62,B60,B61
Howard Street C60
Hulme Street B35
Hulton Street B14
Hunstone Court A28
Hunts Court A20
Indigo Street C43,C44
Irlam Square C54
Irwell Place B12
Irwell Street A45,A46
Irwell View B11
Islington Cottages B6
Islington Grove B4
Islington Square B5,B8
James Place B42
James Street B4,B3
Jay Street B7
Jellys Buildings C30
Jennings Street B47
John Street C32,C27
Johnson Street A42
Jonas Street B65
Kay Court B7
Kays Gardens A65
Kempster Street B68
Kent Place B16
Kersal Moor B57
Kidderminster Court A5
King St A46-A48
King St, Height C54,C55
Kings Head Yard A5
Kirkley Street A63
Lamb La A58,A59,A13
Lancaster Road C63
Langley Rd South C44,C41
Langworthy Rd C62,C17
Laundry Street C45-C47
Laurel Grove B69
Legendre Street A35
Leopold Street C58
Lester Street A74
Lime Place B72
Lindsay Street B49,B50
Linsley Street A47
Lissadel Street C51,C52
Littleton Road C50
Liverpool Street
    B37-B41,B29,C7,C8
Liverpool St (west) C61,C62
Long Street B65
Lord Duncan Street C8
Lower Arlington St A68
Lower Broughton Road
    B58-B62,B57
Lower Islington St B5,B8
Lower Seddon Street B42
Lyth Street B18,B22
Markendale Street B54
Market Street A75
Market Way C38
Marlborough Road B74
Marshall Terrace A70
Martha Street B51,B46,B47,
    B48,B49,B50
Mason Street B6,B5
Massey Place B35
Massey Street B35

Mayan Avenue A75
Meadow Street A31
Meter Street B23
Meyrick Road C38
Middletons Court A5
Middlewood Street B16,B7
Mill Lane C40
Miller Street A18,A19
Montague Street B61
Moore Street B45
Morris Street A45
Mottram Street A61
Mount Pleasant Street A75
Mount Street A69,A70,A67
Mulberry Road C34
Muslin Street B36
Muslinet Street B37
Myrtle Street C9
Nangreave Street B15,B16
Nelson Place B61,B62
Nelsons Buildings B65
New Bailey Street A42-A44,
    A3,A5,A15
New Bury Street B47
New Chapel St C41,C49
New George Street B3
New Richmond
    C18,C19,C20,C22
New Shaw Street B48
New Windsor C11
Newbury Place B73
Newton Street C23
Nightingales Yard A8
North George Street
    A76,A77,A72
North Hill Street A69,A73
North James Henry St A73
North Road C16
Norton Street A36
Nottingham Terrace C57
Nutter Street B47
Oldfield Road B29-B33,
    B25,B37,B51
Olive Mount B72
Orchard Street C48
Ordsall Lane B6-B14,B20
Oxford Street
    B46,B25,B52,B54
Paddington C19
Palmer Street A36,A35
Paradise A18
Paradise Hill A18,A24
Paradise Row A29,A24
Paradise St A23,A24,A47
Paradise Vale A24
Parker Street A48
Parsonage Street B44
Partington Street C5,C13
Paul Street C33
Peel Street C29,C30
Peel Terrace B59
Pendleton Street C48
Peru Street A75,A76
Peru St, Broughton B70
Peter Street C47
Phoebe St B46,B47,B27
Picton Close A56
Picton Street A56,A57
Picton St, Pendleton C31
Pikes Buildings C13
Pilgrim Street B37
Pimlot Street C30,C31,C20
Pine Street C17
Pleasant St A25,A26,A52
Pollitts Buildings C45

Pollitts Row C45
Popplewells Bldgs C6,C7
Primrose Hill C24,C23
Priory B69
Priscilla Street B16
Prospect Place C56
Prospect Street A62
Providence Place B11
Providence Street B24
Pump Street B4
Pump St, Charlestown C48
Pump St, Ordsall B43,B24
Quay Causey A17
Quay Street A38,A12
Quay Street, Broad St C21
Queen St A48,A49,A34
Queen St, Height C15
Radley Street C45
Raglan Terrace B59
Railway Street C45
Ravald Street A51,A52
Raven Street C30
Regent Road B18-B28,B6
Regent Square B19
Regent Street B17,B7
Richmond Hill A52,A73,A74
Richmond Place C3,C29
Richmond Row A71
Richmond Street
    A52,A53,A62,A70
Richmond Street, Pendleton
    C5,C29
Riding Street A44
Rigby St A57,A61,A65,A67
Rigby St, Broughton B73
River Street B62
Robert Hall Street B53,B54
Robert Street C27
Robinsons Buildings A50
Robinsons Bldgs, Weaste
    C59
Rockley Street C52
Rockliffe Street A77
Rodney Street B6,B5,B7
Rolla Court A50
Rolla Street A50
Rosamond Drive A65
Rosamond St A65,A64,A66
Rossall Street C24
Rowland Street B55
Ruthin Street A76
Ruthin Street, High St C35
Ryall Street B51
Ryland Street A25,A30
Sackville Street A60,A59
St Georges Crescent C63
St James Street B54
St Kildas Drive B75
St Mary Street A61
St Simon St A31-A34,A27
St Stephen Street
    A61,A62,A11,A26
Salford Approach A4
Salford Cross A19,A21
Salford Quays B56
Salford Street A26,A27
Salmon Street A28
Sandford Street A26
Sandon St A27,A31,A33
Sandy Lane C16,C17
Sandywell A22,A23
Sandywell Court A22
Sandywell Street A29,A28
Seddon Street B10,B43
Seedley Gardens C23

Senior Street A28
Shaw Brows
    A26,A52,A67,A69,A70
Sherborne Street A33
Ship Court A18
Short St, Broughton B65
Short St, Pendleton C29
Shuttleworth Street C53
Sidmouth Street A57,A56
Sidney Street B5
Siever Street C61
Silk Street A72,A73,A67,A68
Sligo Street C52,C53
Small Street B51
Smethurst Street C25
Smith Street A60,A59
Smith St, Ordsall B54
South Hall Street B10
Sovereign Street C45
Spaw Street A42,A13
Springfield A28
Springfield Lane
    A28,A29,A32
Spring Vale Road C30
Stanley Street A45,A46,A56
Stanley Terrace B67
Stowell Street C60
Strasburg Street C56
Strawberry Bank C51
Strawberry Hill C14
Strawberry Hill Terrace C14
Strawberry Road C51
Streets Buildings A33
Sun Terrace B73
Sunnyside Street B42
Sussex Street B63,B64
Sussex St, Regent Rd B28
Tanners La C35,C16,C28
Tatton St B51-B53,B47,B50
Taylorson Street B46
Temperance Street A77
Temple Place A46
Thomson Street A34
Thorpe Street B46
Thurlow Street C57
Toft Street B16,B17,B8
Tomlinsons Buildings B4
Tontine Street C13,C6
Trafalgar Place B8
Trafalgar Pl, Broughton B69
Trafalgar Street B68
Trafford Rd B54-B56
Trafford Street B53
Trentham St C40,C51,C52
Trinity Way
    A16,A23,A46,A48,A55
Tully Street B73
Turner Street C23
Tysoe Gardens A65
Union Place B17
Union Place, Broughton B62
Union Street A10
Union Street, Broughton
    B62,B63,B59
Union Street, Charlestown
    C49,C18
Union Street (West) B17
University Road C12
Unwin Street C4,C38
Upper Cleminson St A76
Upper George Street A76
Uxbridge St A55,A56,A57
Vale Street A27,A30
Victoria Bridge Street A3
Victoria Place C35

Victoria Street B67
Victoria Terrace C35
Vulcan Street C12
Waddington Street B4
Wallness Bank C13
Wallness Lane C13,C14,C12
Walmer Street B51
Water Street A36,A7,A8
Waterloo Place A56,A57
Watkin Street A31
Weaste Avenue C58
Weaste Lane C59,C60
Weaver Street B36
Wellington Street C43,C48
West Street B49
West Albert Street C9-C10
West Ann Street B37,B41
West Bank Street B32
West Brownbill Street B27
West Burton Street B27
West Charles St B30,B41
West Clowes Street B56
West Craven Street
    B47,B28,B52
West Cross Street B17,B20
West Dean Street B41
West Dixon Street B45
West Duke Street B15
West Egerton Street B26
West Fleet St B9,B30,B31
West George Street C11
West Gore Street B37
West John Street B36
West King Street A46,A48
West Market Street A63
West Park Street B54,B13
West Peel Street B23,B24
West Stable Street B15
West Union St B17,B9,B33
West Wellington St B40
West William Street B36
West Worsley St B49,B50
Wheathill A31
Wheathill Street A31,A26
Whit La C40-C44,C18,C39
White Cross Bank
    A16,A17,A64,B34
Whitfield Terrace B59
Wilburn Street
    B18,B6,B7,B8,B22
Wilford Terrace B59
Wilkinson Place C30
Wilkinson Street A38,A42
William Street A60,A55
Williams Street C42
Williamson Street A27
Willow Street A26
Wilmslow Street C56,C57
Wilna Terrace B41,B40
Wilton Terrace C7,C8
Windsor C11,C12
Windsor Place C10
Windsor St B20,B26,C4
Windsor Terrace C6,C7
Woden Street B42,B12
Wood Street A38
Wood St, Brindleheath C47
Woods Yard C45
Worsley Street A43
Wroe Street A17
Wroes Court A35
York Street A47
York St, Broughton B67
York St, West Gore St B37
Zebra Street B33,B44

Name index

This index includes all the licensees or occupants of pubs mentioned in the three volumes of Salford Pubs. The names are as in directories, licensing records, electoral rolls, census records and newspaper reports, so there may be variations in spelling for the same name.

Page numbers with the letter A refer to Salford Pubs Part One, B to Part Two and C to Part Three.

Abbott Eric B48
Abbott Marjorie B48
Abbott Thomas B64
Abbott William B37
Ackers Elizabeth C21
Ackers John C21
Ackley Richard A15
Ackroyd Oliver A76
Acton Edward A74
Acton Harriet C48
Acton James C53
Acton Samuel B21
Acton Thomas A7
Adams Henry B67
Adams John A17
Adams William B67
Adamson John B22
Addison James C19
Addy Mark B43
Adler Annie A55
Adler John A55
Adshead Timothy B57
Agard Charles A62
Ahern John B45
Ainscow Ann B17
Ainscow George A67
Ainscow James A48
Ainscow Oliver B12
Ainscow Richard A48,B53
Ainscow Roger B17
Ainscow Thomas B30
Ainsworth Betsy A25
Ainsworth James A4
Ainsworth Mary Alice A4
Ainsworth Robert A55
Ainsworth Thomas B17,B41,B43,B47
Ainsworth Walker A19,A25
Aitchison Victor B7
Albiston Roger A7
Alcock David B16
Alcock George A44
Alcock Thomas C15
Aldcroft Isaac C55
Aldcroft John A9,A12,C40
Aldcroft Thomas B23
Aldcroft William A58
Alderson Francis A26
Aldred Alfred A37
Aldred Enoch B19
Aldred James C46
Aldred John C34
Aldred Thomas B19
Aldridge Adam A52,A70
Alexander Mary A9
Allanson Frank C26
Allanson Gladys C26
Allardyce David C8
Allcock Samuel C59
Allcock Sarah C59
Allen Arthur A11
Allen George A57,C37
Allen James A22,C59
Allen John Thomas C59
Allen Joseph A76,B18,C52

Allen Stella A46
Allman Ann B5
Allman John B5
Allman Mary B48
Allmark Elizabeth C10
Allmark Henry B36
Allwood John B29,B30
Alsop Thomas A3,C11
Alton James B65
Alton William A54
Alvey William A69
Ambery Isaac A12
Ambrose George B23
Amphlett Joshua C8
Anderson James A54
Anderson Samuel C33
Anderson William A29
Anderton Richard A67,B18
Anderton Robert B15
Andrews James C59
Andrews John C37
Andrews Richard B40
Andrews Septimus B43
Andrews William C12
Ankers Charles B45
Ankers Henry B21
Ankers John A68
Annesley Ellen B32
Annesley John B32
Annette James C24
Anstead Charles A76
Anthony Caroline B32
Antrobus John B57
Appleby John A21
Appleby Thomas A25
Appleton Elizabeth C25
Appleton John C25
Archer Richard B36
Archer Thomas A76
Archibald Mary B52,C34
Arkwright Frederick C47
Armer John A44
Armitage Henry A63
Armitage Isabella A46,A63
Armitage John B58,B70
Armitage Mary B58
Armitage William A31
Armitt John C51
Armitt Sarah C51
Armstrong James A36,A55,B51
Armstrong Robert A8
Arnfield Arthur A15
Arnold Arthur B62
Arnold Francis C6
Arnold Fred C4
Arnold Joseph A67
Arnold Kathleen C6
Arnsby Harry B26
Arrowsmith John A78
Arrowsmith Samuel A14,A36
Arthur John A9
Ashbury Mary B40
Ashcroft Herbert B75
Ashcroft John B31

Ashcroft Mary B31
Ashcroft Winifred B75
Ashdown Annie B29
Ashton Alfred A68
Ashton Eleanor B33
Ashton Hugh B19
Ashton James A13
Ashton John B33,B65
Ashton Sarah Ann A48
Ashton Thomas B71
Ashworth Charles A26
Ashworth James B72
Ashworth Stanley B66
Ashworth Thomas B25
Ashworth William B37
Askew Edith A63
Askew Florence B29
Aspin Minerva B44
Aspinall Elizabeth B4
Aspinall Lawrence B4
Asprey Peter C45
Asten Richard C49
Astley Eliza B68
Astley Elizabeth A5
Astley James A52
Astley William A5
Aston James A35
Atherley David A50
Atherley Harriet A26
Atherley Henry A26
Atherley Josie A50
Atherley Samuel A31
Atherton Annie B13
Atherton Frederick C14
Atherton James A20
Atherton John B13
Atherton Robert C47
Atherton Tom B34
Atkin Joseph C45
Atkins Alfred B49
Atkins William A63
Atkinson Elizabeth A58
Atkinson Henry A47
Atkinson James A65,C32
Atkinson John B17
Atkinson Richard A58
Atkinson William A14,C7
Attenbury Ann B20
Attenbury John B20
Ault Henry B43
Austin Edward B25
Austin James B15
Avery John B15
Avery Martha A44
Axon Bill B47
Axon Elsie B47
Backhouse Basil B61
Backhouse Mavis B61
Bacon Thomas A62
Baddeley Charles B34
Baddeley George A55,A56,C10
Baddeley James A75
Baddeley William A75
Bagnall George C16

Bagshaw George B73
Bagshaw Lizzie B73
Baguley Hilda C28
Baguley William B7
Bailey Edward A49
Bailey James A26,C11
Bailey John T A43
Bailey Joseph B22
Bailey Mary A46
Bailey William A63,B31
Bain William A67
Bainbridge Elizabeth C6
Bainbridge James B61
Bainbridge Jane B35
Bainbridge John A44
Bainbridge Peter B19,B31,B35
Bainbridge Phoebe B63
Bainbridge Robert A53,A54
Bainbridge Sarah A53,A54
Bainbridge Thomas A59
Baines Thomas C18
Baird William A30
Baker Edward A57
Baker James C40
Baker John A44,A57
Baker Margaret A70
Baker Martha A44
Baker Mary A15,A57
Baker Ralph A15,A69
Baker Ralph jun A15
Baker Richard A50
Baldwin James B34
Baldwin Thomas C58
Balmer James C19
Balmer Sarah B47
Bamber James A49
Bamber John C11
Bamford James C44,C47
Bamford William A47
Bamforth Roy A63
Bancroft George B71
Bancroft Harry B71
Banham George C34
Banham Hannah C34
Banham William C34
Banner Ernest B15
Bannister John C19
Banton William A20
Barber Christopher B60
Bardsley Dorothy A50
Bardsley Edwin A7
Bardsley James A50
Bardsley Samuel A56,C12
Barge Elizabeth A21
Barge Hannah A21,A24
Barge John A24
Barge Robert A20,A21
Barge William A3,A21,A24
Barker Charles B32
Barker John A64,C6
Barker Robert B65
Barker Susannah B22
Barlow Ann C20
Barlow Cornthwaite C52
Barlow David C54
Barlow Edward B36
Barlow Elias A61
Barlow Elizabeth B72
Barlow Ernest C32
Barlow Florence C54
Barlow George A50,C29
Barlow Henry C9
Barlow John A48,A50,A60,A61,C4,C54
Barlow John Nash A26
Barlow Marian C23
Barlow Martha A36
Barlow Mary C16
Barlow Matilda C54
Barlow Michael A38,A70
Barlow Peter C27
Barlow Philip A61
Barlow Richard C20

Barlow Samuel A26,B67
Barlow Sarah B36
Barlow Susannah B67
Barlow Thomas A50,B67,C16,C22
Barlow William C23,C27,C40,C57
Barnes Alfred B15
Barnes Charles A26,B72
Barnes Edward C32
Barnes Ernest C58
Barnes John B17
Barnes Joseph B37
Barnes Laura B72
Barnes Nathan C41
Barnes Thomas A5
Barnes William C41,C42,C54
Barnes Winifred B15
Barnet John B37
Barnett Annie A4
Barnett John B17,B30
Barnett Vincent A63
Barnett William B15
Barnfield Jessie C46
Barr John C34
Barratt Ann A27,B57
Barratt John C27
Barratt Thomas B57
Barrett Alfred C23
Barrett Alice C8
Barrett Charles B65
Barrett Edwin C8,C40
Barrett Jessie B2
Barrett John B40
Barrett Lilian C14
Barrett Mary C23
Barritt John C27
Barritt Thomas A55
Bartington Edward B9
Barton Jane A62
Barton Joseph A75
Barton William A75,B33
Barzillai Martin A49
Bass William B63
Bastow David A53
Bate Mary B25
Bateman Isaac C22
Bateman Louis C54
Bateman Nellie C54
Bates Elizabeth C27
Bates James C34
Bates Joseph C27
Bateson George C22
Battersby Hannah B9,B51
Battersby Sherbrooke B71
Battersby William B46
Batty Harold C13
Batty Margaret C13
Batty William C31
Battye John A34
Baxter Emma C48
Baxter Joseph B67,C40
Baxter Mark A53,C37,C38
Baxter Thomas A4
Bayley John B37
Bayley Moses B56
Beahan John A64,B6,C5
Beamer Ada C22
Beamer Harry C22
Bean Anthony B22
Beardmore Elizabeth B45
Beardow Ada A72
Beardsall Alfred B72
Beatty George A5
Beaty William B26,B50
Beaulah Jemima B55
Bebbington George A60
Bebbington Keith B54
Bebbington Mary A60
Bebbington Nora B54
Beckett Thomas B11
Bedforth Ernest A16,C50
Bedforth Lilian A16,C50
Bedgood John B31

Name	Ref
Bedggood Thomas	B31
Beech Albert	B73
Beech Josephine	B73
Beesley Albert	A22
Beesley Ann	A58
Beesley William	A58
Beeston Frank	B75
Beeston John	A76,C11,C18
Bell Ann	B30
Bell George	C30
Bell Hannah	C51
Bell James	C51
Bell John	B30
Bell Joseph	A54,C29
Bell Leslie	C11
Bell Seth	A49
Bell Thomas	A6
Bellringer Robert	C19
Bennett Charles	B41
Bennett George	B29,B43
Bennett John	A8,A53
Bennett Mr	A10
Bennett Nathaniel	A67
Bennett Thomas	A45,A61,B36
Bennett William	C7,C24
Benson William	C33
Bentham Anne	C11
Bentley Elizabeth	B10
Bentley Hannah	B26
Bentley James	B27,B30
Bentley Margaret	C42
Bentley Rachel	B30
Bentley Robert	C42
Bentley Walter	C7
Benton James	B19
Beresford John	A75
Berry Cicely	C15
Berry Jacob	A53
Berry John	B9
Berry Mary	B43
Berry Thomas	A58,C15,C33
Berry William	B23,B43,B50
Besson Robert	C13
Bestall Harriett	A19
Bestall John	A36
Bestall Thomas	A19,A36
Bestwick Iphis	B41
Bestwick William	B41
Beswick Charles	C8
Beswick Edward	A74,A78
Beswick Levi	A48
Beswick Richard	A63
Beswick Stephen	C32
Beswick Walter	C54
Bethell Arthur	C62
Betley James	A58
Bevan Frances	A28
Bevan Henry	A72
Bevan John	B51
Bevan Robert	A28
Bibby Herbert	B31
Bibby Rebecca	B51
Bickerton Thomas	A58
Biddolph Edmund	B51
Billings James	C43
Billings Mary	C43
Billington Sylvester	C20
Bills Stephen	A69
Bilsborrow William	B58
Binns Albert	B69
Birch Daniel	A46
Birch James	B55,C58
Birch John	A42
Birch Joseph	A38
Birch Margaret	B52
Birchall Benjamin	A31
Birchby James	A16
Birchwood Elizabeth	C63
Birchwood John	C22
Birchwood John Grundy	C63
Bird Joseph	C9
Bird Thomas	A9
Bird William	A9
Birkby Harriet	C13
Birkby Jane	C56
Birkby Teresa	C56
Birkinshaw Agnes	B23
Birkinshaw John	B51,B53
Birtles John Henry	B7
Birtles Thomas	B67
Bishop John	B63
Bisset Robert	B40
Black Alice	C37
Blackburn James	A9
Blackburn John	B19,C30
Blackburn Mary	A9
Blackburn Thomas	C55
Blackley Benjamin	A18
Blackshaw William	A25
Blackwell Mary	A75
Blakeley John	C43
Blakeley Joseph	C31
Blakeley Thomas	C31
Blakeley William	C43
Bland Charlotte	A63
Bland James	A63
Bland Samuel	B52
Blanshard George	B14,B20
Blay Clifford	C58
Blick William	B47
Blinkhorn William	A8,C45
Blood William	C47
Bloomfield Richard	A36
Blore Walter	B71
Blore William	A45
Blundell Alfred	C25
Blundell Arthur	C43
Blythe Agnes	B31
Boardman Alice	A17
Boardman Betty	B58
Boardman Charles	A17
Boardman George	B61
Boardman Harry	C51
Boardman Isabella	B61
Boardman John	A12,A24,C17
Boardman Joseph	A30
Boardman Margaret	C4
Boardman Robert	C51
Boardman Samuel	C4
Boardman Thomas	A14
Boardman William	B58
Bohanna Mary	C32
Bohannah Catherine	C19
Bohler Frederick	B36
Bolland Jane	C40
Bond Henry	A75
Bond John	C29
Bond Joseph	A16
Bond Joseph jun	A16
Bond Martha	C44
Bond Matthew	C44
Bond William	C44
Bone Samuel	B58
Bonnar Sarah	B27
Bonsall Joseph	A58
Bonsall Ralph	A22
Bonsall Richard	B36
Booker George	B15
Booker John	B15
Boon Walter	C13
Bootes Ada	C9
Bootes Stanley	C9
Booth Alice	A6
Booth Annie	B66
Booth Benjamin	A22
Booth Edward	A26,A30
Booth George	C32,C47
Booth Isaac	A6
Booth James	C49
Booth Joe	C54
Booth John	B42,C33,C42
Booth Marjorie	C54
Booth Mary	A30
Booth Robert	B31
Booth Sarah	A36
Booth Thomas	B19,C28
Booth William	C29
Bostock Joseph	A31
Bostock Thomas	A53
Boston John	A65
Boswell William	A19,B73
Bottomley Ann	A74
Bottomley Joseph	A9
Bottomley Samuel	A74
Bouch John	A9
Bould John	A18
Bowden Arthur	C58
Bowden Henry	C57
Bower George	A57
Bower Thomas	A13
Bowers Edna	A74
Bowers James	A74
Bowker James	B57
Bowles Dora	B58
Bowles James	B58
Bowling Elizabeth	C12
Bowling Frederick	C12,C13
Bowman Joseph	A30
Bowring George	C35
Boyd Robert	A57
Boyle Edith	C27
Boyle Joseph	A62
Bracegirdle Ernest	B54
Brackenbury Christopher	A7
Bradburn Alice	C63
Bradburn Henry Whittaker	A23
Bradburn Thomas	C63
Bradbury Abraham	A20
Bradbury Alice	C28
Bradbury Elizabeth	A47
Bradbury James	B60
Bradbury John	A21,A47,B52,C28,C57
Bradbury Thomas	B24
Braddock John	C25
Brade James	B16
Bradford Charles	C33
Bradford Thomas	A70
Bradley Charles	C57
Bradley Isaac	C10
Bradley John	C54
Bradley Laurence	B41
Bradshaw Emanuel	B26
Bradshaw Henry	A30
Bradshaw Matthew	C9,C10
Bradshaw Robert	B36
Bradshaw Thomas	A59
Bradwell Robert	B33
Brady Andrew	B19
Brady Charles	A38,A50
Brady Richard	A10
Brady Thomas	A38
Bramer Albert	C61
Bramer George	B51,C27
Bramer Jane	C61
Bramer Tilly	B51,C27
Bramley George	B56
Brandrett William	B5
Brands John	A67
Branson William	B29
Bray John	A29
Breakell James	B42,B51
Breakell Samuel	A76
Brelsford Solomon	A32
Brennan Catherine	C22
Brennan Charlotte	A33
Brennan George	A61
Brennan Hugh	B10
Brennan Jane	B10
Brennan Matthew	A61
Brennan Patrick	C58
Brennan William	B4
Brennand Savilla	A32
Brennand Thomas	A32
Brentnall Maria	C6
Brereton Amelia	B31
Brereton William	B31,B43
Brian William	B32
Brickill James	A66
Bride James	B18
Bridge James	B31
Bridge John Walter	A54
Bridge Jonathan	A20
Bridgman Francis	B49
Brierley John	A71
Brierley Mary	B17
Brierley Robert	C33
Brierley Squire	C47
Brierley William	C45
Briggs Edgar	C14,C34
Briggs Isaac	B72
Briggs Oswald	B72
Briggs Thomas	A5,A20,B55,B56
Briggs William Alexander	B28
Brightman Dave	B31
Brightman Jenny	B31
Brighton George	B61
Brighton Sarah	B61
Briscoe Mary	A6
Briscoe Robert	A6
Brittain Elizabeth	C53
Brittlebank Robert	A28
Britton Jane	A68
Britton Joseph	A16
Broadbent Dyson	B49,C7
Broadbent Hilda	C38
Broadbent James	A34
Broadbent Wilfred	C38
Broadbent William	A50
Broadhurst Charles	C53
Broadhurst Hugh	A58
Broadhurst Margaret	A58
Broadmeadow Joseph	A58
Brocklehurst Anthony	C32
Bromley Harold	C62
Bromley Lily	C62
Bromley Mary	C51
Bromley Thomas	C51
Bromlow James	C49
Brook James	A10
Brookes Henry	C53
Brookes James	C45
Brookes Peter	C54
Brookes Samuel	A54
Brookes Stanley	C15
Brookes Sydney	C6
Brookes William	C61
Brookfield James	A34
Brooks Claude	A76
Brooks James	B15,C14
Brooks Leonard	C43
Brooks William	C61
Brooksbank Albert	B34
Broom Emma	B11
Broome Joseph	A75
Brotherdale John	A45
Brotherton Ernest	C11
Broughton Benjamin	A77
Broughton Chris	C39
Broughton James	C39
Broughton John	A37,C28
Broughton Margaret	A37,A68
Broughton Robert	A77
Broughton Thomas	A52
Brown Annie	A67
Brown Bessie	C54
Brown Bill	A18
Brown Bolton	A17
Brown Clifford	C54
Brown Elijah	A63
Brown Elizabeth	B16,C11
Brown Gladys	C15
Brown Henry	A30
Brown James	A29,A49,B74
Brown John	A47,B43
Brown Joseph	C13,C15
Brown Lily	C25
Brown Margaret	A68
Brown Mary	A29,A30
Brown Rachel	A17
Brown Samuel	A19,C48
Brown Sarah Ann	A63
Brown Thomas	A8,A61
Brown William	A3,B51,C25,C28
Browne Joan	C3
Browne Martin	C3
Brownhill James	C37
Brownhill John	C43
Brownridge John	B28
Bruckshaw John	B37
Brundreth Thomas	C47
Brunt Violet	C53
Bryan Henry	B21
Bryant Elsie	B59
Buchanan Frederick	A37
Buck John	A9
Buckler Harriet	A25
Buckler Herbert	C58
Buckler Thomas	A49
Buckler William	A25
Buckley Charles	A36
Buckley Dick	A16
Buckley Jack	B61
Buckley James	A14,A36,A37,C30
Buckley John	C50
Buckley Susan	C34
Buckley Thomas	A60,C37
Buckley William	A53,A54
Bullock Elizabeth	B19
Bullock John	A15
Bullock Matthew	C5
Bullock Sarah	C5
Bullock Thomas	C5
Bullock William	B19
Bullough William	A42
Bulman Thomas	C26
Bumby Thomas	C45
Bunter George	A47,B19
Burden Peter	C48
Burdett Josiah	A5
Burgess Andrew	A6
Burgess Jonathan	A21
Burgess Joseph	A30
Burgess Mary	A30
Burgess Thomas	B13
Burgess William	C5
Burke Edward	B3
Burke James	A56
Burke Josephine	A78
Burke Mary	B42
Burke Nicholas	B42
Burke Patrick	A72
Burke Thomas	A78
Burke William	B61,C18
Burland Richard	B9,B21
Burnett Frederick	C51
Burnish Henry	B22
Burns Albert	B34
Burns John	C44
Burns William	C23
Burrows Harriet	B40
Burrows James	A75
Burrows Richard	B42
Burton Frank	B61
Burton Leonard	C4
Burton Thomas	A30,A38,C30
Bury Benjamin	B62
Bury George	A60
Bush James	B25
Bush May	A56
Bush William	A9,A53
Butler Alice	C59
Butler Henry	B33
Butler John	B15
Butler Mary	A18
Butler Nancy	A21
Butler Olive	B33
Butler Robert	C52
Butler Thomas	A18
Butlers Charles	B18
Butters James	B63
Butterworth George	C24
Butterworth Mary	A7
Butterworth William	A7

Buxton James A27,A47,A50,B7,B10
Buxton Thomas A14
Byrne Margaret A74
Byrom Dennis B54
Cahill Andrew C34
Cain Abigail A63
Cain Agnes B22
Cain Anne B60
Cain John B22
Cain Sarah B44
Cairns John C7
Cairns Thomas A11
Calder Matthew A56
Callaghan Alfred B73
Callow Thomas A8
Calvert John A32
Calvert Joseph A7
Cameron Rowland B23
Campbell Daniel B26
Campbell James A13,B74
Campbell Thomas C29
Canavan John C3
Canavan Thomas C3
Cann Maureen B40
Cann Norman B40
Capper Eunice C42
Capper Thomas C42
Carew Michael A25,A71
Carey Ellen A5
Carey James A5
Carline James A71
Carney John A58
Carney Thomas A19,B75
Carrington James B8,B48
Carrington Jane B60
Carrington William A21
Carroll Edward A27
Carroll William B23
Carruthers Alex B63
Carter Alfred B12
Carter Charles C17
Carter Henry B9
Carter James A34
Carter John B15
Carter Mary B12
Carter Peter B50
Carter William A35,A53,B43
Cartlidge James A55
Casewell Alfred C20,C27
Casewell Edward C20,C30
Casewell Thomas C27
Casey Benjamin C50
Casey Patrick C46
Cass Beatrice A76
Cass Cecil A76
Casserley Thomas C61
Cassidy Hannah C56
Cassidy Richard C56
Casson William A58
Caton Henry C52
Catterall Ann B45
Catterall Sarah B41
Catterall Thomas B41,B53,B54
Catterall William B6
Cavanagh Josephine C57
Cavanagh William C57
Cave Henry A35
Cawley James B28
Cawley Margaret A3
Cawley Mary B44
Cawley Thomas B47
Chaddick John A19
Chaddick Mary A19
Chadwick Elizabeth B9
Chadwick James C40
Chadwick John A19,B9
Chadwick Mary A19
Chadwick William A58
Challinor Richard C25
Challoner John A10
Chaloner John C12
Chambers Arthur A68

Chambers James C27
Chandley Joseph A70
Chantler Samuel A8,C16
Chapman Albert C48
Chapman Alfred A31
Chapman Alice C48
Chapman Charles A45
Chapman Henry A18,C48
Chapman James A65,C12
Chapman John B31,B36
Chapman Margaret C27
Chapman Sarah B61
Chapman William B61
Chappell Thomas A72
Charles Agnes A28
Charles Joseph A28
Charleson William A48
Charlesworth James A26
Charlesworth Sarah A26
Charlton Elsie B42
Charlton Mary Ann C51
Charlton Thomas C51
Charters William B19
Chatterton Clara C12
Chatterton Jacob C16
Chatterton Joannah C16
Cheadle Robert B71
Cheetham John A23,A29
Cheetham Thomas C14,C17
Chester Samuel A64
Chesters Arthur C62
Chesters John A10
Chesters Thomas A60
Chesworth John A34
Chetham John A60,B45,C9
Chidlow John A53
Chilton John B44
Chilton Vincent C5
Chorley Robert C63
Chorlton John B40
Chorlton Richard A9
Christopher George A18
Church Deborah B8
Church Rebecca B8
Church William A77
Clampitt Blanche A16
Clampitt Hilda B61
Clampitt James B55,C6,C11
Clare Albert C6
Clare Charles A30
Clare Elizabeth C28
Clare Peter B23
Clark David B19
Clark John A35
Clark Sarah A67
Clark Susannah A19,A35
Clark Thomas B7
Clark William A67
Clarke Alice C8
Clarke Charles B48
Clarke Eunice B30
Clarke Hannah C28
Clarke Harry C13
Clarke John B30
Clarke Jonathan A52
Clarke Thomas C8,C28
Clarke William A44
Clarkson David C15
Clarkson James C52
Clarkson John A53
Clay William B18,C59
Clayton George A7,B29
Clayton John B11
Clayton Robert B62
Clayton Thomas B62
Clayton Thomas Albert B11
Clayton William B2
Cleary John A69
Clegg Edmund C15
Clegg Edward A20,A35
Clegg James B14,B15,B58
Clegg John A35,C61
Clegg Josiah A54
Clegg Mary A54,B8

Cleminson John A63
Cleminson Thomas A69
Clemson John A20
Clerk John C7
Clewes Mary A73
Cliff John B26,B60
Cliffe Charles B66,C3
Cliffe Ethel C13
Cliffe Stanley C13
Clough Henry B57
Clough Jane B42
Clough Joseph B10
Clough Thomas B57
Clough William C20
Clowes Ann B30
Clowes Thomas B30
Coakley Ann A56
Coakley William A56
Coates Alfred B25
Coates Alfred Charles B10
Coates Henry B42
Cobb John A30
Cobb Thomas B40,C12
Coburn Charles A42
Coburn Mary A43
Cockburn David A53
Cocker James A66
Cocker Rachel A31
Coglan James A59
Coldman John B11
Cole Charles A5
Cole Harry C62
Cole Jean C62
Cole William B50
Coleridge Albert C48
Colley Mark C29
Collier Aaron B12
Collier Abraham C42
Collier Catherine C22
Collier Harry B56
Collier Irene C44
Collier Jack C44
Collier James A13,A57,C20
Collinge Priscilla A59
Collinge William B24
Collins Adam B23
Collins Albert C49
Collins James A37,A78,B36,B49,C13
Conlan Michael A22
Conlon Ada B47
Connah William B7
Connell Priscilla B18
Connell William C29
Connolly Andrew B6,B46
Connolly James B7
Connolly Sarah A50
Connolly-Brooks Eileen B75
Connolly-Brooks Walter B75
Connor Agnes B13
Connor Christopher A60
Connor Daniel B45
Connor Henry A51
Connor Jessie A51
Connor John C15
Connor John Smith B7
Connor Peter B72
Connors Ellen C5
Connors Tom B24,C5
Constantine James A16
Constantine John A12
Conway Thomas B72
Cook Alfred A38
Cooke Mary C7
Cooke Thomas B22
Cooken Bernard C35
Cookson Charles B40
Cookson Charles W B40
Cookson James B35
Cookson Rosina B40
Cookson Thomas B70,C53
Coombes Charles B55
Coombs James Henry A17
Cooper Edith A30

Cooper Elizabeth B49
Cooper Georgina B27
Cooper James C39,C43,C54
Cooper Jeremiah B23
Cooper John A34,A53,A74,C13
Cooper Mary Ellen C45
Cooper Richard C19
Cooper Sarah B36,B62
Cooper Thomas A44,B66
Cooper Walter B27
Cooper William B30,B51
Cootes Fanny B29
Cootes Henry B29
Cope Mr A38
Cope Thomas A59
Copestick William A62
Copley Elizabeth A4
Copley John A28
Copley Mary A4
Copper Charles B47
Corcoran Martin C33
Cordwell John C30
Cordwell Martha C20
Cordwell Thomas C52
Cork John B10
Corkill Patrick B7
Cornish Harry A9
Corry Norah B45
Corry Patrick B5,B45
Costello Clara C42
Costello Elizabeth B16
Costello John C42
Cottam Ann B14
Cotterill Thomas B75
Cotton Mary B13
Cottrell John A58
Coulston Alice A63
Coulter John B27
Coulter Mary B27
Coulthwaite Thomas C22
Coupe John A12
Coupe Joseph C18
Coupe Mary C18
Coupe Thomas C18
Court Herbert C4
Cowell John A3
Cowell Mary Ann B5
Cowley Walter B21
Cowley William B25
Cowsill Peter A36
Cox Annie B26
Cox Charles B29
Cox Thomas A15
Coxon Annie B47
Coxon William B47
Crabtree John B57
Craig James B36
Crane Mark C23
Cranshaw Christopher C34
Crapper Charles C27
Crapper George C27
Crawford Elizabeth B52
Crawford George A3
Crawford James B52
Crawford Jane B27
Crawford John B51
Crawford Robert B27
Crawford Tabitha B32
Crawshaw Alfred B72
Crawshaw Richard A56,A57,B34
Crawshaw Thomas A69
Creed Edward C19
Creer William A6
Cregan John B32
Cresswell John A31,A49,A62
Crockett Daniel C47
Croft Fred B71
Croft John A49
Croft Matthew A56
Croft Roy C25
Croft Sarah A16,C13
Crompton James A6

Crompton John A63,B12
Crompton William A73,B12
Cronshaw James A59
Cronshaw Schofield A59
Cronshaw William B63
Crook John B44,C48
Crook Ralph A60
Crookell George C34
Crosbie Sarah B34
Crosby Peter A36
Crosby Sarah A36
Crosby William B7
Cross Thomas A77
Crossland May A37
Crossley Robert C5,C11
Crouch John A15
Crowther Ann C10
Crowther Isaac A36
Crowther Luke C10
Cruikshank William A16
Cryer Samuel A10
Cubbin Edward B4
Cuerdale Edward A68
Cullen Fred C38
Cummins Edward B5
Cummins John A27,B63
Cundiff Joseph B6
Cundiff Thomas B6
Cundy Frank B67
Cunliffe Joyce B41
Cunliffe Richard A68
Cunningham Joseph C25
Cunningham Timothy A51,A69
Curley Thomas B73
Curran Peter A17
Currey Edward B40
Currie James A21
Cussons Thomas A53
Dagnall Henry B9,B17
Dakin William A42,C11
Dale Ernest C6
Dale Richard A51
Dale William A22,B13
Daley Harold B35
Dalglish George B43
Dalglish Robert A57
Dalton Ann A18
Dalton Anthony A55
Dalton Edward C34
Dalton Joe C63
Dalton John A18,A51
Dalton Peggy C63
Dalton Robert A51
Dalton Thomas A19,B17
Dalton Vincent B23
Dalton William B46
Daniels Robert C45
Daniels Sarah C45
Daniels Thomas B31
Daniels William B7
Dann Joseph B43
Danson Charles A49
Danson Martha A55
Darby Harry A46
Darbyshire William B13
Darlington Arthur C44
Daubney George B51
Daubney Maureen B51
Davenport Ellen A13
Davenport Helena B12
Davenport Samuel B43
Davey Harold B47
Davidson Alexander A30,C61
Davidson Edith A30,C61
Davies Andy B35
Davies Arthur C30
Davies Dai C47
Davies Edward A7
Davies Elizabeth B27,C5
Davies George B33
Davies Henry C19
Davies James A21,B74
Davies Jim B64

Davies Jo B35
Davies John A66,B45,C5
Davies John Edward A67
Davies Joseph A42,B12
Davies Muriel A21,B74
Davies Samuel A55,A59
Davies Thomas A29,B31
Davies William A24,A62,B36,C33
Davis John B40
Davison Harper B72
Dawes Elizabeth B60
Dawson Annie B32
Dawson James A6,A49,C48
Dawson Richard C15,C54
Dawson William B49
Dawson Zachariah B57
Day John B15
De Felice Hannah A23
De Felice Joseph A23
Deakin George A12
Deakin James A22
Deakin John A22
Deakin William A22
Dean Harry C38
Dean Herbert C34
Dean James A34
Dean Joseph B29,B40
Dean Martha B13
Dean Vera C23
Delaney John A49
Delaney William B30
Deller James C45
Denson William C58
Denton Annie A32
Denton Charles A32
Denton John B23
Denwood Jonathan C23
Derbyshire Alfred C15
Derbyshire Elizabeth B33
Derbyshire James B3
Derbyshire John Henry B33
Derbyshire Joseph A13
Derbyshire Parker B26
Derbyshire Thomas B25,B33
Derbyshire William B44
Derrington Samuel C16
Dertington Samuel B27
Devaney Bernard B21
Deveney Eliza B27
Devine Henry B16
Dewes Charles A63
Dewhurst Charles B47,C10
Dewhurst Jane A74
Dewhurst John A73,A74
Dewhurst Thomas A62
Dickinson Annie B6
Dickinson George A35,A53,C32
Dickinson John A63
Dickinson Joseph A34
Dickinson William C32
Dickson Margaret B50
Dickson Robert C19
Dickson William B50
Diggins Michael C19
Diggins Pauline C19
Diggle James B61
Diggle Joanna B57
Diggle William B57
Dillon Charles A62
Dineley Joseph B34
Distin William B30
Ditchburn Beryl A56
Ditchburn Roy A56
Ditchfield David C53
Dixon Anne A3
Dixon Charles A11
Dixon Dilys C60
Dixon George B13
Dixon John A68,B65,C59
Dixon Mavis B13
Dixon Thomas A28
Dixon William A3

Dobbie Andrew A11
Dobbins Gerald C19
Dobing Dora A14
Dobing George A14
Dobson John A13
Dobson William B75
Dodd Alfred A16
Dodd Francis A49
Dodd James A49
Dodd John B18
Dodd Joyce A16
Dodd Mabel B59
Dohoney Frances B62
Dohoney William B54,B62
Dolby Elizabeth B45
Don James A32
Donachie John C11
Donaghy Robert C25
Done Edwin C8
Done John B44
Donnelly Jim A44
Donnelly Rita A44
Dooley Alfred A54
Dooley Harold B27
Dooley Walter B27
Dooley William B3
Dorning Henry C34
Dorsey John B29
Dougherty John A68
Doughton James B54,C58
Doughty John C21
Doughty Roger B74
Douglas George A49
Douglas Hance B65
Douglas James B35
Dover James A55
Dowie Walter C59
Dowie William B28
Downes William A74
Downie David C20
Downing Joseph A44
Downing Martha A44
Doyle James A9
Doyle John C48
Doyle William B7
Drake Alice B44
Drake William B3
Drinkwater Thomas C63
Driscoll John B20
Driver John A61
Drummond James B9
Drummond Sarah C5
Duckworth Elijah A27
Duckworth James A18,A27,C25,C27
Dudley Alfred A57
Dudley Richard A78
Dudley William A50,A69,C19
Duffy Edward A60
Duffy Gerald A64
Duffy Hugh A24
Duffy James A64
Dugdell Matthew A38
Dugmore Edwin A48,A62,C30,C55
Dunbar Alexander B19
Dunbavin Catherine C59
Dunbavin George C59
Dunbavin John B63
Dunkerley Benjamin C37
Dunkerley John C23
Dunn Edna A16
Dunn James C53
Dunn William B16,C47
Durrant William C41
Dutton Elizabeth C53
Dutton John B14
Dutton Norman B52,B58
Dutton Richard A75
Dwyer Rose A77
Dyche Jean B40,B49
Dyche Victor B40,B49
Dyer Frederick A17
Dyer John B74

Dyer Margaret B74
Dykes John A29,A54
Dyson George B21
Eades Thomas C35
Earith Arthur B47,B53
Earle Charles Richard C16,C17
Earnshaw Abraham C41
Earnshaw John A34
Eastwood Elizabeth A53
Eastwood Frank B12
Eastwood James A53
Eatock Tom C56
Eatock William B59
Eaton Joseph B28
Eaton William C34
Eatough Francis B27
Eaves William C61
Eberlein Arthur A43
Eccles Henry A11
Eccles John A21,A47
Eccles Thomas B16
Eckersley George B20
Eckersley James C13
Eden Edward C4
Eden Stephen A49
Edge James A42
Edge Richard A13,B58
Edge Robert A26
Edge Thomas A23,A31
Edmondson Alice B27
Edmondson Harriet A23
Edmondson Henry A23
Edmondson James B53
Edmondson Margaret A23
Edmondson Mary A16
Edmunds Robert A65
Edwards Charles A50
Edwards Elizabeth C46
Edwards Fred A22
Edwards James B15
Edwards John A56,A66,C6,C52
Edwards Mary B15,B40
Edwards Richard B10
Edwards Thomas C43
Egan William B51
Eley Caroline B41
Elkin Frederick B14
Elks Henry B15
Elliott Mary A31
Elliott Mr A11
Ellis Albert C33
Ellis Edward B11
Ellis Sarah C12
Ellis Thomas C19
Ellison John A52
Ellison Thomas A52,A74
Ellor Richard C3
Elton Ann B65
Elton Fred B7
Elton James A35
Elvidge George A71
Elwell John B52,C26
Embley Joseph C39
Emerson George B35
Emery Stephen C29
Emery Thomas A72
Emery Vida A72
English John B62,B63
Ennion Harry B28
Ennion Thomas B28
Ennis Elizabeth B46
Ennis Mary B10
Entwistle John A10,A20,A47
Errington Mr B59
Etchells Elizabeth B12
Etchells Lilian C6
Evans Ethel C34
Evans John B25
Evans Joseph A48
Evans Margaret A70
Evans Roger A54
Evans Thomas A12,A73,C41

Evans William B74
Eves William B22,B52
Exley Kathleen C46
Eyres James B19
Eyres Simeon B19
Fagan Daniel B40
Fagan Ellen B40
Fairbank John A50
Fairbrother Betty A5
Fairbrother Robert A4,A5
Fairclough Alexander C29
Fairless Edward C28
Fallon William B24
Fardell Edward A60
Farnsworth George B6
Farnworth Edmund A32
Farrall William B13
Farrand Alfred B49
Farrand Frederick B43
Farrand James C22
Farrand Mr A22
Farrar Frederick B11
Farrar Henry A48
Farrar James C61
Farrar Margaret C61
Farrar William A49
Farrell Alfred B56
Farrell Charles C8
Farrell James A77
Farrell John B22,C13
Farrell William B55
Farringdon Mary A59
Farringdon Thomas A59
Farrington Lawrence B16,B17
Faulkner Alice B29
Faulkner James A34,B10
Faulkner Matthew A29
Faulkner Richard C45
Faulkner Walter B29
Fawcett Sam C10
Fawcett Thomas B75
Fearn George A48
Fearnhead Martha C49
Featherstone Francis A29
Featherstone George A28
Featherstone Joshua A27
Featherstone Susannah A28
Feeley Barbara B15
Feeney Ann C24
Feeney Edwin C24
Feetham John C26
Fell Joseph C61
Fell William A26,A51
Fenn John B21
Fenna Edward B40
Fenna Elizabeth B40
Fenna Henry A3,A50,A62,B29
Fennessey John A50
Fenton Annie A20
Fenton Arthur A20
Fenton James A54
Fenwick William B64
Ferguson James A69
Fernely Albert B13
Fernely Bertha B13
Ferns James A68
Ferrey John C27
Ferrey John W C27
Ferris Mary B60
Few Charles A17
Fidler Edward B3
Fidler Elizabeth B3
Fielding Elsie C9
Fielding John C9
Fielding Philip B68
Fildes Joel A12
Fildes John B67
Finch Thomas A68
Findley Michael B4
Finnegan Thomas B65
Finney Charles B23
Finney Harriet A47
Finney Martha C50
Finney Samuel A51

Fish Barnet A38
Fish John C40
Fish Mary C16
Fish William C16
Fishbourne Harriet A53
Fisher Andrew C61
Fisher George B45,C31
Fisher John A73,B53
Fisher Sarah A47,B37
Fisher William B37,C29
Fishwick Alice B3
Fishwick James B3
Fishwick Walter C7
Fishwick William A12,A46,B3
Fitton Henry B62
Fitton James A68
Fitzgerald Colin B49
Fitzgerald Elsie B73
Fitzgerald Evelyn B6
Fitzgerald John A36
Fitzgerald Roy B73
Fitzgerald Thomas B6
Fitzpatrick Bernard C56
Fitzpatrick Francis B32
Fitzpatrick Walter A48
Fitzsimmons John A68,B49
Flanagan Patrick B42
Fleet John B51
Fleet Mary B51
Fleming Elizabeth C26
Fleming John C48
Fleming Michael C46
Fletcher Fred B55
Fletcher James C17,C24
Fletcher Jessie B47
Fletcher John A6,B44
Fletcher Joseph A8
Fletcher Richard B29
Fleury William B68
Flynn James A64
Foden Jane A36
Foden Joseph B60
Follows Leonard B37
Ford Alice B70
Ford John A50
Forster Clifford B10
Forster Kathleen B10
Forster Matthew B21
Foster Ann A31
Foster Annie C34
Foster Edwin A15
Foster Eliza C41
Foster Henry A42
Foster John A3
Foster Margaret C34
Foster Mary A31
Foster Matthew A10
Foster Richard A31,C53
Foster Robert A31
Foster Samuel B60
Foster Thomas C34,C41
Fothergill Elizabeth A69
Fothergill Forrester A62
Fothergill William C25
Foudy Patrick A34
Foulds Maggie B26
Foulkes Elizabeth A59
Foulkes Henry A49
Foulkes James C25
Foulkes Thomas C43
Fowler Philip A11
Fowler Thomas C45
Fox Alfred A68
Fox George A3
Fox James A43,A68
Fox John A67,A68
Foy Edward A31
Foy Eliza A31
France Ezra B8
Francis Joseph B46,C12
Frankcomb Charles B58
Frankland John C25
Franklin Herbert A14
Franks Michael B22

Fraser Donald C35
Frazer John B24
Frechette Annie A44
Frechette Frederick A44
Freeman John A34
French Alfred A77
French Thomas B24
Frier George A64,B63
Frier Hilda A64,B63
Frith Robert B29
Frost John A64
Frow John A70
Fryer Benjamin A75
Fryer Frank C58
Furniss William C58
Gadd Alfred B13
Gadd Clara B26
Gahan Charles B53
Gallagher James B36
Gallemore Annie A29
Gallimore John B33
Galloway John A42
Galloway Timothy A48
Galvin Arthur B15
Gardiner Thomas C23
Gardner John A52
Gardner Nicholas B52
Gardner Thomas C23
Garnett Christopher C48
Garnett Frederick B12,B47
Garrity Peter C25
Garside Abraham B25,C3
Garside George B25
Garside Samuel C33
Gartside Isaac C32
Garvey Michael B3
Gaskell Benjamin A74
Gaskell Sarah Jane C57
Gaskell Thomas B7
Gatehouse Herbert A67
Gatley Ellen B66
Gatley Josiah A38
Gatley Martin C52
Gatley Tom B66
Gaunt William B60
Gaynor James A60
Gaynor John A60,A75
Gaynor Maria A60
Geddes Wellwood B16
Gee Edith A51
Gee George A63
Gee Harry B47
Gee James A64
Gee John B23
Gee Percy C18
Gee Thomas A4,A48
Gemmell William B42
Gendall Edwin C20
Gendall John B24
Gendall Kate B24
Gennoe Margaret B9
Geoghegan Frederick A15
George Hugh A61
German Thomas B48
Gerrard George C59
Gerrard John A36
Getliffe Harry B12,B31
Getliffe Mary B46,C43,C47
Getliffe Samuel B46
Gibbon James C34
Gibbons James A8
Gibson Alfred A4
Gibson Clarence C22
Gibson Edward B49
Gibson Elizabeth A4
Gibson James B35
Gibson Richard B56
Gibson Robert B15
Giffard William A43
Gilbody Abner A29
Gilbody Sarah A29
Gilchrist Thomas A36
Gilfillan George C9
Gilkinson Joan B31

Gilkinson Norman B31
Gill John A44
Gill Thomas A77
Gillies Alexander C21
Gillingham Harold C30
Ginder Thomas A62,C33
Gleave Peter B46
Gleave Thomas B46
Gledhill James Rea B58
Gledhill Miles B27
Gleeson Denis A67
Gleeson Edward A69
Glennon Norah A78
Glover Ellen B40
Glover Hugh A9
Glover James C60
Glover Myra B28
Glover William B28
Goacher Annie B63
Godbert John C43
Godwin Gladys B14
Godwin Walter B14
Goldsmith Samuel C15
Goodall Edward B51
Gooden James B20
Gooden John B28
Goodfellow George B63
Goodfellow James A29
Goodman James B21
Goodwin Abraham A74
Goodwin Emma A68
Goodwin Thomas C4,C5,C9
Goodwin William A31
Goostry John A16
Gordon John A47
Gordon Joshua B43
Gordon Richard A28
Gordon William B34
Gore John A34
Goring William A44
Gorst George B18
Gorton James C59
Gorton John B21
Gorton Thomas C59
Gould Audrey C43
Gould Fred C43
Gould Herbert B44
Gould Walter A3
Gouldin Annie B44
Gouldin Charles B44
Grace Edward C7
Graham Hannah C23
Graham Thomas B70
Grainger Annie C51
Grant Benjamin A63
Grant Catherine C10
Grant Thomas C10
Grant William B68
Gray George B26
Gray William A67,B9
Grayson Danny C60
Graystock Elizabeth A75
Greasby Charles B49
Greatorex Amorel C26
Greaves George B67
Greaves James B2
Greaves Jane B2
Greaves Thomas A46
Greaves William A68
Green Benjamin A47,B29
Green Charles B51
Green Dorothy A74
Green Enoch B12
Green Frank B70
Green Herbert B30
Green James
A27,A60,A74,C47
Green John C5,C41
Green Joseph A64,A68,B30
Green Leonard A45
Green Rebecca B48
Green Walter C9
Greenfield Joseph A48
Greenhalgh Alice B42

Greenhalgh Emily A13
Greenhalgh James A72
Greenhalgh John A13,A58
Greenhalgh Joseph B47,C43
Greenhalgh Martha B5
Greenhalgh Mary A16
Greenhalgh Thomas C23
Greenhalgh William B31,C54
Greenshields John A59
Greenwich Mary Ann A5
Greenwood Albert A43,A73
Greenwood Alice B60
Greenwood Gertrude A43
Greenwood Holland A43
Greenwood James C7,C54
Greenwood Jane C7
Greenwood John
B23,C16,C17
Greenwood Samuel A54,C12
Greenwood William B27,B40
Gregory Bernard C22
Gregory Henry C35
Gregory James A69,B29
Gregory John
A7,B41,B75,C31
Gregory Joseph A7
Gregory Joshua A57
Gregory Lilian B25,C60
Gregory Mildred B41
Gregory Robert C60
Gregory William B53
Gregson Mrs S A A27
Gregson Samuel A27
Gregson Tom B31
Grey Thomas B75
Greystock Henry A60
Gribbin Eugene A64,B34
Gribbin Thomas A64
Grice William B32
Griffin Nora C30
Griffith William B32
Griffiths Edward B25
Griffiths John B25,B47
Griffiths Mona B47
Griffiths Thomas C37
Grimshaw Elizabeth A55
Grimshaw George A45,C32
Grimshaw Jacob A55
Grimshaw Jane C32
Grimshaw Joseph B62,C34
Grimshaw Martha A45
Grimshaw Thomas A63
Grimshaw William
A37,A45,A68,C14
Grindrod John C61
Grocott James A11
Groves Henry C35
Grundy Elizabeth Clara A57
Grundy John A57,C33
Grundy Ralph C30
Guildford Ada B55
Guildford Francis B55
Guy Catherine C21
Guy Thomas A49
Haberer George B37
Hackett John C33
Hackin George A13
Hackin James A20
Hackin Margaret A20
Hadfield Ellen B32
Hadfield Ernest C12
Hadfield James A33
Hadfield Joseph A78,C51
Hagen Thomas A77
Hague Margaret A20
Hague William A44
Haigh Abraham B13
Haigh Benjamin A28
Haigh Joseph C34
Haines Edward B55
Haithwaite George B26
Hale Matthew A50
Hale William A9
Hall Alfred B12

Hall Amelia C32
Hall Amery A14
Hall Ann A14
Hall Dennis C41
Hall Edward A58,A75
Hall Ellen B71
Hall Frank B51
Hall George A7
Hall James A8
Hall Jane A14,C20
Hall John B71
Hall John Henry B36
Hall Joseph A56,B51,C24
Hall Kathleen A76
Hall Malcolm A75
Hall Mary Alice C6
Hall Mary Jane B26
Hall Moses C31
Hall Richard B29
Hall Robert B25,B71,C60
Hall Samuel B3
Hall Sydney C6
Hall Thomas A75
Hall William B5,B27,B40,B53
Hallam Richard B17
Halleran Francis A34
Halligan John B24
Halliwell George B43
Halliwell John B5,B48,B49
Halliwell Mary Ann B43
Hallows Ann A14
Hallows Edward C56
Hallows Thomas A14,B8
Hallsor Amelia B8
Hallsworth Frances A22
Hallsworth James A22
Hallsworth Samuel A50
Halsall John C10
Hambleton William A60
Hamer Emma B63
Hamer James B63
Hamer John A70,B48
Hamer William C17
Hamilton Edward B9
Hamilton John A73
Hamilton Samuel A23
Hamlett Peter B11
Hammond Alfred B42
Hammond Matthew B20
Hampson Charles B16
Hampson Edward B34
Hampson Elizabeth B13
Hampson Franklin B16
Hampson Frederick B33
Hampson George A48
Hampson James C23
Hampson Jessie C59
Hampson John
A55,B11,B72,C28
Hampson John Willie B25
Hampson Richard A42
Hampson Samuel A10
Hampson Thomas C55
Hampson William C10,C48
Hancock James A25
Handley James A70
Handley Mordecai B32
Handley Robert A74,C61
Handley Thomas B59
Hankers Jane B37
Hankers William B37
Hankinson Alice C20
Hankinson Martha A36
Hankinson Robert C20
Hanlon Michael C28
Hannah John A69
Hannan William B13
Hannay Andrew A24
Hannay David A24
Hannay George C56
Hanrahan Michael A77,B10
Hanson George C12
Hanson Thomas C13
Hanvey Daniel C57

Hardcastle Margaret B2
Hardiman Edward A3
Harding Francis B2
Harding James A
Harding Thomas A8,A3
Hardisty Ann C2
Hardisty Cornelius A20,A3
Hardisty John C20,C5
Hardman Betty B7
Hardman George A3,C43,C4
Hardman Hannah C4
Hardman James B7
Hardman John C4
Hardy Edward B3
Hardy Frederick William B1
Hardy James A49,A5
Hardy John C4
Hardy Louis B5
Hardy Margaret A52,C4
Hardy Maria C4
Hardy Martha C4
Hardy Mary C4
Hardy Richard C5
Hargrave Ann A3
Hargreaves Barbara B7
Hargreaves George C4
Hargreaves Gertrude C3
Hargreaves Henry C6
Hargreaves James C4
Hargreaves Jane C4
Hargreaves John A76,C21
Hargreaves Joseph B36
Hargreaves Richard B5
Hargreaves Robert B11,C17
Hargreaves Stephen B72
Hargreaves Thomas A52,C13
Hargreaves William B2
Harley Amy A77
Harley Joseph A77
Harley William A77
Harper Robert A45
Harper Timothy A30
Harper William B57
Harreston Walter B48
Harriman Benjamin B33
Harris Annie B3
Harris James A74,C51
Harris John B3
Harris Joseph A13
Harris Robert A47
Harrison Barbara C43
Harrison Catherine B13
Harrison David C9
Harrison Edward A43
Harrison Elizabeth A55,A56
Harrison Ethel B47
Harrison George B17
Harrison Hamlet B30
Harrison Hannah B71
Harrison James B36
Harrison John A29,B17
Harrison Josephine C9
Harrison Mary B50
Harrison Ralph A49
Harrison Robert B13
Harrison Samuel B50
Harrison Sarah A54
Harrison Sid C25,C41,C47
Harrison Thomas C26,C43
Harrop Harriet B69
Harrop John B69,C22
Harrop Robert A36
Hart Joseph B51
Hart Samuel B63
Hart Violet C20
Hartcliffe William A76
Harte Michael C27
Harter Ezekiel B25
Harter Rachel B41
Harter Samuel B41
Hartley Joseph A31
Hartley Lawrence C62
Hartshorn Ezekiel A56
Hartwell Elizabeth A28

Name	Ref	Name	Ref	Name	Ref	Name	Ref	Name	Ref
Hartwell Richard	A28	Hewatt William	B72	Hitchen Richard	C21	Horrocks John	A7,B29	Hunstone Samuel	A49
Harvey Alfred	A38	Hewitt John	A37	Hitchen William	C13	Horrocks Richard	C52	Hunstone William	A28,A49
Harvey Charles	B50	Hey Ellen	B9	Hitchin George	B13	Horrocks Samuel	B29	Hunt Elijah	A8
Harvey Thomas	B50	Heyes George	B23	Hobday Dorothy	B28	Horrox Daniel	A27	Hunt Michael	A20
Haslam George	C62	Heyes John	B30	Hobday James	B28	Horsfall Elizabeth	A37	Hunt Robert	A28
Haslam Hannah	C40	Heyes John Knott	C21	Hobson Agnes	A48	Horsfall John	A37	Hunt William	A35
Haslam James	B68	Heyes Matilda	B30	Hobson John	A48,C16,C57	Horsley Jane	B15	Huntbatch Richard	C34
Haslam John	B16	Heyes William	A47	Hobson Joseph	A48	Horton Frederick	A65	Hurst Ann	B73
Haslam William	A6	Heys John	A17	Hobson Martha	A48	Hoskins Mary	A58	Hurst Elizabeth	A49
Hassall Ellen	A19	Heyward George	C18	Hobson Ralph	C45	Hough William	A57	Hurst George	C20
Hassall John	C10	Heywood Emma	C24	Hobson William	C16	Houghton John	B9	Hurst James	A7
Hassall William	A19	Heywood Ernest	B33	Hockenhull Gweneth	B33	Houghton Margaret	A8	Hurst Joseph	A45
Hatton family	A4	Heywood James	C24	Hockenhull Norman	B30,B33	Houldsworth James	A66	Hurst Thomas	B73
Hatton John	A6	Heywood John	C24	Hodges David	B5	Houldsworth William	A62	Hussey James	B65
Hauty Mary Ellen	A51	Heywood Peter	A55	Hodges Frederick	B5	House Ephraim	B70	Hutcheson William	A72
Hauty Thomas	A51	Heywood Ronald	C28	Hodges Mary	A71	Housen Ephraim	B70	Hutchinson Alfred	B64
Hawkins Richard	A63	Heywood Sarah	C28	Hodgkinson Elizabeth	A73	Howard Annie	C52	Hutchinson Edith	C5,C10
Hawksworth Mary	B4	Heyworth Joseph	A70	Hodgkinson John	A49	Howard Edwin	B36	Hutchinson Frank	C19
Hawksworth William	B4	Hibbert Henry	A67	Hodgkinson William	B75	Howard John	C24	Hutchinson George	C48
Haworth James	B13	Hibbertson James	A12	Hodgson Elizabeth	B22	Howard Joseph	A38	Hutchinson Henry	B50
Haworth Robert	A59	Hicks John William	C60	Hodgson Phyllis	A31	Howard Sarah	B51	Hutchinson John	A44
Haworth William	B13,C18	Hicks Joseph	B3	Hodgson Samuel	A31	Howard Thomas	C37,C46	Hutchinson Joseph	A27
Hawthornthwaite William	C3	Hickson Dorothy	B73	Hodgson Thomas	C15	Howarth George	A43	Hutchinson Sarah	A44
Hay James	B45	Hickson Herbert	A69	Hodgson Walter	B13	Howarth Gilbert	B36	Hutchinson Thomas	C49
Hay Walter	A28	Hickson Matthew	A19	Hodson Thomas	A76	Howarth James	B3,C41	Hutchinson William	C5,C10
Haycock Vincent	B72	Hickson Walter	B73	Hoey William	B44	Howarth Mary	B3	Hyde Harry	B60
Haydock John	A74	Higgen Charles	B42	Holcroft Jane	B72	Howarth Richard	A50	Hyde James	A38
Haydock Thomas	A56	Higgin John	A11	Holcroft John	B72	Howarth Thomas	A11,A43	Hyde John	A68
Hayes Benjamin	A72	Higginbottom James	B21,C9,C28	Holden Charles	C13	Howarth William	A77,C19	Hyde Margaret	B60
Hayes Jack	A56	Higgins Cyril	C9	Holden Elizabeth	C13	Howe Frances	B54	Hyde Mary	A29
Hayes John	A11,B55,B56,C47	Higgins Lavinia	C9	Holden James	C17,C37	Howell John	C40	Hyde Rachel	C61
Hayes Matilda	B16	Higgs Joan	B45	Holden John	C17,C26	Howell Samuel	B51	Hyde Robert	C8
Hayhurst William	C8	Higgs William	A20	Holden Joseph	A67,B66	Hoyes Ernest	B37	Hyde Sarah	A38
Haythornthwaite Edward	B67	Higham Florence	C4	Holden Mary	C13	Hoyland Lewis	B27	Hyde Thomas	A38
Haywood Samuel	B27	Higham Frances	C22	Holden Sarah	C17	Huddart Hannah	B2,C8	Ingham Benjamin	C16
Heaford Helen	B50	Higham James	A72,C22,C50	Holden Thomas	A11,A59,B25	Huddart Jonathan	B2	Ingham Herbert	B53
Heaford Michael	B50	Higham John	C3,C4	Holder Henry	C18	Huddleston William	B3	Ingham James Warren	A2
Heald Elsie	C35	Higham Margaret	B40	Hole Lionel	A51	Hudson Edith	B21	Inman Charles	C35
Heaney Charles	B2	Higham Richard	B40	Holehouse George	C6	Hudson Ernest	C44	Inman Emmanuel	B75
Heaney Doris	A17	Higham Sarah	C4	Holiday Joshua	A77	Hudson Esther	C60	Inman Georgina	C35
Heaney Hannah	B2	Highfield William	A47	Holland Ellen	C58	Hudson Fred	C60	Irlam John	A4
Heaney Thomas	A17	Hignett Ruth	C44	Holland George	B19,B35	Hudson Henry	A13	Irlam Martha	C14
Heap Albert	C5	Hignett Thomas	C44	Holland James	A9	Hudson Isabella	A13	Irlam Thomas	A66,C14
Heap George	B9	Higson Elizabeth	B41	Holland John	A29,B47	Hughes Annie	C46	Irving David	B65
Heap Robert	B56	Higson George	A23,A24	Holland Mary	A29	Hughes Charles	B27	Isherwood Henry	B70
Heath Harold	B13	Higson Josiah	B66	Hollingsworth Isabella	A50	Hughes David	B8	Isherwood James	B21
Heath John	A14	Higson Thomas	C34	Hollingsworth John	A19	Hughes Eliza	B8	Isherwood John	B33
Heathcote Robert	A34	Hilditch Jane	A18	Hollingworth William	B75	Hughes Fanny	A74	Isherwood Martha	B70
Heathcote Samuel	C41	Hill Ann	B63	Hollins John	A58	Hughes Frederick	B10	Ivill James	B46,B66
Heaton Charles	C17	Hill Daniel	B63	Holmes Cecil	B50	Hughes Harriet	B44	Ivill Norah	B66
Heaton Elizabeth	B19	Hill Edward	B55	Holmes Edna	C28	Hughes Henry	B10	Jackson Alfred	B69
Heaton George	B19	Hill Elizabeth	B16	Holmes Francis	A54	Hughes James	C3	Jackson Alice	B70
Hebblethwaite Thomas	C13,C56	Hill Frederick	C20	Holmes Frank	B59	Hughes John	A50,B23,B49	Jackson Charles	A23
Heblethwaite John	B48	Hill George	B16,C3	Holmes John	C28	Hughes Marjorie	B30	Jackson Charles Gilbert	C28
Heckman James	A72	Hill Margaret	B35	Holmes Robert	A26	Hughes Martha Ann	B23	Jackson Edwin	B70
Heenan Albert	B13	Hill Reuben	B74	Holt Douglas	C19	Hughes Richard	A53	Jackson Frederick	B58,C12
Heenan Lily	B13	Hill Rose	C3	Holt Emily	C19	Hughes Thomas	A9,A37,A66,C24	Jackson Hannah	A25
Heggie Robert	B26	Hill William	A51,A60,B35	Holt George	A60			Jackson Henry	B10,B41
Helme Thomas	B16	Hilton George	A9	Holt James	A59	Hughes William	A47	Jackson Herbert	C13,C53
Helsby Norman	C21	Hilton William	B21,C18	Holt Jane	A75	Hulland George	C23	Jackson Irene	C53
Hemm Charles	A29	Hind Alfred	C9	Holt Joseph	A66,A71	Hulland William	C33,C40	Jackson Isaac	B37
Henderson Duncan	B64	Hind Harry	B54	Holt Thomas	A33,A75	Hulley Benjamin	A28	Jackson J	A17
Henderson Joseph	A75	Hind Joseph	C61	Hood George	B40	Hulme Avril	A16	Jackson James	A29,B4
Hennell Richard	A54	Hind Margaret	B26	Hood James	A63	Hulme Elizabeth	A5,B10	Jackson Joan	B58
Hennessy Herbert	A31	Hindle James	C8	Hood Martha	B40	Hulme Harriet	B35	Jackson John	A58
Henshall George	C19	Hindle Nellie	B11,C8	Hooper Albert	A34	Hulme Henry	B35	Jackson Maria	B13
Henshall Isabella	B72	Hindle Sarah	A19	Hope Alice	C3	Hulme James	C6,C12	Jackson Martha	A55
Henshall John	A12	Hindley Elizabeth	C41	Hope Cornelius	C3	Hulme John	C41	Jackson Mary Ann	B22
Henshall Thomas	B30	Hindley George	C54	Hope Daniel	B26	Hulme Martha	A5	Jackson Mary Emma	B9
Henshall Timothy	C4	Hindley Harriet	B51	Hope Edmund	B51	Hulme Mary Ann	B35	Jackson Richard	A36
Henson Herbert	C57,C60,C63	Hindley Joseph	C15	Hope Elijah	C44	Hulme Neville	A16	Jackson Robert	A25
		Hindley Mary	C15	Hope Jane	B51	Hulme Oliver	B10	Jackson Sarah	B50
Hepper Anthony	C35	Hindley Richard	B15	Hope John	C3	Hulme Thomas	A21	Jackson Thomas	A26,B33,C37
Hepplestone Hannah	A38	Hindley Samuel	C41	Hope Richard	B36	Hulmes John	B3		
Hepplethwaite John	B53	Hinds Doris	C48	Hope William	C52	Hulse Isaac	A47	Jackson William	B13,C15
Hepworth Lees	B46	Hinds George	C48	Hopkinson John	A50	Hulse James	B51,B53	James Alice	C62
Herbert Harry	C22	Hine Robert	A47	Hopwood Matthew	A58	Hulton David	A72	James Arthur	C62
Herdman Edward	A47	Hinman Janet	C21	Horlock Derrick	A78	Hulton Frank	A53	James Jane	A51
Hertford Charles	B74	Hitchen Charles	B28,B48	Horn Frederick	B13	Hulton Franklin	A72	James John	A52
Hesford Thomas	A23	Hitchen George	B22,B61	Hornby Richard	B49	Hulton James	A72	James Lily	B44
Hesketh John	A61	Hitchen John	C21	Hornby Thomas	A52	Hulton Julius	A72	James William	A28
Hestford Albert	C47	Hitchen John Paul	C21	Horner John	B44	Humphreys Henry	B17,B21	Jameson James	B16
		Hitchen Joseph	B7	Horrocks Ann	B29	Hunstone Alice	A28	Jardine Leslie	B54
				Horrocks James	A49	Hunstone Mary	A49	Jeffs Harriet	C51

Jelly Frederick C30	Jones William A32,A59,B74	Killon Doris A14,B63	Lazonby William A53	Linney Thomas C26	
Jelly Harriet C30	Jordan Henry B9	Kilner David A12	Leach Abraham B29	Litherland Richard A73	
Jelly Sarah C30	Jordan Thomas C11	King Frederick C6	Leach Charles A25	Litherland Walter A46	
Jelly William C30	Joughin William A9	King James A6,B51	Leach Joseph A67	Lithgow Hector C58	
Jenkinson John B71	Joyce Celia B63	King William B29,B30	Leach Susannah B61	Little John B31	
Jenkinson William B36	Joyce Martin B63	Kinnaston John A9	Leach Thomas A30	Little Mary Ellen B31	
Jennings Edwin A37	Joynes Ernest B66	Kinsey Ralph A53	Leadbetter William B60	Little Violet B31	
Jennings John B73	Joynt J Scott B58	Kinsey Sarah A53	Leater Elizabeth C5	Littlemore George B66	
Jervis Thomas B4	Jump Peter C59	Kinsey William B31	Leater Henry C5	Littlewood Arnold A37	
Jobson Joseph A18	Justice William A3,A22	Kirby Annie B27	Leater James C6	Littlewood Fred A70	
Jobson Robert A67,B17	Kain John B67	Kirkby Thomas A74	Leater Thomas C13	Livesey Alfred B24	
John Thomas C29	Kay Edward A37	Kirkham Margaret B70	Leatherbarrow George B65	Livesey Joseph A58,C37	
Johnson Alan B12,B13,B54	Kay Elijah C53	Kirkman Alice B27	Leatherbarrow Robert A16	Livesey Richard B23	
Johnson Alice A25	Kay Ellen C20	Kirkman Fred A77	Ledsham William A73	Livesey Sam A3	
Johnson Amy A28	Kay Hannah A37	Kirkman Peter A54	Ledsome William C18	Lloyd George B60	
Johnson Arthur A3	Kay James C20	Kirkman Robert C30	Lee Albert B6	Lloyd Harry A72	
Johnson Charles B60,C24	Kay John A46,A72,B21,B72	Kirkman Thomas B27	Lee Annie B22	Lloyd John B54	
Johnson Edward A77	Kay Lawrence Rostron A20	Kirkwood Charlotte C53	Lee Ernest C63	Lloyd Theophilus A57	
Johnson Elsie C4	Kay Margaret A72	Kirton Ann C12	Lee Harold B7	Lloyd Thomas	
Johnson Emily B23,C4,C6	Kay Mary C53	Kirton Charles C12	Lee Henry B12	A28,A56,B40,B44	
Johnson Esther C15	Kay Peter C11	Kitchen Ellen A72	Lee Joseph A58	Lloynd George A10	
Johnson Florence C35	Kay Rebecca C11	Kitchen John A72	Lee Samuel A61	Lobban James B33	
Johnson Frederick B42	Kay Richard A17	Kitchen William A73	Leech James A17	Lockett James B72	
Johnson George B36,C15	Kay Robert A45	Kitson George A62,B67	Leech Joel A26	Lockhart William A72	
Johnson Gerald C58	Kay Thomas B7	Kitson William B51	Leech Peter A4	Lofthouse Henry A48	
Johnson Iris	Kay William C12	Knight James B44,C20	Leeming Joseph A23	Loftus Mary Jane B13	
B11,B12,B13,B54	Kean Abigail A68	Knight Nancy A16	Lees Jacob B8	Loftus Thomas A70	
Johnson James A8,A15,	Kean Thomas A68	Knight Samuel C52	Lees Richard C53	Lomas Charles B33	
A25,B21,B26,B36,C15	Kearney John A57	Knight Thomas C30	Lees Robert A12	Lomas Clara A31	
Johnson John	Kearton Christopher A63	Knott Abraham B69	Lees Samuel B15	Lomas James B50,B56	
A48,B36,B43,B57,C4	Keates Edgar B60	Knott Alfred B8	Lees Sarah B4	Lomas Kathleen B56	
Johnson John Alfred C4	Keenan Elizabeth C10	Knott Brian B54	Lees Thomas C42	Lomas Robert A31	
Johnson Joseph A60,C52	Keeton John A60	Knott Daniel B37	Lehane Anne A28	Lomas Theresa B67	
Johnson Josiah B10	Kehoe John James B45	Knott Jean B54	Lehane Daniel A28	Lomas Thomas B67	
Johnson Martha B41	Kehoe John S B45	Knott John C6	Leicester James jun B58	Lomax Richard A14	
Johnson Mary Ellen B32	Kelley Tom A65	Knott Joseph A60	Leicester James sen B57	Long Frank B6	
Johnson Matthew B43	Kelly Agnes B49	Knott Mary B69	Leicester William A3	Long James B50	
Johnson Richard A53,B16	Kelly Ann B22	Knowles Jane A55	Leigh George B61	Longshaw Edwin B7	
Johnson Samuel B27	Kelly Edward B42,B61	Knowles John A55	Leigh James A69,C11	Longworth John B57,C22	
Johnson Thomas	Kelly Eileen C7	Knowles Joseph B20	Leigh John C18	Longworth Thomas A76	
A48,B9,B32,C5,C15	Kelly Henry B22	Koppel Jessie B27	Leigh John Thomas B20	Lord Edmund C23	
Johnson William C6,C30	Kelly James C3,C6	Kynaston Richard B64,B68	Lennon Arthur C26	Lord Frederick B50	
Johnston Annie C9	Kelly Joseph A42,B49	Kynaston Sarah Ann B64	Lennon Ethel C17	Lord Jeremiah A37	
Johnston Barry A21	Kelly Maria B7,B33	Laithwaite Jane A25	Lennon James C17	Lord John B50,C16	
Johnston William	Kelly Mary C21	Laithwaite Jonathan A25	Lennon Joan C26	Lord Joseph A18	
A44,C9,C56	Kelly Matthew A66	Lakin Francis B48	Lennon John A37	Lord Lawrence A35	
Johnstone William C56	Kelly Peter B9,B20,B24	Lamb Elizabeth A28	Leonard Ellen B36	Lord Reuben C16	
Jolly Alan C55	Kelly William A64,B7	Lamb Jane A34	Leslie Andrew A75	Lord Samuel B30,C16	
Jolly Derek B20	Kelsall John B37	Lamb John A34,C62	Leslie James A55	Lord Thomas C52	
Jolly Doris C55	Kelsey George B26,B43	Lamb Thomas A27	Lester James B33,B53	Loseby Dorothy B50	
Jolly Edward B30	Kelsey Harold C37	Lambert Elizabeth C28	Lever Edwin A59	Loseby Harry B50	
Jones Alfred B23	Kelsey Martha B26	Lambert James A54	Lever George C37	Lovett Joseph A51	
Jones Ann B15	Kelsey Thomas A64,A65	Lambert Joseph B40	Lever Harold C41	Lovett Peter A51	
Jones Ann Alice C10	Kemp Harold C61	Lambert Thomas	Lever Joseph B16	Lowcock Sam A20	
Jones Arthur B64	Kemp James C61	C27,C28,C34,C51	Lever Mary Ellen B45	Lowe Alfred A28	
Jones Benjamin B15	Kemp Jeremiah C16	Lancashire Robert A73	Lever Muriel C41	Lowe Frederick A75	
Jones Blanche A25	Kemp Nancy C16	Lancaster James A22,B48	Lever Thomas B16	Lowe James B9	
Jones David Thomas A14	Kemp Samuel A37,A49	Lancaster John A17	Lever William	Lowe John C7	
Jones Edith B24	Kemp Thomas C19	Lancaster Joseph A44	A54,A71,B33,B45	Lowe Peter B37	
Jones Edward B36	Kendall William A62	Landers Jane B13	Leviston Robert A73	Lowndes Edward C45	
Jones Edward Beech C31	Kennedy Annie B47	Lane William A67	Lewis Albert C43	Lowndes Margaret C46	
Jones Eliza B46	Kennedy Charles B24	Lang Alice A67	Lewis Alice C40	Lowndes Richard C46	
Jones Elizabeth A23	Kennedy Elizabeth C54	Lang Ann B35	Lewis George C19,C49	Lowthian Richard A48	
Jones Frederick C57	Kennedy Thomas C54	Lang Ben A11,A42,B14	Lewis Harold B53	Lucas George B72	
Jones George A28,B11,C31	Kenney Michael A30	Lang James C18	Lewis Henrietta B12	Lucas John A57	
Jones Hannah B64	Kenny Arthur B36	Lang Schofield A67	Lewis John C51	Lucas William A77	
Jones Harriet A37	Kensett Joseph B30	Langford Thomas C49	Lewis Samuel B4	Lundy Henrietta C51	
Jones James B15,B63,C37	Kent Sam A3	Last Arthur A35	Lewis Vina B11,B53,C8	Lundy William A78,C51	
Jones John	Kenworthy Emma A75	Last Elizabeth A35	Leyland Elizabeth A78	Lunn John B32	
A21,A58,B67,C23	Kenyon Edward A29	Latham William B72	Leyland Ernest A78	Luty Albert B20,B50	
Jones John William B46	Kenyon James C28	Lavender J C A25	Lidgett George A67	Luty Ernest C13	
Jones Joseph A23,C30	Kenyon Samuel A17	Lavery John C18	Lightburn James A28	Luty James C37	
Jones Louisa A52	Kenyon William A49	Law Margaret B17	Lightfoot Clifford C6	Luty John C13	
Jones Mary B55	Kerfoot James A50	Law Thomas B17	Lightfoot Lilian C6	Luxford Edward B55,B69	
Jones Nathan A25	Kerrell George B23	Law William A48,B17	Lindley Elizabeth A56	Lynch Benjamin A50	
Jones Peter C10	Kerrigan Mary Jane B25	Lawler Andrew C24	Lindsay George B50	Lynch Joseph C40	
Jones Reuben A32	Kershaw Alice C26	Lawless John B64	Lindsay George Frederick	Lyon James A10	
Jones Richard A56,B10	Kershaw Hilda A31	Lawless Sarah A23	B50	Lyon John A10,A14	
Jones Robert A31,B14	Kershaw James A9	Lawley Charles A37	Lindsey George B66	Lyon Joseph A26	
Jones Sarah A73	Kershaw Mary C26,C34	Lawrence John B51	Lindsey Jesse B7	Lyons Anthony B32	
Jones Thomas A46,B10,C53	Keyzey Gerald A72	Lawrence Thomas A64	Linford James A75	Lyons Betsy B6	
	Kilby Raymond C22	Lawton George A3	Linnett James A21	Lyons Bridget B71	
	Kilgour James C32	Lawton Henry B18	Linney George A57	Lyons Frederick C33	
	Killon Arnold A14,B63	Lazenbury William C17	Linney Norman C26	Lyons John A26,C34	

Name	Ref	Name	Ref	Name	Ref	Name	Ref	Name	Ref
Lyons Michael	B71	McVeigh James	A72	Mason Robert	C59	Millington John	A35	Mulligan Charles	A22
Lyth John	A9	McWilliams Thomas	A47	Massey J	A66	Millington William	A28	Mulligan Thomas	A57
Lyth William	B20,B21,C4	McWright John	A71	Massey Samuel	A51	Mills Alexander	B55	Mulliner John	B35
Macadam Allan	C37	Madden Lilian	B48	Massey Walter	B9,B26	Mills Alice	B25	Mulroy James	C37
McArdle Mary	A20	Madeley David	A56	Massey William	B15	Mills Charles	A14	Mulroy John	C37
Macarty Emma	C48	Madeley Elizabeth	A45	Mather Betsy	B7	Mills Charles B	C18	Munday Roy	B46
Macarty Joseph	C48	Madeley Harriet	C3	Mather Charles	A24	Mills Esther	B71	Mundy John	A64,B2
McBaide Annie	A32	Madeley Robert	C3	Mather James	B35	Mills Frank	A14	Mundy Stephen	B2
McBride Marion	B41	Maguire Daniel	A38	Mather Jane	A63	Mills Harry	B71	Mundy William	A56,C25
McBrierley Jane	A22	Maguire James	A45	Mather John	A63,C35	Mills Henry	A60	Mundy William jun	A56
McCabe James	B33	Mahoney Maria	B35	Mather Joseph	B65	Mills John	B46,C38	Murch John	A26
McCallum Christopher	B60	Maiden Thomas	B33	Mather Mildred	B65	Mills Joseph	C7	Murdon William	C38
McCarthy Edwin	B43	Makin Charles	B47	Mather Robert	A45	Mills Mary Ann	B25	Murphy David	B37
McCarthy Emily	C37	Makin Elizabeth	B47	Mather Samuel	B7,B16	Mills Walter Jack	C31,C37	Murphy Edward	C21
McClelland Sarah	B5	Makin John	A46,B31	Mather Thomas	A9,A12	Mills William	A63,A68	Murphy James	B25
McCluskey John	C15	Makin Joseph	A14	Mather William	A45	Millward Florence	B21	Murphy John	A63
McConnell Christopher	C52	Makin Obadiah	B10	Mathieson John	C28	Millward Samuel	C9	Murphy Joseph	B52
McCormick Catherine	B45	Makin Robert	A17,B31	Matley William	A51	Millward William	B21	Murphy Michael	A9,A57
McCormick Fred	B56	Makin Samuel	A29	Matthews Abraham	C47	Milne James	B75	Murray Elizabeth	B67
McCormick James	A68	Makin Thomas	C25,C51	Matthews Edward	A60	Milroy William	B47	Murray John	C4
McCormick John	A20	Malley Arthur	A31	Matthews Gerald	B27	Mitcham George	C31	Murrell Lilian	B40
McCormick Mary	A20,B65	Mallinson Edward	A24	Matthews Isaac	C47	Mitchell Alfred	A51	Murrell Samuel	B40
McCraith James	A29	Malone Emily	C16	Matthews James	C22	Mitchell Alice	A51	Mycock Mary	B26
McDermott John	B13	Malone John	A17,C16	Matthews Patricia	B27	Mitchell Henry	A43,A61	Myerscough Richard	C27
McDermott Michael	C27,C30	Malpas Joseph	C37	Matthews Thomas	A60	Mitchell Horace	A63	Nash Walter	C57
McDermott Richard	B23	Mann Abraham	B71	Matthews William	B63	Mitchell James	A9,A78	Naylor Elizabeth	A65
McDonald Daniel	A67	Mann Edward	B74	Mawdsley Benjamin	C11,C42	Mitchell John	B28,C18	Naylor James	A65
McDonald Ethelbert Leo	B21	Mann Ethel	B74	Mawdsley Dorothy	C46	Mitchison James	A58	Naylor Mary	A65
McDonald John	B55	Mann Mrs	C20	Mawdsley Evan	A57	Moffitt John	C11	Naylor Richard	A65
McDonald Peter	A59	Mann Robert	B29	Mawdsley John	C34	Monks Thomas	B23	Naylor William	B34
McDonald Timothy	C53	Mann William	C20	Maxwell Emma	C10	Monks William	A59	Neal John	A51
McDonough James	B50	Manning George	B52	Maxwell Joseph	C10	Moody William	B16,B65	Neary Joseph	C38
McDonough John	A34	Mannix Michael	B15,B22	May James	C27	Moorcroft David	A23	Needham Alice	B33
McDonough Lilian	B50	Mannix Sarah	B22	May Richard	B15	Moore Abraham	B23	Needham George	B33
McDougall Margaret	C22	Mappin Herbert	B75	Mayall Robert	B3	Moore Arthur	A50	Needham John	B17
McFadden Samuel	B65	Marchant Ada	A53	Maychell James	C58	Moore Thomas	B34,B45	Needham Joseph	B17
McFarland John	C41	Margison John	B44	Maycock John	A60,B34	Moore Valentine	A10	Nelson George B	B28
McFarland Malcolm	C41	Mark Joseph	A44	Maycock Mary	B34	Moores James	A27,B37	Nelson Henry	A19,A29
McFarlane James	B68	Markland Ann	B46,C48	Mayer Ellen	A47	Moores Sam	C40	Nelson Horatio	C48,C53
McGhie Arthur	C55	Markland Bill	B66	Mayne Richard	B44	Moores William	C62	Nelson Mary	A19
McGillon Gerard	B27	Markland Elizabeth	B42	Mayor John	A77	Moorewood Andrew	A12	Netherton Thomas	B16
McGowan Christopher	B73	Markland Henry	B42,B45	Meadowcroft James	B64	Moorhouse William	A74	Neville William	A21
McGowan Leslie	C57	Markland James	C48	Mee Richard	A20	Moorman James	C28	Newell Albert	B48
McGowan Stephen	B3,B26	Marland Audrey	C30	Megson Grace	A7,B53	Moreton Jane	C58	Newsham Joseph	C8
McGrath John	B51	Marland Edward	B63	Megson Hannah	B8	Moreton Samuel	B37	Newsome George	C34
McGrath Michael	B50	Marland Frank	C43	Melia James	C7	Moreton William	C56,C58	Newsome John	C29
McGreevy Ann	B18	Marland Kenneth	C30	Mellor Ann	C13	Morgan Daniel	B52	Newton Agnes	A78
McGreevy John	B18	Marland Nellie	C43	Mellor Elizabeth	B58,C18	Morgan Hannah	C27	Newton Edmund	A78
McGuinness Hannah	B40	Marlor John	B61	Mellor George	C46	Morgan Louise	B52	Newton John	A78
McHale Francis	B30	Marlor Robert	B50	Mellor Jim	A17	Morley Annie	B4	Newton Robert	B31
McHale Herbert	C7	Marriott John	B50	Mellor John	B14,C13	Morley John	B25,B46	Newton Samuel	A48
Machin Michael	B24	Marriott Thomas	C42	Mellor Joseph	A56	Morris Edward	B41	Newton William	B29
McHugh James	B7	Marrs Vera	C53	Mellor Margaret	A50,B31	Morris Ellen	C42	Nicholls Mary Jane	C8
McIntosh Walter	A75	Marrs Wilfred	C53	Mellor Ronald	B31	Morris George	C19	Nicholls Thomas	C8
McIntyre Duncan	C53	Marsden Emma	C23,C25	Mellor Thomas	C18	Morris Hannah	B37	Nichols Harry	B56
McIntyre Edward	C61	Marsden George	B17	Mellor Vera	A17	Morris Joseph	B25	Nichols John	C8
McIntyre John	C22	Marsden Richard	B47	Melody Michael	A21	Morris Susannah	A34	Nichols William	C8
McKenna Bernard	A35	Marsden William	A68,B72,B73	Menzies William	A12	Mort Lewis	A32	Nicholson Alice	C29
McKenney Alexander	A78	Marsh Ellen	B22	Mercer Joseph	A56	Mort Mary	A45	Nicholson Eleanor	A68
Mackin Michael	B24	Marsh John	A9,B20,B23,C34	Mercer Margaret	C47	Mort William	A45	Nicholson Henry	C29
McKinna David	A13,B50	Marsh Robert	A16	Mercer Samuel	C47	Morton James	B26	Nicholson Jane	A62
McKinna Peter	B74	Marsh Wallace	B16	Merrick James	C15	Morton John	B35	Nicholson Joseph	A47
McKinna Robert	C22	Marsh William	A55,C12	Merritt William	B30	Morton Mike	C60	Nicoll William	C7
McKnight John	A55,B73	Marshall Henry	C44	Merten Harry	B70	Morton Pauline	C60	Nightingale William	A7
McLean John	B63	Marshall James	C21	Metcalf Christopher	B34	Morton William	B69	Nixon John	A36
Maclean John	B74	Marshall John	A44,A50	Metcalf Deborah	B34	Moss Henry	A58,C22	Nixon Joseph	B73
McLellan John	B18	Marshall Wally	A72,B70	Metcalf Ellen	B34	Moss James	A3	Noakes Joan	B50
McLoughlin James	A25,A45,C35	Marsland Norman	C7	Metcalf George	B34	Moss John	A8	Noble Harry	B27
McManus James	B15,B27,B73	Marston James	B31	Metcalf Thomas	A13,A14	Mottershead William	C8	Noden Thomas	A75
McManus Teresa	B27	Martin Annie	B24	Micklewright Ellen	A77	Mottram Edward	A54	Nolan Frank	B30,B37
McMillan John	B31	Martin Elizabeth	A33	Micklewright John	A77	Mottram John	A11	Nolan John	B64
McMorrow Thomas	C21	Martin George	A54	Middleton Alfred	C8	Mottram Samuel	A11	Nolan Peter	A34
McMullen Len	B20	Martin John	A12,A22,A37	Middleton Emily	B37	Mottram Susannah	A11	Noonan John	B47
McNabb James	A4	Martin Joseph	A33	Middleton Hugh	B47	Moult Isaac	A22	Norbury Ada	B23
McNally Annie	B6	Martin Lily	B44	Middleton Percy	C37	Moulton David	A63	Norbury John	A77
McNally Patrick	B6	Martin Margaret	B36	Miles Jane	C51	Mounsey Isabella	B15	Norbury Sam	A53
McNeill Jim	A21	Martin William	A48,B13	Miller Harold	B33	Moylan Michael	A65	Norbury Thomas	C9
McNicholl David	A60	Martinscroft Samuel	C52	Miller Jack	A18	Much Edward	B13	Norbury William	A28
McNicholls Esther	B53	Martland Thomas	A35	Miller Joseph	A48	Mugglestone John	B37	Norris Abraham	B43
McNicholls George	B53	Martland William	B24	Miller Reuben	B33	Muldoon Elizabeth	B53	Norris Catherine	A30
McQueen James	B15	Marvin Charles	A13	Millett James	B23	Muldoon Robert	B53	Norris Elizabeth	B16
McRitchie Margaret	C35	Mason John William	B26	Milligan Agnes	A33	Mullaly Arthur	A16	Norris Henry	A30
		Mason Joseph	B29	Millington Florence	C19	Mullard Mary	B24	Norris John	B16
				Millington James	C19	Mullen Dennis	B23	North Robert	C30

Name	Ref
Norton Charles	B14
Nunnerley Nathaniel	C18
Nuttall John	A42
Nuttall Thomas	B74
Nuttall Wilf	C48
Nutter George	A76,C21
Nuttley William	B16
Oates James	A70
Oates Thomas	C21,C58
O'Brien Elizabeth	A48,B53
O'Brien Joseph	C47
O'Brien William	A48,C7
O'Donoghue Elsie	B55,C56
O'Donoghue Kenneth	B55
O'Donoghue Marion	B55
O'Donoghue William	C56
Ogden Ann	C31
Ogden Annie	C18
Ogden Eric	B54
Ogden Geoffrey	B57
Ogden Isaac	C31
Ogden Joseph	C26
Ogden Margaret	B54
Ogden Samuel	B17,C45
Ogden Stanley	C18
Ogden Thomas	B52
Okell Elizabeth	B30
Okell Joseph	B30
Okell Peter	A15,B30
Okell William	A53
Old Ernest	A56
Oldfield John	A22,B32
Oldfield Thomas	A24
Oldham Adam	B57
Oldham Elizabeth	C3
Oldham Thomas	A27
Oliver Samuel	B54
Ollier Matthew	A8,B41
Ollier William	B57
Openshaw Albert	A31
Openshaw Alfred	C19
Openshaw John	C19
Openshaw Timothy	B47
Oram Jane	C20
Oram William	C20
O'Reilly Elizabeth	B42
Orme Samuel	A17
Orme William	B4
Ormrod John	B52
Orrell James	B36
Orton John	B12
Orton William	A77
Osborne Frank	C61
Osborne Joseph	A20
Outhwaite Harriet	B53
Overall Anne	A10
Overall Thomas	A10
Owen Alfred	B60
Owen Eliza	A35
Owen James	B32
Owen John	A57,B62,C58
Owen Lewis	C24
Owen Thomas	A29
Owen William	A50
Owens Ann	B2
Owens David	B21
Owens Marie	B21
Padgett William	A42
Page Edwin	A38
Page Elizabeth	B43
Page George	A65
Palfreyman Charles	A36
Palin Ann	C23
Pallister Vincent	A11
Palmer Annie	B13
Palmer Fred	B13
Palmer George	C12
Palmer James	B71
Pardon Eleanor	A32
Park William	A6
Parker Charles	C30
Parker Esther	C30
Parker Mary Emma	B68
Parker Richard	A13,C37
Parker Samuel	A52
Parker Stephen	B61
Parker Thomas	B37
Parker Walter	A53
Parkes Marjorie	C56
Parkes William	A26
Parkin Thomas	C17
Parkinson Charles	C60
Parkinson George	A77
Parkinson James	C40
Parkinson Jimmy	C13
Parkinson Joseph	B30,C21,C52
Parkinson Mary Ann	A77
Parkinson Ralph	C7
Parkinson Rowland	B29
Parkinson William	A53,B43
Parnell Edna	B13,C21,C37
Parnell Wilfred	B13
Parnell William	A67
Parry David	A77
Parry Edward	C20
Parry William	C27
Parsons Alan	C55
Parsons Thomas	B70
Partington Albert	B54
Partington Caroline	B59
Partington May	B54
Partington William	A7
Parton John	A19
Parton Paul	A19
Pass Horace	C21
Pass William	B57
Patterson John	A68
Patton Thomas	B47
Pawsey Thomas	A24
Paxton Nellie	B63
Payne Thomas	B60
Peacock William	A5
Peake William	C57
Pearce Elizabeth	C33
Pearce James	C33
Pearce Robert	A9
Pearson Henry	A52
Pearson Isabella	A75
Pearson James	C14
Pearson Joseph	B69,C42
Pearson Mary	B65,B69
Pearson Mary Jane	C52
Pearson Nora	B42
Pearson Thomas	A42,B42
Pearson William	A72
Peat Edwin	C53
Peatfield Jonathan	A34
Peatfield Margaret	A34
Pedley James	A30
Pee Enoch	C43
Peel Catherine	A60
Peel Henry	A10
Peers Mary	A59
Pemberton Arthur	A75,A76
Pemberton May	A76
Pendlebury Andrew	B34
Pendlebury Thomas	A55
Pendleton Thomas	B57
Penkethman Thomas	A57
Penkett George	C23
Pennington Elizabeth	A53
Pennington John	A53,C42
Penny Stephen	B49
Penwarden Charles	C18
Peover Thomas	C25
Percival Hannah	B44
Percival Nathan	A31
Perkins Ann	B58
Perkins Jane	B58
Peters George	B26
Peters Winifred	B26
Petrie Joseph	B13
Petrie William	B46
Pheasey William	A50,C32
Phelps James	C23
Phillips Ada	C43
Phillips Clifford	B19
Phillips Edith	B74
Phillips John	C43
Phillips Thomas	B75,C3
Phippin Robert	A61,A67
Pickman James	B41
Pidd Ann	C9
Pidd Watson	C9
Pierce Elizabeth	A4
Pierce John	A4,A70
Pierce Margaret	A70
Pierpoint Eliza	B50,B51
Pierpoint William	B50,B51
Piggott Ellis	A8
Pike Elizabeth	A25
Pike John	A25,A47
Pike Thomas	A47,C62
Pilkington John	B42,B65
Pilling Edmund	B51
Pilling James	B45
Pilling John	C40
Pitt Frank	A75
Pitts Samuel	A5
Plaister Ronald	C47
Plaister Ruth	C47
Plant Betty	B46
Plant Cyril	B46,C20
Plant Edward	A71
Plant William	A71
Platt Uriah	A58
Poizer James	A68
Pollard Ellen	B9
Pollard Hugh	B9
Pollard James	A74
Pollard Ruth	B14
Pollard Samuel	A52
Pollard Sarah	B53
Pollard Walter	A56
Pollard William	B53
Pollett John	B57
Pollitt Gertrude	B70
Pollitt James	A56
Pollitt Jane	A56
Pollitt John	A26,C53
Pollitt Louie	C53
Pollitt William	A2
Pomfret Alice	B53
Poole Mark	C23
Pope Eva	B35
Pope George	C43
Pope John	C43
Pope Mary	C23
Pope Vincent	C23
Port James	A53
Porter Benjamin	C8
Postlethwaite William	A6
Potter Elizabeth	B69
Potter George	A61
Potter Mary	B40
Potter Septimus	A14
Potton William	A65
Potts Charlotte	A38
Potts Samuel	A33
Pover Richard	A37
Powell Eliza	A7
Powell Thomas	A52
Powell William	B66
Power John	B46
Powner John	A64
Poynter Elizabeth	B36
Pratt John	A48,C34
Prescott Charlotte	A46
Presley John	A25
Pressler George	B47
Pressler Georgina	B47
Preston Francis	B70
Preston John	B65
Preston Margaret	A36
Preston Rose	B70
Preston William	A32
Prestwich Ann	C23,C40
Price Catherine	C30
Price Dorothy	A16
Price John	A44
Price Leonard	A16
Price Mary	A33
Price Michael	A60
Price William	A51
Prince Albert	C32
Prince William	B25
Pritchard Fred	A4
Probert Edward	C54
Probert George	C55
Probert Lilian	B13
Procter Albert	B40
Procter Ellen	A54
Procter Ernest	B47
Proctor Alice	C53
Proctor John	B53
Proctor Joseph	C53
Proctor Thomas	A49
Proe John	C22
Pugh Billie	A21
Pullen Henry	B16
Pullin Wilfred	B37
Pye Henry	C20
Pye Mary	C20
Quigley Sarah	B48
Quinlan John	C4
Quinn Thomas	A16,B17
Quinn Walter	B73
Quinn William	B46
Quinton John	B73
Radcliffe Richard	A3
Raffald John	A5
Rainey Mary	C32
Rainey Samuel	C32
Rainford Jane	A8
Rainford Roger	A55
Rainsford John	A10
Ralphs Harry	C30,C31
Ralphs Mary Jane	C31
Ramsbottom Jane	C23
Ramsbottom William	C23
Ramsden Robert	C13
Ramwell Willoughby	B23
Randall Albert	C26
Randall Eva	C26
Ratcliffe Edith	C49
Ratcliffe John	A38,A53
Raven Charles	A73
Ravenscroft Jonathan	A47
Raw Joseph	B11
Rawlinson Ellen	A28,C61
Rawlinson George	C61
Rawlinson William	A29
Rawson Richard	B8
Raymond Florence	C34
Raymond James	C34
Rayner Mary Jane	A71,B16
Raynor Henry	C43
Raynor James	A7
Read Bernard	B67
Read Edward	B5
Read George	A73
Read James	A68
Read John	A13,A53,A58
Reckless Joseph	B31
Reddin Anna	C23
Redford Edith	C14
Redford James	A18
Redford John	B25
Redford Mary Kathleen	C49
Redford Sarah Ann	C14
Reece Charles	B21
Renninson Ellen	A22
Renshaw George	C19
Renshaw James	A69
Renshaw Joseph	B13
Renshaw Lynda	B13
Reynolds Eliza	A71
Reynolds Ernest	A26,A71
Reynolds William	B20
Rhapps Jack	C33
Rhodes George	A51
Rhodes Naomi	C9
Richards Harry	A31
Richards Henry	A60
Richards James	A42
Richards May	B2?
Richards William	A5?
Richardson Ebenezer	A?
Richardson F W	A?
Richardson George	B2?
Richardson Henry	B2?
Richardson James	B2?
Richardson Joseph	A3?
Richardson Thomas	A7?
Richardson William	B73,C4?
Richmond Jackie	C?
Richmond Mary	B5?
Ricketts David	C5?
Riddell William	B3?
Ridings Ann	B3?
Ridings Joseph	B3?
Ridley Jenny	B6?
Ridley John	B4?
Ridyard Peter	A3?
Rigby Alfred	C5?
Rigby Charles	A3?
Rigby Jane	B4?
Rigby John	B3?
Rigby Joseph	B4?
Rigby May	C5?
Riley Alfred	A2?
Riley Clare	A7?
Riley Herbert	C2?
Riley James	A13,A2?
Riley Joseph	B?
Riley Mary	A6?
Riley Robert	A66,C4?
Riley Samuel	A6?
Riley Thomas	A7?
Riley William	A2?
Rimmer Alfred	C3?
Rimmer John	A4?
Rimmer Mary	C3?
Rimmington Charles	A5?
Rinman William	A1?
Ritchie John	A6?
Rivett Barbara	B4?
Rix Edward	A5?
Rix Ted	A2?
Roberts Alan	C6?
Roberts Ann	A1?
Roberts Charles	C1?
Roberts Edward	C2?
Roberts Ellen	C31,C3?
Roberts Florence	C1?
Roberts Henry	A2?
Roberts Hugh	B1?
Roberts James	A?
Roberts James Oswald	B6?
Roberts John	A15,B49,B52
Roberts Joseph	A3?
Roberts Mary	A5?
Roberts Mary Ann	B4?
Roberts Maurice Joseph	C1?
Roberts Robert	A54,A7?
Roberts Samuel	A7?
Roberts Stanley	B6?
Roberts Thomas	C3?
Roberts Veronica	C4?
Roberts Wilfred	C4?
Roberts William	A6,A35,C34,C4?
Roberts Winifred	B6?
Robertson Alexander	B6?
Robey Arthur	B50,C62
Robinson Alfred	B41,C5?
Robinson Alice Jane	C5?
Robinson Charles	A3?
Robinson Dugald	B1?
Robinson Eileen	C6?
Robinson Elizabeth	A3,C5?
Robinson Henry	A37,C6?
Robinson James	B4,B58,C6?
Robinson John	B6?
Robinson Joseph	A54,A5?
Robinson Richard	A77,C5?
Robinson Samuel	A2?
Robinson Sarah	A20,B2?
Robinson Stanley	C6?

Robinson Thomas A16,A18,A20,B25,B48,B60
Robinson William A15,A36,A63
Robson William A65
Roden William A36
Rodgers George B70
Roe James B10
Roe Thomas A13
Rogerson Albert C22
Rogerson Eliza C22
Rohan Elizabeth C61
Rooney Elizabeth A57
Rooney Richard A55
Roose Stephen C42
Roscoe Abraham C43
Roscoe Agnes C43
Roscoe Charlotte C54
Roscoe Frank C43
Roscoe George C41
Roscoe James A22,C49
Roscoe Richard A22
Roscoe William B43,C48
Rose Mary B41
Ross Daniel B34
Ross Donald B5
Ross Edwin B52
Ross John A2
Ross William A33
Roth Kathleen C16
Roth William C16
Rotherham Timothy C13
Rothwell Hilton A64
Rothwell James A75
Rothwell John C54
Rothwell Naomi C20
Rothwell Peter A49
Roughley William A18
Rourke Matthew A61
Rouse Elizabeth A44
Rouse George A44
Rouse Joseph A51
Rouse Robert B35
Rowbotham James A59
Rowland Charles A17
Rowland David B25
Rowland Eddie B62
Rowlands Charles A37
Rowlands Harry A53
Rowlands Kathleen A53,B53
Rowlinson James A78
Rowlinson Jane A78
Rowson Arthur A57
Roylance John A34
Royle Henry B25
Royle James C33
Royle John C31
Royle Ralph B25
Royle Samuel B9
Royle Thomas B58
Royle William A70
Rudd Betsy B9
Rudd Grace B49
Rudge Samuel C47
Rudman Albert A26
Rudman Charles A55,A67,B66
Rudman Florence A26
Rudman Louise A67
Rudman Samuel A55,B54
Rudman Sarah A67
Rudolph Frederick C26
Rushforth William B20
Rushton John A45,B4
Rushton Mary C53
Rushton Thomas B4
Rushton William B17
Rushworth William B19
Russell Robert B33
Russon William B10
Rutter Ann A52
Rutter Joseph A52
Ryan James A13,C53
Ryan Lilian A13

Ryan Malachi C48
Ryan Mary B7
Ryan Richard B7
Ryder John B53
Ryder Samuel B44
Rydings Carrie A31
Rydings Wilfred A31
Rylance John A14
Rylance Thomas A14
Ryland Annie A50
Sale John Vose A30
Salkeld James A9
Salkeld Mrs A9
Salt Charles A43
Salt Hilda C29
Salt William A29
Saltmarsh Denis A47
Saltmarsh Violet A47
Sample Arthur A30
Sanders Thomas C40
Sanderson Agnes C7
Sanderson Daniel C7
Sanderson Irene A28
Sanderson William A28
Sandford George B63,B74
Sandford Nathan A34
Sandford Valentine A17
Sandiford Hannah B17
Sandiford Thomas A57
Sandilands Ivor A28
Sandilands Winifred A28
Sands Harriet A25
Sargeant John A8
Sargeant Maria A8
Sargent Robert B33
Satterthwaite Elizabeth B43
Savage Harry A44
Saville Richard A22
Saxon Alice A49
Saxon Betty A8
Saxon James A8
Saxon Robert A36
Scadding Henry B61
Schneider Charles C52
Schofield Alice A4,A16
Schofield Amos B11
Schofield Edward A68
Schofield Elizabeth C27
Schofield James C27
Schofield John C27
Schofield Major A3
Schofield Millicent C25
Schofield Mr A7
Schofield Sarah B27
Schofield Thomas A4,A37,B66
Scholes John B29
Scholes Richard B15
Scholes Samuel C34
Scholes Sarah C34
Scorer Henry B63
Scott Adam B5
Scott Beryl B50
Scott Charlie B74
Scott Colin B50
Scott Ellen C43
Scott Henry A18
Scott John C40
Scott Robert B64
Scott Squire C43
Scott Walter C13
Scully Elizabeth B42
Seal John B44,C51
Seddon Hannah C49
Seddon Priscilla A64
Seddon Robert C10
Seddon Thomas A58
Seddon William A64,A72,C27
Sedgwick Sarah A66
Sedgwick William A66,A67
Seed Ann C28
Seed Arthur C50
Seed Joan C50
Seel Gertrude A73

Seers Roy A44
Sellen Thomas B19
Sellers William A23
Senior Mary Ann A62
Settle Elizabeth A70
Settle James A74
Settle John A74
Settle Thomas A74
Settle William A70
Severn Charles B60
Shakespeare William H A68
Sharp Frank B42
Sharp Isabella B75
Sharp Jessie B42
Sharp Thomas A54
Sharp William A6
Sharpe Philip B56
Sharples Aaron A49
Sharples James C54
Sharples John A6,A24
Sharples Joseph B6
Sharples Mary B3
Sharrocks Mary A19
Shaughnessy James B3
Shaw Agnes A33
Shaw Edith Clara B70
Shaw James A35,A48
Shaw John B48,C5
Shaw Jonathan C34
Shaw Joseph B8
Shaw Matthew B43
Shaw Mrs B64
Shaw Peter A15
Shaw Robert B64
Shaw Thomas A62,B21
Shawcross William A17
Sheard Edith B75
Sheard John B10
Sheard Thomas C34
Shedwick William B33
Sheehan Duncan B46
Sheen Martin A60
Sheen Richard C42
Sheeran Edward B2
Sheldon Clifford C57
Sheldon Myra C57
Shenton Thomas A11,A13
Shepherd Henry A27
Shepherd John B60
Shepherd Marjorie A20
Shepherd Mary B71
Shepherd Samuel A20,C44
Shepherd Thomas C57
Shepherd William A58
Sheppard Samuel A47
Sheridan William C47
Shields James A20
Shindler Ezra B32
Shires Herbert A56
Shore James C14
Shorthouse John C57
Shortman Dorothy C49
Shortman John C20,C38,C49
Shuker George B61
Siccombe Robert A70
Siddall William C23
Sidebotham Thomas A10
Sidlow James B20,B21
Simm Alfred B3
Simm Henry B7
Simmonds Ferdinand B36
Simmonds Mary Ellen A44
Simmons Arthur B73
Simmons Ellen A77
Simmons Fanny B73
Simmons James B73
Simmons John A60
Simpson Ann C31
Simpson Hannah B40
Simpson Joseph A52
Sims John A77
Sinclair James C37
Sinclair Joseph C5
Sinclair Stafford C6

Sincup Lily B40
Singleton Abraham B59
Singleton Elizabeth C54
Singleton John C54
Sinker Francis A47
Sinker John A47,A67
Sixsmith John A36
Skellorn Sarah B4
Skellorn William B4
Skidmore Joseph A49
Slack Charles A76
Slack Richard B34
Slack Samuel A49
Slater Daniel B7
Slater William A49
Sleath James B28
Sloane Edith B19
Sloane Hannah B32
Sloane James B32
Sloane William B19,C24
Smales John A56
Smales Winifred A56
Smallshaw Joseph A18
Smallshaw Sarah A18
Smart Colin B51
Smart Edgar B9
Smeeton Herbert C41
Smeeton Sidney C57
Smeeton Thomas C56
Smelt Jane A14
Smelt Robert A14
Smelt William A14
Smethills Frederick B41
Smethills Harry B46
Smethurst Robert B49,C6
Smith Alfred C52
Smith Alice B49
Smith Annie A66
Smith Arthur B46,B50
Smith Benjamin A68
Smith Charles A22,C47
Smith Cyril B47
Smith Eleanor B50
Smith Elizabeth A37,B24
Smith Ellen B41
Smith Emily B37
Smith Emma B75
Smith Frank C26
Smith Frederick B20
Smith George A26,A70
Smith Grace A10
Smith Harold B33
Smith Harry C35
Smith Henry A19,A54
Smith Jeremiah A23
Smith Joan C52
Smith John A70,B37,B50,B61,C53
Smith John William A14,A44
Smith Jonas B4,C7
Smith Joseph A17,A71
Smith Josephus A52
Smith Kathleen A65,B50
Smith Margaret A52
Smith Martha B47
Smith Mary A17,B37
Smith Olive C46
Smith Richard A49
Smith Robert C25
Smith Robert Canning A66
Smith Rose B61
Smith Samuel A49
Smith Thomas B75
Smith Thomas Sampson A20
Smith Walter C46
Smith William B16,B34,C31,C53
Smithson George B62
Smithson Joseph C17
Snape Amelia B17
Snape Elsie C23
Snape Henry A9,B21
Snape Mary A9
Snape Robert B17

Snee Sarah B26,B44
Snee Thomas B26,B44
Sneyd Mary C44
Sneyd William C44
Soar William C49
Solby Frank B30
Sorton John B43
Sorton Mary B16
Southern Samuel C50
Southward Ferguson C19
Speakman Ambrose B4
Speakman Harold A20,B46
Spence Arthur C11
Spence William B60
Spencer Charles B49
Spencer William B36
Spiby Albert A57
Spilsbury Henshaw C7
Spivey Emma C31,C32
Spivey Samuel C31,C32
Sproston Frederick C21
Sproston Josephine C21
Stafford Sarah C61
Staines Mary B33
Standley Samuel B51
Standring Frank B14
Standring James B65
Stanford James B15
Stanier Jane A64
Stanley Clifford C57
Stanley Edward C31
Stanley Ella C57
Stanley Henry C31
Stanley James A10
Stanley Margaret C31
Stanley Samuel A23
Stanley William A6
Stansfield William C32
Stanton Thomas C40
Starkey Arthur B12
Statham Joseph C18
Statham Mary C18
Statham Robert A26
Stead Richard A63
Steele Fanny B51
Steele George B46,B52
Stelfox John B75
Stephens Frederick C47
Stephens Maria C11
Stephens Thomas C11
Stephenson Arthur B61
Stephenson Eliza A42
Stephenson James C61
Stephenson Mary B72
Stephenson William A65
Stevenson Arthur B17
Steward John B27
Stewart Donald C19
Stewart Elizabeth C19
Stewart Lewis C4
Stirrup John A12
Stirrup Stuart A12
Stirrup Thomas A56
Stirrup William A58
Stoakes Norman A16
Stocks Frank A34
Stoddard Fred C30
Stokes Hannah A45
Stokes Harry B68
Stone James A49
Stone John A49,A50
Stone Thomas A18,A29
Stone William A73
Stonehouse Nellie B11,C8
Stonehouse Samuel C8
Stones Philip C49
Stonier Caroline B42
Stott Henry B41
Stott Isaac A9
Stott James C51
Stott John A10,A35
Stott Mary A10
Stott Thomas A62
Stott William B33

Name	Ref
Strafford Harry	C17
Strafford Mary	C17
Strafford Thomas	A10
Strath Mary	A54
Strath Minnie	A27
Street Mary	C24
Street Samuel	A33
Stretch John	A3
Stretton Henry	A9
Stretton Peggy	A9
Strickland Joseph	A66
Stringfellow Charles	C18
Stringfellow Charlotte	C18
Stringfellow Noah	C42
Strong Angela	B73
Stuart Clara	A43
Stuart William	A43
Sudren James	A46
Sullivan Bartholomew	A16,A28
Sullivan Daniel	C24
Sullivan John	A65
Summers George	B58
Sutcliffe Ann	B18
Sutcliffe John	A74,B16,B66
Sutcliffe William	A20,A74
Sutton Thomas	A42
Swain Elizabeth	B68
Swain John	A3
Swan Samuel	B8
Swann James	C38
Swarbrick Eliza	B30
Swarbrick Emily	A31
Swarbrick James	B51
Swarbrick John	A31,A58,C24
Swarbrick Squire	B52,B53
Swarbrick Thomas	A60
Sweetman Henry	A71
Sweetman James	A71
Swift Alfred	B47
Swift Arthur	C26
Swift Gladys	C56
Swift James	C56
Swindells Thomas	A9,A47
Swindells William	B24
Swindlehurst Thomas	A43,A58,B48
Swires Robert	A8
Sykes Jabez	C30
Sykes Oliver	A62
Sykes Thomas	A8,B61
Taafe Christopher	B22
Tabbron Thomas	A52
Tansey George	A55
Tarrant John	A42
Tate Samuel	C27
Tatler Edward	C41
Tatler Frances	C41
Tatlock Richard	B50
Taylor Abraham	A33
Taylor Albert	B10
Taylor Annie	C3
Taylor Arthur	A47,B63
Taylor Deborah	A16
Taylor Douglas	C18
Taylor Edward	C3
Taylor Elsie	C39
Taylor Emma	C13
Taylor Esther	B25
Taylor Florence	B69
Taylor Frank	B25,B41
Taylor Fred	A56
Taylor George	B47
Taylor Harry	C39
Taylor James	A77,B10,C13,C25
Taylor Jean	B10
Taylor Jessie	B47
Taylor John	A16,A75,B11,B12,B49,B50
Taylor Joseph	A76
Taylor Llewellyn	B63
Taylor Mary	A26,B10
Taylor Rachel	A8
Taylor Robert	B18
Taylor Samuel	B61
Taylor Sarah	B10
Taylor Thomas	A8,A28,A55,B9,B17,B47
Taylor Tom	B43
Taylor Victor	B69
Taylor Walter	B73
Taylor William	A24,A74
Teece Enoch	C6
Telford Alexander	A62
Telford Harold	B20
Telford Percy	C60
Telford Thomas	B20,B51
Templeton Harry	B67
Thackwray Catherine	A9
Thackwray Frank	A9
Thackwray Joseph	A70
Thaell Isaac	A28
Thaw Sarah	B8
Thickett Frederick	A31
Thickett Joyce	A31
Thomas Alice	C53
Thomas Betty	B53
Thomas David	A65
Thomas Emma	A55
Thomas Evan	C61
Thomas Frederick	C53
Thomas James	A9
Thomas Margaret	B67
Thomas Martha	C61
Thomas William	A66,C25
Thomason John	C32
Thomason Peter	C3
Thompson George	B50
Thompson Henry	A13
Thompson James	B58
Thompson John	B15,B41
Thompson Richard	A30
Thompson Samuel	A62
Thompson Thomas	B62
Thompson William	A47
Thompstone Charles	B62
Thorley James	C58
Thorley Lot	B8
Thorley Philip	B8
Thornhill Alice	C8
Thornhill Ann	A17
Thornhill Henry	C8
Thornhill James	A17
Thornhill Joseph	A59,B53
Thornley John	B8
Thornton Edward	C34
Thornton James	A29
Thornton Sarah	A29
Thornton Sydney	C44
Thorp John	A55,B69
Thorp Rebecca	B7
Thorp William	A61,B14,B42
Thorpe Frederick	A37
Thorpe Irene	A37
Thorpe John	A20,B67,C18,C24
Thorpe Mary	C24
Thorpe Robert	B33
Thorpe Thomas	A22,A36
Threlfall James	A18,B7,B63
Threlfall Mary Ann	B7
Thurstan Thomas	A14
Thurstan Zillah	A14
Tickle William	B6
Tighe Francis	B75
Tildesley Thomas	C31
Tildsley Henry	C27
Till Cornelius	A51
Tilling Leslie	B33
Times William	C6
Tinker Margaret	B61
Tinsley Thomas	A76
Tipping George	B41
Tipping William	A22
Titterington James	C12
Tittle Annie	B51
Tobin John	B21
Todd Albert	C60
Todd John	A75,B9
Todd Sarah	A75
Tole Margaret	A66
Tomkinson William	A76
Tomlinson Caroline	C40
Tomlinson Edward	A18
Tomlinson Elizabeth	A34
Tomlinson Ellen	A37
Tomlinson Henry	C30
Tomlinson Horace	A67
Tomlinson Joseph	C31,C49
Tomlinson William	A37
Toms Susannah	B44
Tonge Agnes	B20
Tonge Ann	B24
Tonge Edward	A36
Tonge Elizabeth	A10
Tonge John	A10
Tonge May	C19
Tonge Rachel	A13
Tonge Robert	A13
Tonge Sarah	A10
Tonge Thomas	A13,B9
Tonge William	B30
Topper Samuel	C33
Topper Walter	C20
Topping Beatrice	A60
Torkington Samuel	B42,B53
Towers Mary	A46
Towers Samuel	A46
Towers Thomas	A18
Towers William Crookall	A43
Towler Harry	A14,B41
Townsend Clarence	C52
Townsend Elizabeth	A21
Townsend George	A24
Townsend Joseph	A60
Townsend Mrs	A24
Townsend William	A25,B31
Townson Edward	B9
Townson George	A58
Tracy Joan	B30
Tracy John	B30
Trafford Alice	C41
Travis Elizabeth	C33
Travis John	B48
Travis Peter	C17
Travis Richard	C49
Travis Sarah	C49
Tristram Henry	A57
Trotter James Watson	B59
Trow Hannah	C46
Trow John	C12
Trow Thomas	C47
Tucker Harold	C49
Tucker Richard	A45
Turgoose Thomas	B40
Turner David	B36
Turner Edmund	A69
Turner George	C35
Turner James	A61,B4
Turner John	A64,C12,C35
Turner Mary	B47,C35
Turner Simeon	B22
Turner William	B23,B32,C32,C35
Turtle Thomas	B20
Turton Benjamin	A20
Turton John	A61
Turton Walter	C33
Twamley Robert	C56
Twigg John Henry	A64
Twist Agnes	C8
Twist William	C8
Tyrrall William	B15
Tyson Grace	A54
Tyson John	B29
Underwood Thomas	A61
Underwood William	A6
Unsworth Henry	B11
Unsworth Martha	A26
Unsworth Peter	A17
Upton Thomas	B61
Urmson Thomas	B51
Vale Henry	A71
Valentine Albert	B20
Valentine Edward	B20,C47,C48
Valentine James	C37,C46
Valentine James H	A22
Valentine Jessie	B20
Valentine Jim	B20,C47
Valentine John	B7,C46,C47
Valentine Joseph	A30,B27,C15
Valentine Robert	C16
Valentine Sarah	B7
Valentine Thomas	C35
Varey Charles	B33
Varlow Matthew	A65
Vaughan David	B30
Vaughan Elizabeth	B30
Vaughan John	C27
Vause Frederick	A47
Vause John	C13
Verity Joseph	B36
Vernon Charles	A61
Vesey James	B20
Veysey James	A14
Veysey Phoebe	A15
Vickers William	A53
Vigerstaffe Leslie	A64
Vigerstaffe Patricia	A64
Waddington William	B17
Wade Daniel	A75
Wade John	B21
Wagner Florence	C4
Wagner Joe	C38
Wagner Joseph	C4
Wagstaffe John Rhodes	C11
Wagstaffe Thomas	C11
Wain Emma	C24
Wainhouse Edward	B9,B49
Wainhouse John	B9,C58
Walch James	A70
Walker Abraham	B17
Walker Alfred	C8,C32
Walker Elizabeth	A37
Walker Frances	B11
Walker Francis	B63
Walker George	A6,A23,A42,C25,C4
Walker Hannah	A
Walker James	A59,C
Walker Jane	
Walker John	A54,A72,A73,C14,
Walker John H	
Walker Josephine	C8
Walker Nora	C50
Walker Richard	B5
Walker Robert	A58,B46,C53
Walker Ruth	B70
Walker Sarah	C45
Walker Thomas	A37,C40
Walker Wilfred	B11
Walker William	B53,B70
Wall Ellen	B11
Wall Lawrence	B11
Wall Michael	B11
Wall Tom	B11,B12,B14, B54,C8,C21
Walley Emma	C4
Walley John	C4
Walley John Edwin	B8
Wallington Susannah	B66
Wallis Elizabeth	A65
Wallwork James	B34
Wallwork John	B35
Walmsley Robert	B52,B58
Walmsley Thomas	C40
Walsh Benjamin	A24
Walsh Elizabeth	A29
Walsh Frank	C52
Walsh Martha	B32
Walsh Richard	A72
Walsh Susannah	A24
Walter John	A49
Walters Alfred	A11,B63
Walters Arthur	C8
Walters Elsie	C32
Walters Richard	A62
Walthew Agnes	B10
Walton John	C33,C45
Walton Sarah	B17,B18
Walton William	C53
Walwyn James	C35,C50
Warbrick John	A54
Warburton Edgar	B46
Warburton Harry	B66
Warburton Joseph	B21
Warburton Peter	C24
Warburton Thomas	B59
Ward Elizabeth	C25
Ward Ellen	B50
Ward Eric	B26
Ward Eva	A74
Ward Frank	B42
Ward George	B65
Ward James	A63,B30,B50,C3
Ward John	A64
Ward Michael	A63
Ward Nellie	B42
Ward Robert	A64
Ward Thomas	B5
Ward William	A27,C25
Wardell Ann	A25
Wardle Annie	B30
Wardle James	B23
Wardle Susannah	B23
Wardle William	B37
Ware John	A9
Warham Arthur	C7
Waring Sarah	A62
Warner George	A5

Warren Jane A11
Warren John A11
Warren Nigel C50
Warwick Edwin A64
Washington Alice B15
Washington George B17
Waterhouse George C12
Waterhouse Joseph C50
Waters George B72
Waters May B23
Watkin John B52
Watkins Edward B24,B49
Watkins Harry B54
Watkins Thomas A15,A59
Watmough William C8
Watson Charles B59
Watson Charlie A13
Watson Edith A70
Watson Frank A70,C25
Watson Frederick B36
Watson George B34
Watson Gordon C49
Watson John B57
Watson Margaret C49
Watson Mary B34
Watson Richard B57
Watson Samuel C35
Watson Thomas B48
Webbon Fred C62
Webbon Frederick C57
Webbon Nellie C62
Webster George A74
Webster Hugh B27,B41
Webster John A17
Webster Maria B41
Wedley Alfred B30
Welby Dominick A15,B6
Welch Charles A11,B49
Welch Florence A51
Welch William A10
Welsby Thomas A76
Welsh Edmund A54
Welsh Sarah A77
Welsh William A77
West Albert C38
West Robert A63
Westbrook Charles C37
Westbrook Frances C37
Weston John A55
Westwood Charles B20
Westwood Elizabeth B20
Westwood Emily B20
Whaley Frederick A9
Whalley Alfred B51
Whalley Benjamin C61
Whalley Ellen A55
Whalley Harry B16,B63
Whalley Irene B44
Whalley Robert A55
Whalley Sidney B44
Wharf Henry C10
Wharf Joseph C9
Wharmby Alice B68
Wharmby Hannah B68
Wharmby William B68
Wharton Elizabeth A66
Wharton Joseph A65
Wharton William A65
Whatmough John A71
Wheatcroft Edward A6
Wheeldon William A49
Wheeler Lena C38
Whelan Annie A71
Whitaker George C11
Whitby William C40

White Elizabeth B2
White George C35,C43
White John A34,B2,B49
White Thomas A43
Whitehead Donald A11
Whitehead Dorothy B27
Whitehead Edward B42
Whitehead Hannah B35
Whitehead James B35
Whitehead John B35
Whitehead Mark B53
Whitehead Mary A61
Whitehead Richard A61
Whitehead William B24,B35
Whitehouse Annie A73
Whiteley John C6
Whiteley Ward C6
Whiteley William B56
Whittaker Abraham A16,C4
Whittaker Elizabeth B73
Whittaker Ellen B34
Whittaker George
A77,B34,C26
Whittaker Henry A31
Whittaker James B51,C4
Whittaker James Fletcher C4
Whittaker John B62
Whittaker John Sawley
A14,C26
Whittaker Joshua A17,C10
Whittaker Levi C21
Whittaker Mary B63
Whittaker Mary Ann A31
Whittaker Peter B73
Whittaker Richard A77
Whittaker Thomas B11,C37
Whittaker Thomas Goodwin
C4
Whittaker William
A31,A76,B12,B72
Whittingham Mrs A21
Whittle John A12
Whittle Peter A75
Whittle Richard A21,A22
Whitworth Eric C62
Whitworth Gwen C62
Whitworth James C25
Whitworth Thomas A12
Whyatt Elizabeth A35
Whyatt John C27
Whyatt Joseph A35
Wickman Bridget C53
Wicks John B9
Wigan Hannah A6,A34
Wigan John A6
Wigglesworth William B29
Wightman Henry A45
Wilcock James C33
Wilcock John B62
Wilcock Joseph A71,C58
Wilcox Samuel B11
Wild George Albert A50
Wild Herbert B16
Wild John C7
Wild Joseph A33
Wilday William A65,C59
Wilde Charles A35
Wilde Elizabeth C7
Wilde William C21
Wilding Thomas C37
Wilding William
A33,A62,A68,A74,C34
Wildman William C32
Wiles Charles B75
Wiles Zillah B75

Wilkes Clarence C3
Wilkes Thomas C8
Wilkinson Dora C10
Wilkinson Elizabeth C14
Wilkinson Frances B47
Wilkinson Fred A64
Wilkinson George C8
Wilkinson Hannah A38
Wilkinson Harriet B72
Wilkinson Henry B31
Wilkinson James A77,B17
Wilkinson John C51
Wilkinson Kenneth A14
Wilkinson Margaret A14
Wilkinson Norman A67,C10
Wilkinson Sarah A73
Wilkinson Thomas A38,C33
Wilkinson William A38,B72
Wilks Annie C15
Wilks Edward B52
Willan Susannah B8
Willcock Sarah C58
Willetts Alfred B69,C18
Willetts Bessie B69,C18,C53
Willey John A7,B19
Williams Ada B60
Williams Alexander C20
Williams Ann C33
Williams Billy B19
Williams Charles B47
Williams Daniel B34
Williams Edward C33
Williams Ellis B27
Williams Emma A46
Williams Enoch C44
Williams Fred B11
Williams John
A25,B30,B33,C25,C26,C51
Williams Lilian B33
Williams Mary B27
Williams Peter A60
Williams Rhys B8
Williams Richard A29,C9
Williams Robert B27,C44
Williams Sarah C20
Williams Thomas
A68,B10,C20
Williams William A15,B17
Williamson Charles C34
Williamson James A18,C54
Williamson John B29
Williamson Richard A32
Williamson Thomas B11
Willis Walter A60
Willmott Robert A50
Willoughby Mary C12
Wills Elizabeth C53
Willsdon Walter C17
Wilson Albert C40
Wilson Andrew A77
Wilson Annie B22,B63
Wilson Ben A70
Wilson Bessie A70
Wilson Edith C40
Wilson Edward C61
Wilson Frances A7
Wilson Henry A33
Wilson Herbert A70
Wilson James A53,B63
Wilson James Hetherington
C32
Wilson John
A48,A59,B17,B22,C16
Wilson Joseph A77,B51
Wilson Joshua A60

Wilson Mary A48
Wilson Matthew A65
Wilson Richard A7,A72
Wilson Thomas
A56,B10,B26,B36
Wilson William A30
Wiltshire Isaac C23
Winder Doris A67,B62
Winder Emily B30
Winder Matthew B62
Windley Ann C5
Windley John C5
Winskill William B62
Winstanley George A45
Winstanley Joseph A31
Winstanley Marjorie B25
Winston John A36
Wiseman Ellen B41
Wiseman Sherwood A25
Witham Clyde B63,C31
Withers James A57
Withers Joe A22
Withington Ann C29
Withington James C42
Withington John C29
Withington Joseph
B25,B37,C20
Wolstencroft Hannah C20
Wolstencroft William A57
Wolstenholme Charles A35
Wolstenholme Jacob A47
Wood Alice B34,B49
Wood Arthur B47
Wood Benjamin A52
Wood Charles A46,B29
Wood Charlotte A57
Wood Emily B65
Wood Ethel B44
Wood Francis A17
Wood James A19,A68,A71
Wood Jesse B35
Wood Jessie B35
Wood John
A31,B35,B70,B73,C12,C45
Wood Lilian C13
Wood Marion B73
Wood Paul B41
Wood Robert A33
Wood Samuel M B68
Wood Stephen B65
Wood Thomas
A3,A4,A58,B34,C61
Wood Thomas J B47
Wood William
A14,A26,A37,A57
Woodall John A58
Woodcock James A33
Woodcock John B49
Woodhead Claire C29
Woodhead Herbert B67
Woodhouse Henry B57
Woodhouse Mary A38
Woodhouse William B11
Woodland Robert A26
Woodruff George A3,A54
Woodruff Samuel A54
Woods Jane B35
Woods Ralph A70
Woods Thomas B35
Woodward Thomas C4
Woolley James A45,A63
Woolley William A12
Woolrich Joseph A78
Wordsworth Frederick A69
Wordsworth George A27

Wordsworth Thomas C13
Worrall Elisha B32
Worrall John B36,B41
Worrall Stanley C7
Worrall Winifred C7
Worsley family A6
Worsley Martha B46
Worsley Thomas C4,C17
Worthington Alfred B34
Worthington Amos B36
Worthington Charles B61
Worthington Isaac
B61,B68,C40
Worthington James C28
Worthington John B47
Worthington Joshua A71
Wray Charles B52
Wrench Stephen A66
Wright Arthur C34
Wright Clara B12
Wright David B64
Wright Frank B31
Wright Geoffrey A47
Wright George B60
Wright Henry A42
Wright Herbert B45
Wright James A56,C27
Wright Jane A42
Wright John B12
Wright John William A72
Wright Nellie B34
Wright Peter B17
Wright Richard B13,B20
Wright Samuel B40
Wright Thomas A53
Wright William B13,B26,B36
Wroe Elizabeth C39
Wroe Fanny C25
Wroe Grayson C39
Wroe James A17
Wroe James Cooper C39
Wroe John B57
Wroe Reuben A6,A20
Wroe Samson A62
Wynn Thomas A26
Yardley Samuel B65
Yarwood James B64
Yarwood John B52
Yates Albert A62
Yates Benjamin B31
Yates Ellen C20,C44
Yates Ged C20,C25,C30,C44
Yates George B43
Yates Gerald A65
Yates Henry A25
Yates James C58
Yates John
A29,A65,C17,C30,C33
Yates Moses C54
Yates Peter A5
Yates Richard A26
Yates Robert B21
Yeadon Edward A74
Yeadon Martha A74
Yorke Josephine A13
Yorke Kenneth A13
Youd Elizabeth B3
Youd Tommy A46
Young Elizabeth A13,A60
Young Francis B35
Young Jane B71
Young Lydia C55
Young Samuel C55
Youngman Benjamin A8

Pub Index

The numbering of buildings on Salford's streets and roads altered in the course of the nineteenth century and nearly all the licensed houses saw at least one change of address. Until the 1840s, streets were numbered consecutively up one side and then down the other. After the modern (odd numbers on one side, even on the other) system was adopted, there continued to be adjustments in numbering to take into account newer rows of houses which filled the gaps in the building line of the developing streets and roads. In a few cases, street numbering was reversed; going from west to east instead of east to west, for example. When the alignments of older lanes and roads were altered, new names and numbering sometimes followed.

In this index, only the later address, usually settled on towards the end of the nineteenth century, is given for each pub. For pubs that didn't survive that long, the last known address is given. In cases of earlier or alternative names, the street numbers the buildings had at that time (if they had them) are used.

The page number of the main entry for each pub is given first. Italics refer to illustrations. To save space, the words Hotel, Inn, Tavern and Arms have usually been omitted.

Page numbers with the letter A refer to Salford Pubs Part One, B to Part Two and C to Part Three. The letter P after an address refers to Pendleton; LB to Lower Broughton, HB to Higher Broughton.

ABERCROMBIE 96 Chapel St   A10
ADELPHI RIVERSIDE Crescent
                          B35,A78
ADELPHI TAVERN 69 Arlington St
                      A67,A55,A72
ADMIRAL NELSON 36 Chapel St A9
ALBERT 87 Bury St P   C33
ALBERT 11 New Bailey St   A43
ALBERT 55 New Bailey St A42,A43
ALBERT 203 Oldfield Rd   B33,B62
ALBERT 184 Regent Rd   B25,B12
ALBERT 8-10 Short St LB   B65,B65
ALBERT 14 West Dixon St   B45,C38
ALBERT 269 Whit Lane   C44,C44
ALBERT PARK 4-6 Duke St B67,B67
ALBERT PARK 19-21 Fenney St B71
ALBERT PARK Gt Clowes St   B67
ALBERT VAULTS 169 Chapel St
                      A13,A12,A42
ALBION 217 Cross La   C9
ALBION 1 Cross St P   C29
ALBION 27 Essex St   B17
ALBION 49 Lissadel St   C52
ALBION 99 Lwr Broughton Rd   B60
ALBION 126 Ordsall L B11,B12,B10
ALBION 4 Small St   B51
ALEXANDRA 1-3 Barlows Rd   B41
ALEXANDRA 26 Chapel St P
                         C31,C31
ALEXANDRA 125 Lwr Broughton Rd
                          B61,B60
ALMA 151 Oldfield Rd   B33
AMALGAMATED 92-4 Gloucester St
                          B45,B46
AMALGAMATION 48 Chapel St A6
AMATEURS ARMS 11 Bexley Sq A62
ANCHOR Chapel St   A12
ANCHOR Gravel La   A34
ANCHOR & GRAPES Chapel St A12
ANGEL 357 Chapel St   A17,A17
ANGEL Gravel Lane   A34
ANGEL Greengate   A18
APOLLO 12 Cook St   A58
APOLLO 7 Cross Lane   C6
ARBUCKLES Salford Quays   B56
ARLINGTON INN 2 Mount St   A69
ART TREASURERS INN 77-79
  Lwr Broughton Rd   B59,B60
ASHLEY BROOK Liverpool St   C62
BALTIC FLEET 52 Shuttleworth St
                         C53,C52

BALTIC FLEET 1 Sunnyside St
                     B42,B42,B33
BANK OF ENGLAND 72 St Simon St
                             A33
BARLEY MOW 1 Ford St   A64
BARLEY MOW 8 Hope St   B36
BARLEY SHEAF 97 Chapel St
                      A10,C62
BATH 16 Corporation St   A75
BATH 5 North George St   A76
BATH Stanley St   A45,A44
BAY HORSE 77 Broad St   C22,C22
BAY HORSE 122 Greengate   A23
BAY HORSE 8 Hope St   B36
BAY HORSE 119 Ordsall La   B10
BEAR Chapel St   A17
BEARS PAW Chapel St   A17
BEDFORD 41 Bedford St   A30
BEE HIVE 14 Brooks St   A77,A28
BEE HIVE 61 Bury St P   C33
BEE HIVE 33 Gold St   C33
BEE HIVE 74 Holland St   C48
BEE HIVE 3 Kempster St   B68
BEE HIVE 91 Lwr Broughton Rd B60
BEE HIVE 7 Stanley St   A45,A61
BEE HIVE 6 Tontine St   C13
BEE HIVE 22 Watkin St   A31
BEE HIVE 22-24 West Worsley St
                         B49,B49
BEE HIVE 13 York St   A47
BELFAST & FLEETWOOD HOUSE
  120 Chapel St   A12
BELL Greengate   A19
BELL TOWER 357 Chapel St   A17
BEXLEY 10 Bexley Square   A63
BIG FIDDLE 12 William St A60,A60
BILLY & DARBY Back Salford   A18
BIRD IN HAND 3 Back Borough St
                     C49,C50,C49
BIRD IN HAND Bloom St   A59
BIRD IN HAND 11 Boundary St B16
BIRD IN HAND 9 Brindleheath Rd
                             C47
BIRD IN HAND 104 Bury St &
  37 Sidmouth St   A56,A57
BIRD IN HAND Chapel St   A17
BIRD IN HAND 32 Regent Rd   B21
BIRD IN HAND St Stephen St
                      A61,A56
BLACK BULL 172 Chapel St   A8
BLACK FRIAR 13 King St   A48,A48
BLACK HORSE 58 Chaney St   C32

BLACK HORSE 15 Crescent
                     B34,B34,A60
BLACK LION 65 Chapel St   A9,A7
BLACKSMITHS 20 Bury St   A53
BLACKSMITHS Greengate   A22
BLACK SWAN 206 Chapel St   A6
BLAIR ATHOL 11 Bridgewater St
                         A29,A30
BLEACHERS & CARRIERS
  11 Bolton St   A46
BLUE ANCHOR Chapel St   A12
BLUE BELL 4 Arlington St
                      A67,A68,A68
BLUE BELL 1 Bloom St   A60
BLUE BELL 22 Brown St   A37,A38
BLUE BELL 124 Greengate   A23
BLUE BELL 13 Lamb La   A58
BLUE BELL 4 Sovereign St   C45
BLUE BELL 1 West Gore St   B37
BLUE BOY 80 Greengate   A21
BLUE CAP 80 Greengate   A21
BLUE LION 14 Cook St   A58,A46
BOARS HEAD 10 Bank St   B75
BOARS HEAD Cockpit   A29
BOARS HEAD 16 East Stanley St A31
BOARS HEAD Halstead St   B75
BOAT HOUSE 35 Everard St   B43
BOAT HOUSE 2 Oldfield Road
                     B29,C53,C62
BOATSWAIN 82 Chapel St   A13
BOILERMAKERS 178 Chapel St A10
BOILERMAKERS 55 Hope St   B36
BOLTON PACKET HOUSE
  95 Oldfield Rd   B29
BOROUGH 6 Borough St   C50,C22
BOROUGH 5 Brewery St   A66
BOROUGH 1 Encombe Pl   A77,A80
BOROUGH 386 Regent Rd   B20
BOWLING GREEN Broughton   B57
BOWLING GREEN Frederick St P C18
BOWL OF PUNCH 81 Chapel St   A9
BRASS HANDLES Edgehill Cl   C38
BRASS TALLY Liverpool St   C62
BRAZIERS 54 Hodson St   A53,A52
BREWERS 13 Boond St   A50
BREWERS 12 Brewery St   A66
BREWERS 42 Ordsall La   B8
BREWERS 36 Queen St   A49
BREWERS 42 Ravald St   A51
BREWERS 34 Regent St   B21
BREWERS 46 Silk St   A73,A75
BREWERY TAP 1 Worsley St   A43

BREWERY TAVERN 12 Adelphi St
                         A78,A78
BRICKLAYERS 110 Broughton Rd
                             A26
BRICKLAYERS 148 Ordsall La
                   B12,B11,A55,A62
BRICKLAYERS 15 Richmond St A53
BRICKMAKERS 47 Chapel St   A7
BRIDGE 46 Broughton Rd
                 A24,A25,A21,A29
BRIDGE 152 Broughton Rd A27,A27
BRIDGE 64 Greengate   A20
BRIDGE 238 Lwr Broughton Rd
                     B61,B62,B61
BRIDGE 27 New Bailey St A42,A38
BRIDGE 22 Regent Rd
                     B20,B21,B20,B9
BRIDGE 83 Springfield La   A29
BRIDGE 17-19 Strawberry Rd   C51
BRIDGE Windsor   C12
BRIDGEWATER 11 Bridgewater St
                             A29
BRIDGEWATER 112 Ordsall La   B10
BRITANNIA Bank La   C55
BRITANNIA 102 King St   A48
BRITANNIA 68 Ordsall La   B7,B6
BRITANNIA 229 Whit La   C43,C42
BRITISH FLEET Broad St   C22
BRITISH FLEET 187 Oldfield Rd B?
BRITISH QUEEN 119 Bury St
BRITISH QUEEN 28 Ellor S C25,C25
BRITISH QUEEN 41 Gravel La
                     A34,A35,A34
BRITISH ROLLA 2 Collier St   A50
BROADWAY 30 Broadway B56,B56
BROUGHTON 135 Blackfriars Rd
                     A26,A25,A31
BROUGHTON 10 Chapel St HB B75
BROUGHTON 271 Gt Cheetham St E
                         B73,B74
BROWN BULL 187 Chapel St
                      A14,A15
BROWN COW 14 Gravel La   A34
BROWN COW 34 Oldfield Rd
                     B33,B33
BROWN COW 101 Silk St   A72,A73
BROWNCROSS Browncross St   A42
BRUNSWICK 147 Ordsall La
                     B10,B25
BRUNSWICK 32 Union St &
  16 Gallemore St   B63,B60
BUCK 108 Cross La   C8,B11,C38
BUCK 31 Mount St   A69,B15
BUFFALO 14 Bloom St   A59
BUILDERS Barrow St   B4
BULLS HEAD 55 Derwent St   B42
BULLS HEAD Ford St   A63
BULLS HEAD 19 Garden La   A50
BULLS HEAD 47 Greengate
                   A19,Acover,C50
BULLS HEAD 44 Hampson St
                     B15,B15,C62
BULLS HEAD 62 Regent Rd   B21
BURNS TAVERN 215 Chapel St   A7
BURY'S ARMS 5 Arlington St   A67
BUSH 28 Brown St   A38
BUSKERS 40 King St   A47
BUTCHERS 43 Chapel St   A6
BUTCHERS 44 Cross La   C4,C5
BUTCHERS Ford St   A63
BUTCHERS 33 West Worsley St
                     B49,B50,A68
BYROMS Littleton Rd   C50
CALENDERERS Greengate   A18
CAMBRIA 86 Lwr Broughton Rd B59
CAMBRIDGE 160 Regent Rd B23,B24
CAMBRIDGE 169 Sussex St   B64
CANAL TAVERN 73 Oldfield Rd B29
CANON Greengate   A18
CANTEEN Regent Rd   B18,B19,A7
CANTERBURY 12 Chapel St A3,A3
CARDERS 1 Norton St   A36
CARDIGAN 43 George St B3,B3,B11
CARLTON 31 Camp St   B69,B69

CARPENTERS 52 Phoebe St B47
CASTLE Cheadle Ave C50
CAT & CUSHION 178 Chapel St A10
CATHEDRAL ARCHES Chapel St A3
CATTLE MARKET HOTEL
52 Cross La C4,C5,*C4*
CATTLE MARKET TAVERN
55 Cross La C5,*C5*,B24
CEMETERY 320 Eccles New Rd C58
CHAMPION Unwin St C38
CHAPEL ST VAULTS Chapel St A64
CHEQUERBOARD Robert Hall St B54
CHIQUITOS Salford Quays B56
CHURCH 5 Albert St C34,*C33*
CHURCH 235-7 Cross La
C10,*C10*,A68
CHURCH 27 Derby St B44,*B44*
CHURCH 28 Duke St B67
CHURCH 1 Ford La P C39,*C39*,C43
CHURCH 1 Ford St A64,B6
CHURCH 121 Hilton S B72,B73,*B72*
CHURCH 380 Regent Rd B26
CHURCH 10 Richmond St A52
CHURCH 117 St Simon St
A31,A32,*A32*
CHURCH Whit La C42
CIRCUS Blackfriars St A36
CLARENCE 57 Clarence St B67
CLARENCE 3 Ford St A64,B6
CLARENCE 202 Greengate A25
CLARENCE 28 King St A47
CLARENCE 125 Whit La C42,*C42*
CLARENDON 25 West Market St A63
CLAY HALL GARDENS Highfield Rd
C23
CLIFTON 30 Hampson St B15
CLOCK FACE 202 Chapel St A3
CLOCK FACE Oldfield Rd B33
CLOCKMAKERS 202 Chapel St A3
CLOGGERS 30 Shuttleworth St C53
CLOGGERS 33 Whit La C41
CLOUGH 220 Ordsall La B13,*B13*
CLOWES 42 Trafford Rd B55,*B54*
COACH & HORSES 30 Chapel St A9
COACH & HORSES 116 Chapel St
A13
COACH & HORSES 350-352
Eccles New Rd C58,C59,*C58*
COBDEN Peter St C47,C48,*C48*
COMMERCIAL Booth St A9
COMMERCIAL 149 Ordsall La B10
COMMERCIAL 35 Rockley St
C52,C53
COMPASSES Chapel St A17
CONCERT 36 Chapel St A9
COOMASSIE 53 Florin St
C35,C37,*C37*,A12,A25
COOPERS 1 Ford St A64
COPPERHEADS 187 Chapel St
A14,A15
CORNERHOUSE Greengate A21
CORNER HOUSE 2 Liverpool St B37
CORPORATION Broughton Rd A27
CORPORATION 3 Chapel St A2
CORPORATION 120 Chapel St A12
CORPORATION 7-9 Cross La C6,*C6*
CORPORATION 1 Market St A75
COTTON TREE 2 Gore St A44
COTTON TREE 25 James St B4
COURT TAVERN 11 Bexley Sq A62
COW & CALF 14 Gravel La A34
CRAVEN HEIFER 43 Cross La C5,*C5*
CRESCENT INN 13 Crescent B34
CRESCENT 20 Crescent
B34,B35,*B35*
CRICKETERS 10 Fenney St B71,C47
CRICKETERS Ford St A63
CROMWELL 49 Regent Rd B22
CROOKED BILLET 71 Chapel St A9
CROSS GUNS Ravald St A52
CROSS KEYS 81 Broad St
C22,*C22*,B59
CROSS KEYS 4a Broughton Rd P
C40

CROSS KEYS 91 Broughton Rd
A25,C35
CROSS KEYS 27 Brown St A37
CROSS KEYS 15 Garden St
B63,*B63*,B60
CROSS LANE TAVERN 1 Ellor St,
Cross La C6,C24
CROWN 24 Blackfriars St
A36,A37,*A36*
CROWN 44 Chaney St C32
CROWN 33 Ellesmere St B48
CROWN 71 Ellor St C25,B27
CROWN 207 Ellor St C28
CROWN 142 King St A48
CROWN Pendleton C17
CROWN 39 Regent Rd B22
CROWN 56 Regent Rd B23
CROWN 53 St Simon St A33,A34
CROWN 2 St Stephen St A61
CROWN 66 West Worsley St B50
CROWN & ANCHOR 55 Bury St
A54,*A53*
CROWN & CUSHION 72 Chapel St
A13
CROWN & MAYPOLE Ford La C19
CROWN & WESTMORLAND &
CUMBERLAND HOUSE
24 Blackfriars St A36
CRYSTAL PALACE 22 Watkin St A31
CUMBERLAND 11 Bloom St A60
CUMBERLAND 23-25 Peru St
A75,A76,A69,A71
CUMBERLAND HOUSE
34 Ellesmere St B48,*B48*
CUSTOM HOUSE 100 Chapel St
A10,A11,*A10*
DENBIGH CASTLE 49 Queen St A49
DENBIGH CASTLE 28 Rosamond St
A65
DERBY 33 Derby St B44,*B44*
DERBY 37 Derby St B45,*B45*,C42
DERBY 46 Hope St B35
DERBY New Bailey St A44
DERBY 205-7 Oldfield Rd B33,*B32*
DERBYSHIRE HOUSE 97 Ellor St
C28,C37
DOCK & PULPIT 1 Encombe Pl A78
DOG Chapel St A17
DOG 92 Chapel St A10,A14,C56
DOG 30-32 Lissadel St C51
DOG & BEAR Chapel St A17
DOG & LAMB Chapel St A14
DOG & PARTRIDGE 355 Bolton Rd
C55
DOG & PARTRIDGE 44 Chapel St A5
DOG & PARTRIDGE 166 Chapel St
A11
DOG & PARTRIDGE 25 Davies St
A30,*A31*
DOG & PARTRIDGE 15 Harrison St
C34,*C34*
DOG & PARTRIDGE 106 King St A48
DOG & PARTRIDGE 86 Ordsall La B9
DOG & PARTRIDGE Richmond Place
C3
DOG & PARTRIDGE 38-42 Silk St
A72,A73,*A74*
DOG & VOLUNTEER 30 Chapel S A5
DOLPHIN 169 Chapel St A10
DOVER 17 Fenney St B70,B71,*B71*
DOVER CASTLE Highclere Ave
B74,A36
DOVER CASTLE 2 Palmer S A36,B74
DROVERS 1 Cross La C6
DRUIDS 11 Bloom St A60
DRUIDS 60 Greengate A20,*A21*
DRUIDS 34 Liverpool St B40
DRUIDS 56-58 Ordsall La B9,B11
DRUIDS CALL 442 Regent Rd B27
DRUIDS HARP 39 Whit La C41
DRUIDS HOME 21 Silk St
A72,*A73*,C60
DRUIDS REST 11-13 Pimlot St
C30,C31,*C30*,C37

DUCHESS OF EDINBURGH
374 Liverpool St C61,*C61*
DUCHY 84-86 Brindleheath Rd
C47,*C47*,B20
DUCHY 2 East Market St A63
DUKE 122a Liverpool St B41,*B41*
DUKE OF CAMBRIDGE
71 Regent Rd B28
DUKE OF CLARENCE
34 Gravel La A34
DUKE OF DEVONSHIRE
13 Everard St B43
DUKE OF EDINBURGH
29 Chapel St A5,A6,*A5*
DUKE OF EDINBURGH 51 Tatton St
B52,*B52*,A18,A43,B58
DUKE OF LANCASTER
2 East Market St A63,A46
DUKE OF SUSSEX
169 Sussex St B64,*B64*
DUKE OF WELLINGTON
51 Greengate A22
DUKE OF YORK 101 Bury St
A56,*A56*
DUKE OF YORK Marlborough Rd
B74,*B74*,A29,B8
DUKE OF YORK 186 Regent Rd
B19,*B19*
DUKE OF YORK 48 York St B67,*B68*
DUKES HEAD Liverpool St B41
DYERS 169 Chapel St A13,A60
DYERS 72 Greengate A20
DYERS 64 Laundry St C46,B20
DYERS 120 Ordsall La B11,*B9*
DYERS Ravald St A52
DYERS 6 Tontine St C13
EAGLE 19 Collier St A49,*A49*
EAGLE 6-8 Duke St B67
EAGLE 52 Phoebe St B47
EAGLE (& CHILD) 3 Regent Rd B24
EAGLE & CHILD 177 Chapel St
A8,A36
EAGLE & CHILD Pendleton C17
EAGLE & CHILD Water St A36,A8
EARL OF CHESTER
155 Blackfriars Rd A27,B5
EBOR INN 93 Sussex St B64
EDINBURGH ALE VAULTS
3 Chapel St A2
EDINBURGH CASTLE
3 Chapel St A2,A3
EDINBURGH CASTLE
48 Greengate A20
EGERTON 14 Gore St A44,*A43*
EGERTON 256-8 Ordsall La B13
EGERTON Trafford Rd B55
EIGHT BELLS Chapel St A8
ELEPHANT & CASTLE
22 Hodson St A53
ELEPHANT & CASTLE
21 Whit La C41,*C40*
ELLESMERE 32 Ellesmere St B48
THE END 205 Cross La C4
ENGINE DRIVERS 49 Tatton St B51
ENGINEERS 55 Chapel St A7,*A5*
ENGINEERS 162 Greengate A23,A24
ENGRAVERS 36 Bury St A54
ETWALL HOUSE 109-111 Ellor St
C26,*C26*
EXCELSIOR 90 Broughton Rd A26
FACTORY TAVERN 15 George St
B2,*B2*,C63
FALCON 144 Cross La C8,*C9*
FALCON 143 Oldfield Rd B33
FARMERS 90 Broughton Rd A26,A31
FARMERS 41 Lissadel St C51
FARRIERS ARMS 7 Bombay St
A57,A74
FATTY ARBUCKLES Salford Quays
B56
FAWNS HEAD 34 St Stephen St
A61,B42
FEATHERS 241 Chapel St A3

FEATHERS 40 Laundry St
C45,C46,*C45*
FINNEYS 66 Greengate A21
FIREMANS REST 25 West Market St
A63
FISHERMENS HUT 19 Chapel St
A4,*A4*,A5
FIVE ALLS 101 Oldfield Rd B33
FLAT IRON Market Way C38
FLAX TAVERN 13 Flax St A74
FLEMISH WEAVER Broadwalk C38
FLOWER POT 29 Chapel St A8
FLOWER POT Pendleton C15
FLYING DUTCHMAN 36 Greengate
A19,*A19*
FLYING DUTCHMAN Salford Quays
B56
FLYING HORSE 114 Greengate
A22,A23,*A23*
FLYMAKERS ARMS 13 Green Bank
A52
FOOTBALLERS 7 John St C32
FOREIGNERS HOTEL Chapel St A17
FORESTERS 15 Booth St P C29,*C29*
FORESTERS 26 Boundary St B16
FORESTERS Bridgewater St A30
FORESTERS 88 Bury St A56
FORESTERS 18 George St B2
FORESTERS 72 King St A48
FORESTERS 37 Lissadel St C52
FORESTERS 29 Ordsall La B8,B9
FORESTERS 388 Regent Rd B26
FORESTERS 1 Rockliffe St A77
FORESTERS 34 Sidmouth St A57
FOUNDERS 31 New Windsor
C11,C12,*C11*
FOUNTAIN HEAD 11 Wheathill St
A31
FOUR HORSESHOES 181 Ellor St
C28,*C28*
FOX 11 Brownbill St A76
FOX 63 Bury St A54
FOX 4 Green St C47
FOX 119 Hope St B37,B16
FOX Liverpool St B41
FOX 331-5 Regent Rd B27,*B27*
FOX & GOOSE Pendleton C17
FOX'S VICTORIA MUSIC HALL
2 Chapel St A3
FRANKIE & BENNYS Salford Quays
B56
FREEMASONS 13 Spaw St
A42,*A37*,C13
FREE TRADE 57 Clarence St B67
FREE TRADE 19 New George St B3
FRIENDSHIP 16 Broughton St
A52,A70
FRIENDSHIP 4 Lester St A74,A75
FRIENDSHIP 35-37 Middlewood St
B16,B37
FRIENDSHIP 18 Quay St A38
FRIENDSHIP 34 Regent Rd B21
FRIENDSHIP 20 St Stephen St
A61,*A62*
FRIENDSHIP 21 Springfield La A28
FRIENDSHIP 85 West Union St B17
FRIENDSHIP 269 Whit La C44
FUSILIERS 1 Ellor St, Cross La
C6,C7,A46,C24
GARDENERS Broken Bank B34
GARDENERS Cannon St A72
GARDENERS 9-11 Pendleton St
C48,C49,*C48*
GARRICKS HEAD 72 St Simon St
A33
GAS TAVERN 13 Lamb La A58,A59
GAS TAVERN 324a Regent Rd
B25,*B25*
GENERAL HAVELOCK
124 Regent Rd B23
GENERAL PEEL 48 King St A48,B53
GENERAL PEEL 42 Trafford St
B53,A48
GEORGE 22 North George St A77

GEORGE THE FOURTH 2 Albion St C11,C42
GLADSTONE Tatton St B53
GLASSHOUSE 268 Regent Rd B26
GLOBE 10 Barrow St B4
GLOBE 48 Bury St A55,A54,A53
GLOBE 12-14 Corporation St A75
GLOBE 70 Cross La C8
GLOBE 60 Greengate A20
GLOBE 61-63 Regent Rd B21,B21
GLOBE 31 Union St LB B63
GLOUCESTER 160 Regent Rd B24,B24
GOLDEN ANCHOR Chapel St A12
GOLDEN GATE 43 Cross La C6
GOLDEN LION Chapel St A9
GOLDEN LION Every St A66,A67
GOLDEN LION 11 Johnson St A42
GOLDEN LION Pendleton C17
GOLDEN MALT 39 St Stephen S A62
GOLDEN QUOIT 22 Watkin St A31,B12
GOOD INTENT 11 Sackville St A60
GOOD SAMARITAN 23 Oldfield La B29
GOODWILL 41 Adelphi St A78
GRAPES Chapel St A12
GRAPES 16 Cross La C3,C3,C38
GRAPES 320 Eccles New Rd C58,C58
GRAPES 36 Gore St A45,B74
GRAPES Pendleton C17
GREAT BRITAIN Broughton Rd A27
GREEN BANK 64 Ravald St A52
GREEN DRAGON Chapel St A10
GREEN MAN Pendleton C17
GREEN VALE 22 Bedford S A27,A28
GRESLEY 89 Ordsall La B9
GREY HORSE 44 Davies St A30
GREY HORSE 6 Hankinson St C23
GREY HORSE Irwell St A46
GREY HORSE White Cross Bank B34
GREY MARE 3 Cannon St A71,A72
GREY MARE 386-8 Eccles New Rd C59,C59
GREYHOUND 103 Broad St C20,C21,C21,B11,B12
GREYHOUND 238 Tatton St B52
GREYHOUND 7 Woden St B42,B43,B43
GRIFFIN 205 Chapel St A15,A15
GRIFFIN 298 Lower Broughton Rd B57,B58,B57
GRIFFIN 30 Queen St A49
GRIFFIN & TURF Kersal B58
GROSVENOR 95 Gt Clowes St B66,B67,A55
GROVE 32 Brewery St A66,A67
GROVE 66-68 Church St P C37,C37,C38
GROVE 26 Eccles New Rd C56,C56
GROVE Islington Gr B4,B5,B5,A27
GROVE 128 Regent Rd B22,B23,B22
GROVE 50 Strawberry Hill C14
GROVE 63 West Worsley St B50
GROVE HOUSE 162 Ellor St C27,C28,C34,C51
HALF WAY HOUSE 19 Hothersall St B65
HANGING GATE 248-50 Tatton St B52,B53
HANKY PARK 95 Gt Clowes St B66
HANRAHANS Salford Quays B56
HARD BACKED NAN'S Broughton B57
HARE & HOUNDS 74 Broad St C18
HARE & HOUNDS 17 Deal St A58
HARE & HOUNDS 18 Deal St A58
HARE & HOUNDS Water St A36
HARMONIA 64 Greengate A20,A21
HARP INN 11 Sackville St A60
HARROW Broughton B58
HAT & FEATHERS 22 Boond St A50
HAT & FEATHERS Queen St A49

HATTERS 64 Broughton Rd A25
HAVELOCK 2 Allen St C34,C35
HAVELOCK 49 Chapel St A7
HAWK 1 Middletons Court A5
HAYFIELD 37-39 Hayfield St C37,C28
HEARTS OF OAK 44 Arlington St A68,A77
HEARTS OF OAK 6 Hampson St B15
HEATHER BELL 24 Bloom St A59
HEATHER BELL 25 Hulme St B35
HEN & CHICKENS 12 Ordsall La B8
HIGHER SHIP Chapel St A6
HIGHLAND LADDIE 14 Booth St C29
HIGHLAND LADDIE Pimlot St C31
HOBSONS CHOICE 34 Oldfield Rd B33
HOPE Eccles Old Rd C63
HOPE & ANCHOR Chapel St A12
HOPE & ANCHOR 34 Gravel La A34
HOPE COTTAGE 275 Broad St C23
HOPE PLACE TAVERN
  1 Stevenson St, George St B3,A71
HORSE & GROOM 19 Oldfield Rd B31
HORSE & JOCKEY 259 Broad St C20,C20
HORSE & JOCKEY 1 Ellor St,
  Cross La C6
HORSE & JOCKEY Greengate A22
HORSE & JOCKEY 50 Ordsall La B9
HORSE & JOCKEY 70 Silk St A73
HORSE & JOCKEY
  67 West Worsley St B50,B52
HORSE & JOCKEY
  White Cross Bank B34
HORSE SHOE 2a Back Hope St B70
HORSE SHOE 309-11 Broad St C16,C17,C17,C35,C38
HORSE SHOE 34 Coke St B75,B75
HORSE SHOE Greengate A18
HORSE SHOE 77-79 Lower
  Broughton Rd B60,B54
HOUSE THAT JACK BUILT
  Newbury Place B73
HUSSAR 40 Ordsall La B7
HYDE PARK CORNER 126 Silk St A72,A72
I HOPE I DON'T INTRUDE INN
  4 Broughton Rd A23
INDEPENDENT ODDFELLOWS
  ARMS 141 Broad St C19
INN OF GOOD HOPE Eccles Old Rd C63,C63
IRISH CROWN Pendleton C17
IRON BRIDGE 29 Greengate A20
IRON WORKS 4 Broad St C21
IRWELL CASTLE 60 Broughton Rd A25
IRWELL CASTLE 10 Gt Clowes St B66,B66
IRWELL CASTLE 251 Whit La C43,C43
IRWELL 40 East Robert St A30,A30
IRWELL 10 Gt Clowes St B65,B66
IRWELL 152 Ordsall La B11
ISLINGTON Islington Sq B5
JACOBS WELL 104 Ellor St C27
JOINERS Barrow St B4
JOINERS 24 Brunswick St A65,A64
JOINERS 17 Bury St A53
JOINERS 198 Ellor St C28,C28
JOINERS Pendleton C5
JOLLIES 23 Oldfield Rd B30
JOLLY CARTER 190 Chapel St A7
JOLLY CARTER 23 Gravel La A35,A35
JOLLY COBBLER 137 Oldfield Rd B32
JOLLY CROFTERS 175 Chapel St A11
JOLLY HATTERS & BLUE CAP
  80 Greengate A21
JOLLY MILLER Gravel La A35

JOLLY POTTERS 111 Greengate A18
JOLSONS BAR Langley Rd S C18
JUBILEE Tatton St B53
JUBILEE 39 Whit La C41,C41
JUST ANOTHER 7 John St C32
KENDAL HOUSE 17 New Bailey St A44
KERSAL CELL Littleton Rd C50
KERSAL HOTEL 216 Moor La B58,B57
KERSAL MOOR Kersal B58
KETTLEDRUM Heywood Way C38
KEYSTONE Market Way C38
KILDAKIN St Kildas Drive B75
KINGS 11 Bloom St A59,A59
KINGS Corporation St A75
KINGS 164 Ellor St C27
KINGS 85 Oldfield Rd B29,B30,B29
KINGS 49 Queen St A49
KINGS 51 West Craven St B47,B48
KINGS 34 Whit L C18,C17,C38,C48
KINGS HEAD 34 Chapel St A4,A5
KINGS HEAD Pendleton C18
KINGS HEAD 15 Ravald St A51,A51
KING WILLIAM IV
  10 East Ordsall La B7,B7
KING WILLIAM IV
  6-8 Springfield La A28,A29,A24
LAMB 142 Chapel St A13,A14,A13
LAMB 25-27 Hankinson St C23,C24
LAMB & BRITISH STANDARD
  136 Chapel St A14
LAMPLIGHTERS 33 Gold St C33
LANCASTER HOUSE
  125 Oldfield Rd B31
LANGWORTHY 176 Langworthy Rd C62,C62,A10
LARK INN 25 Derwent St B42
LEAMINGTON INN 11 Taylorson St B46,B46,A58
LEGS OF MAN Greengate/Gravel La A20
LEGS OF MAN & IMPERIAL
  WREATH 71 Gravel La A20
LIMA Peru St A76
LINER Trafford Rd B56
LIN MILL TAVERN
  3 Broughton Rd P C40
LIVE & LET LIVE 48-50 Liverpool St B40
LIVE & LET LIVE 312-314 Regent Rd B26
LIVE & LET LIVE 281 Whit La C43
LOCOMOTIVE 80 East Ordsall La B8
LONDON & NORTH WESTERN
  205 Cross La C4,C3,C9,C38,C55
LONDON TAVERN 198 Chapel S A17
LORD EGERTON 27 West Craven St B47,Bcover
LORD NAPIER 64 Ellesmere St B49
LORD NELSON 91 Chapel St A9,A10,A9
LORD NELSON
  25-27 Shuttleworth St C53,C51
LORD RAGLAN 114 Regent Rd B25
LOWER SHIP Chapel St A4
LOWRY Langley Road South C44
LUCKS ALL 99 Oldfield Rd B32
MAGNET 48 Arlington St A68
MALT & HOPS Queen St A49
MALT SHOVEL 39 Bury St A53,A54
MALTSTERS Ravald St A52
MANOR 10 Church St A64,A65,A65,C30
MARINER Liverpool St C62
MARK ADDY Stanley St A45
MARKET HOUSE 4 Kirkley St A63
MASONS Chapel St A17
MASONS 68 Chapel St A7,B53
MASONS 207 Ellor St C28
MASONS 13 Green Bank A52
MASONS 2 North George St A76
MASONS 109 Robert Hall St B53,A7,B11

MAYPOLE 11 Ford La C19,C1
MECHANICS 22 Arlington St A6
MECHANICS 4 Bloom St A5
MECHANICS Bury St A
MECHANICS 16 Garden La A50,A51,A
MECHANICS 47 Wilburn St B18,A
MIDDLETON 106-108 Orchard St
MILITARY 176 Regent Rd
MILK HOUSE 7 East Stanley St A30
MILLSTONE 16 Bury St
MINERS 29-31 Chapel St P C31,C32,
MONARCH BREWERY VAULTS
  146 Regent Rd
MOONRAKERS 229-231 Chapel A15,A16,
MOONRAKERS Phoebe St
MORNING STAR 6 Regent St
MOULDERS 44-46 Brindleheath C47,
MOULDERS 93 Bury St A55,
MOULDERS 62 Cannon St A71,
MOULDERS 35-37 Chaney St C32,C
MOULDERS 122 Chapel St
MOULDERS 178 Chapel St
MOULDERS 15 Clowes St
MOULDERS 3 King St
MOULDERS 53 St Simon St
MOUNT 53 Mount St A70,A
MOUNT 18 Rosamond St
MULVANEYS St Stephen St
MUSEUM 13 Primrose Hill C
NAGS HEAD 388 Regent Rd B
NAN'S Broughton B
NAPIER & BALTIC FLEET
  1 Sunnyside St B
NATIONAL 4 Carter St A
NAVIGATION 101 Oldfield Rd B
NEGRO'S HEAD Gravel La A
NELSON 285 Chapel St A16,
NELSON 62-66 Ellor St C25,C26,C2
NELSON 282 Ordsall La B13,B1
NELSON 55 Springfield La A
NEW BRIDGE 38 Hampson St B
NEW CATTLE MARKET Cross La C
NEW INN 2 East Church St A34,A3
NEW INN 28 Phoebe St B46,B4
NEW INN 8 Rodney St B
NEW KINGS ARMS 51 Whit La C4
NEW LEGS OF MAN 206 Chapel St A
NEW LEGS OF MAN 87 Greengate A2
NEW MARKET 138 Chapel St A1
NEW ROAD INN 100 St Simon St A33,A3
NEW SHIP 151 Blackfriars Rd A26,A27,A2(
NEW TOWN HALL 215 Broad St C22,C5(
NORTHUMBERLAND HOUSE
  11 Bloom St A6(
NORTHUMBERLAND HOUSE
  147 Chapel St A13,A6(
NORTHUMBERLAND HOUSE
  47 Derby St B45,B45,A6(
NORWEST 205 Cross La C4
NOTTINGHAM 43 Chapel St P C31
NUMBER FIVE 115 Hope St B36
NUMBER FOUR 72 Hope St B35
OAKWOOD Lancaster Rd C63,B2,B21
ODDFELLOWS 52 Broster St A30
ODDFELLOWS 350 Eccles New Rd C58
ODDFELLOWS 7 George St B2,B3
ODDFELLOWS 2 Harrison St C34
ODDFELLOWS 107 Hope St B36
ODDFELLOWS 24 King St A47
ODDFELLOWS 85 Oldfield Rd B32

ODDFELLOWS Rigby St | A57
OLD ARMCHAIR 29 Muslinet St | B37
OLD BOARS HEAD
27 Bridgewater St | A29
OLD BRITISH FLEET
187 Oldfield Rd | B30
OLD CLOCK FACE 27 Essex St | B17
OLDFIELD LANE COFFEE HOUSE
73 Oldfield Road | B29
OLDFIELD LANE INN
Oldfield Lane | B29
OLDFIELD ROAD HOTEL
73 Oldfield Road | B29
OLDFIELD ROAD TAVERN
29 Oldfield Rd | B31,A46
OLD FORD TAVERN 21 Ford La | A74
OLD HOUSE AT HOME
50 Cannon St | A71
OLD HOUSE AT HOME
26-28 Middlewood St | B16,*B16*
OLD HOUSE AT HOME 4 Pimlot St
C30,*C29*,C20,C25,C44
OLD HOUSE AT HOME
43-45 Regent Rd | B21,C63
OLD HOUSE AT HOME
4 Rigby St | A57
OLD HOUSE AT HOME
103 St Stephen St | A62,B12
OLD HOUSE AT HOME
254 Whit La | C44,*C44*
OLD KINGS HEAD 34 Chapel St
A5,B55
OLD NELSON 285 Chapel St
A16,C27
OLD OAK 38 Garden La | A50
OLD PINT POT Crescent | B35
OLD PRIORY 6 Laurel Grove
B69,B70,*B69*
OLD PUMP HOUSE Salford Quays
B56
OLD QUEEN ANNE 151 Chapel St
A12,A13
OLD SCHOOL 13 King St | A48
OLD SHEARS 53 Greengate
A19,A20,*A20*
OLD SHIP Chapel St | A6
OLD SHIP 17 Chapel St | A4,*A4*
OLD VETERAN 1 Duxbury St
C60,*C60*
OLIVE BRANCH 7 Briggs St
A70,*A70*,A69,A78
ORDNANCE 62 Regent Rd | B21
ORDSALL 217 Ordsall La
B12,B13,*B12*
ORDSALL GARDENS Ordsall La
B14,A11
ORDSALL LANE TAVERN
21 Ordsall La | B8,B74
ORIGINAL 14 Lwr Broughton Rd
B59,*B58*,C22
ORIGINAL PINK TAVERN
68 Bury St | A55
ORIGINAL THREE PIGEONS
21 Cross La | C7
OSBORNE 38 Eccles New Rd
C56,C57,*C55*,A10
OXFORD 11 Bexley Sq A62,A63,*A63*
OXFORD 2 Walmer St | B51,B52
PACK HORSE Bolton Rd
C14,C15,*C15*
PADDOCK Cross La | C7,*C7*
PAINTERS 10 Sackville St | A60
PALACE OF MUSIC 44 Chapel St A5
PALATINE 45-47 Edward S B65,*B65*
PAPERMAKERS 1-2 Clifden Place
B73,*B73*
PARADISE 25 Paradise Row A29,B74
PARK Fenney St | B70
PARK 47-49 Tatton St | B51
PARK 84 West Park St
B54,A55,B11,B12
PARK DAIRY 5 Fenney St | B70
PARK ROYAL 61-63 Regent Rd | B21
PAUL PRY 136 Greengate | A23,A24

PEDESTRIAN 70 Broughton Rd | A25
PEDESTRIAN 21 Cook St | A58
PEEL PARK 270 Chapel St | A17
PEEL PARK 1 Hough La | B60
PEEL PARK COTTAGE
29 Wallness Rd | C13,C14
PEEL TAVERN 1 Hulme St | B35
PEEL TAVERN 2 West Peel St | B24
PEEPING TOM 408 Regent Rd
B26,B27,*B27*
PEN & WIG 23 New Bailey St | A43
PERSEVERANCE 8 Laundry St
C46,C47
PHEASANT 9-11 Primrose Hill | C24
PHEASANT & SHROPSHIRE
HOUSE 17 East Ordsall La | B7
PHOENIX Chapel St | A4
PICKWICK 132 Oldfield Rd B33,B12
PIED PIPER Broadwalk | C38
PIER 6 Salford Quays | B56
PILGRIMS REST 16 West Gore St
B37
PINEAPPLE 4 West Worsley St
B49,*B49*
PINK TAVERN 68 Bury St
A55,A18,B12
PLASTERERS 41 Springfield La
A28,A29
PLEASANT 44 Chapel St | A5
PLOUGH Broughton | B57
PLUMBERS 3 Gold St | C33
PLUMBERS 20 Gore St | A45
PLUMBERS 104 Greengate | A18
PLUME OF FEATHERS Pendleton
C17
POETS CORNER
99 Lwr Broughton Rd | B60,*B59*
POLLARDS 24 Hampson St | B14
POLYTECHNIC 14 Greengate
A18,B52
PONTACK 235 Regent Rd | B27,B28
PORTLAND 55 Doddington St | B48
POST CHAISE Top Salford | A17
POST OFFICE 23 Hilton St B72,*B72*
POTTERS INN 111 Greengate | A18
PRINCE ALBERT VAULTS
165 Chapel St | A13
PRINCE OF WALES 18 Bloom St A59
PRINCE OF WALES 135 Broad St
C21,C22
PRINCE OF WALES 41 Hodge L C61
PRINCE OF WALES 1 Hope St
B36,*B36*
PRINCE OF WALES 1 Jennings St
B47,B48
PRINCE OF WALES 230 Lower
Broughton Rd | B61
PRINCE OF WALES 19 Oldfield Rd
B31,*B30*
PRINCE OF WALES 165 Oldfield Rd
B30,B31
PRINCE OF WALES 34 Pimlot St
C30,C31
PRINCE OF WALES & YORKSHIRE
HOUSE 165 Oldfield Rd | B30
PRINCE OF WALES FEATHERS
20 Windsor | C12,C13,*C13*,C38
PRINCESS TAVERN
100-102 Ordsall La | B9,*B8*
PRINTERS 30 Bridgewater St | A29
PRINTERS Broughton Rd | A25,A26
PRINTERS 139 Broughton Rd | A27
PRINTERS 25 Bury St P | C33
PRINTERS 30 Chapel St | A8
PRINTERS 47 Chapel St | A7
PRIORY 29 Gardner St | C50,*C50*
PRIORY 45 Gardner St | C50,C35
PRIORY 136 High St | C35,*C35*,A3
PUDDLERS 49 Lissadel St | C52
PUMP HOUSE Salford Quays | B56
PUNCH BOWL 81 Chapel St | A9,*A8*
PYED BULL Chapel St | A14
QUAY HOUSE Salford Quays | B56
QUEEN ADELAIDE Gore St | A45

QUEEN ADELAIDE 14 Queen St | A49
QUEEN ANN Greengate | A18
QUEEN ANNE 143 Chapel St | A12
QUEENS Bloom St | A59
QUEENS Broughton Rd | A27
QUEENS 68 Chapel St | A12
QUEENS 100 Chapel St | A11,A12
QUEENS 110 Chapel St | A11,*A11*
QUEENS 98 Florin St | C35
QUEENS 34 Gravel La | A34
QUEENS 304 Ordsall La
B14,B11,B42,B46
QUEENS 20 Regent Rd | B22
QUEENS 74 Regent Rd | B20
QUEENS 14 Sidney St | B5
QUEENS 21 William St | A60
QUEENS HEAD Chapel St | A12
QUEEN VICTORIA 48 Bury St | A55
QUIET WOMAN Queen St | A49
RACECOURSE Littleton Rd C50,A19
RACEHORSE Kersal | B58
RAILROAD TAVERN Cross La | C3
RAILWAY 6 Albion St | C13
RAILWAY 8 Barlows Rd | B41
RAILWAY 38 Broughton Rd P | C40
RAILWAY 205 Cross La | C3,C9,C55
RAILWAY 217 Cross La | C10,*C10*
RAILWAY 19 Gore St | A44
RAILWAY 4 Greengate A18,*A18*,A19
RAILWAY 29 Lissadel St | C51
RAILWAY 1 Liverpool St | B37,*B37*
RAILWAY 23 New Bailey St | A43
RAILWAY 2 Ordsall La | B8,B55
RAILWAY 47 Wilburn St | B18,*B18*
RAILWAY & DROVERS
49 Oldfield St | B30
RAILWAY HOUSE 185 Oldfield Rd
B31,*B31*
RAILWAY MUSIC SALOON
26 Boundary St | B16
RAINBOW 29 Chapel St | A6
RAVEN 9 Chapel St | A3,*A2*,C35
RED BULL Chapel St | A14
RED COW 78-80 Albion St
C13,*C84*,A42
RED DRAGON 20 Crescent | B34,B35
RED LION 279 Bolton Rd
C53,*C53*,B29,C62
RED LION Broughton | B58
RED LION 4-6 Cannon St | A72
RED LION 1 Chapel St | A3
RED LION 241 Chapel St | A16
RED LION Pendleton | C17
RED LION 2 Pimlot St | C30,*C29*
RED ROSE 52 Cross La | C4,*C4*
RED WHITE & BLUE
148 Regent Rd | B23
REFRESHMENT ROOMS
Salford Station | A43,B18
REGATTA 6-8 Regent Rd | B21,B22
REGENT HOTEL 263 Regent Rd | B28
REGENT VAULTS 148 Regent Rd B23
RETFORD 137 Broad St | C20
RICHMOND BREWERY INN
103 Broad St | C20
RIFLEMAN 136 Chapel St | A14
RIFLEMAN 17 New Bailey St | A44
RING O'BELLS 10 Booth St | A37
RING O'BELLS 5 Brindleheath R C47
RING O'BELLS 23 Bury St
A53,A8,C37
RING O'BELLS Chapel St | A8,A53
RING O'BELLS Crookell St | B43
RISING SUN 244 Chapel St | A3
RISING SUN 30 Greengate | A20
RISING SUN Pendleton | C17
RISING SUN 24 Quay St | A38
ROB ROY 2 Arlington St
A67,*A68*,A69,A71,A78
ROB ROY 116 Blackfriars Rd | A26
ROBIN HOOD 86 Chapel St | A8
ROBIN HOOD 43 Lissadel St | C52
ROBIN HOOD Pendleton | C17
ROBIN HOOD 209 Regent Rd | B25

ROBIN HOOD 136-138 St Simon St
A31,A32,A33,*A33*
ROBINSON CRUSOE
3 New Bridge St | A28
ROCK 1 Tatton St | B51
RODNEY Rodney St | B6
ROEBUCK 31 Chapel St | A8
ROLLING MILL 21 Laundry St | C45
ROPEMAKERS 14 Chapel St | A6
ROPEMAKERS 29 Gravel La | A35
ROPERS 14 Chapel St | A6
ROSE & CROWN 49 Broad St
C18,C19,*C18*,C11
ROSE & CROWN 48 Chapel S A6,A8
ROSE & CROWN 63 Gravel La | A35
ROSE SHAMROCK &THISTLE
1 New Chapel St | C49
ROUND O'BEEF 74 Greengate
A21,A22
ROVERS RETURN 91 Chapel St
A9,A10
ROVERS RETURN Guy Fawkes S B54
ROVERS RETURN 47-49 Tatton St
B51
ROYAL 48-50 Chapel St | A6,*A6*
ROYAL 139-143 Church St P
C37,C38,A53
ROYAL 433 Eccles New Rd C57,C58
ROYAL 52 Phoebe St | B47
ROYAL ALBERT 26 Bury St | A54
ROYAL ALBERT
99-101 Liverpool St | B40,*B40*
ROYAL ARCHER 86 Chapel St
A8,B61
ROYAL ARCHER 103 Lower
Broughton Rd | B61,*B60*,A8,B60
ROYAL ARCHER 75 Ravald St | A52
ROYAL COMMERCIAL
48-50 Chapel St | A6
ROYAL DUKE OF CORNWALL
70 Broughton Rd | A25
ROYAL FORESTERS 1 Rockliffe St
A77
ROYAL HUNT 60-62 Robert Hall St
B53
ROYAL OAK 48 Arlington St | A68
ROYAL OAK Chapel St | A17
ROYAL OAK 13 Chapel St HB
B74,B75
ROYAL OAK 85 Chapel St | A9
ROYAL OAK 45 Cross La | C7,*C2*
ROYAL OAK 34 Garden La | A50,A47
ROYAL OAK 94 Greengate | A22
ROYAL OAK 1 Hall St | C13,B35
ROYAL OAK 40-42 Hankinson St
C24,*C24*
ROYAL OAK 55 Hilton St | B72
ROYAL OAK 14 Norton St | A36
ROYAL OAK 100-102 Oldfield Rd
B32,C21
ROYAL OAK 52 Ordsall La | B9
ROYAL OAK Waterloo Place | A57
ROYAL OAK 14 West William St
B36,B37
ROYAL OAK 55 Whit La | C42,*C41*
ROYAL OAK 13 Wilna Terrace | B41
ROYAL RIFLEMAN 74 Bury St | A55
ROYAL SOVEREIGN Chapel St | A6
ROYAL THISTLE 32 Cannon St | A70
ROYAL VETERAN Irwell St
A45,A46,*A45*,C7,C45
ROYAL VETERAN
14 West Cross St | B17,B18
RUNNING HORSES 215 Chapel S A7
RUNNING HORSES 29 Greengate
A18,A19,A35
RUNNING HORSES Kersal | B58,B57
RUTHIN ARMS Broughton Rd | A24
SABRE Taylorson St | B46
SADDLE 63 Chapel St | A7,A8
ST JAMES Markendale St
B54,*B54*,A50,B60
ST JAMES Phoebe St | B47
ST JOHNS 8 Mason St | B6,A64

ST LUKES 120 King St A47,*A47*,A27,A50
ST PHILIPS 23 Oldfield Rd B30,*B30*
ST SIMONS Springfield La A32
ST STEPHENS 53 St Stephen St A61,*A61*
SALFORD ARMS 146 Chapel St A14,*A14*
SALFORD ARMS 70 King St A48
SALFORD ARMS Ordsall La B13
SALFORD ARMS 10 Sackville St A60
SALFORD BOROUGH ARMS 5 Brewery St A66
SALFORD DINING ROOMS 36 Chapel St A5
SALFORD HOTEL 44 Chapel St A5
SALFORD TAVERN 39 Chapel St A9
SALFORD TAVERN 88 Chapel St A14
SALFORD VAULTS Gore St A14
SALISBURY Trafford Rd B55,B56,*B56*,A5,B8,C50
SANDY LANE TAVERN Pendleton C17
SANDYWELL HOUSE 59 Greengate A23
SEEDLEY 70-72 Church St P C37
SEEDLEY GARDENS Highfield Rd C23
SEVEN STARS 1 Market St A75
SEVEN STARS 176 Regent Rd B26,*B26*
SHAKESPEARE 6 Crowther St B43
SHAKESPEARE 21-23 Goodiers La B50,B51
SHAKESPEARE 22 Gravel La A35
SHAMROCK 31 Barrow St B3,B4
SHEARS 53 Greengate A19,A20,*A20*
SHIP Back Salford A18
SHIP Chapel St A6
SHIP 17 Chapel St A4
SHIP Cross La C10
SHIP 2-6 Eccles New Rd C55,C56,*Ccover*,*C55*,C10
SHIP 110 Ordsall La B10,A47,A50
SHOVEL & BROOM 68 Elton St B64
SIR COLIN CAMPBELL 296 Regent Rd B23,*B23*,B26
SIR RALPH ABERCROMBIE 96 Chapel St A10
SOLDIERS REST 122 Regent Rd B22
SPINNERS 191 Chapel St A11
SPINNERS 4 Oldfield Rd B29
SPORTS Belvedere Rd C38
SPORTSMAN 48 Arlington St A68
SPORTSMAN 21 Cross La C7
SPORTSMAN 20 Regent Rd B22
SPREAD EAGLE 26 Chapel St A3,A4,C11
SPREAD EAGLE 162-166 Regent Rd B23,*B22*
SPRINGFIELD TAVERN 2 Springfield La A28,A77
SPRING VALE TAVERN 4 Tanners La C35
SQUEALING PIG Peru St A76
STAFF OF LIFE 19 Brown St A37
STAFF OF LIFE 56 Chapel St A7
STAFF OF LIFE 144 Ellor St C27
STAFF OF LIFE 40 Windsor Bridge C12,*C12*,B46
STAG 129 Hodge La C61,*C60*
STAG 26 Oldfield Rd B31,B32,*B32*
STAG 138 Tatton St B52
STAG & PHEASANT 16 Rosamond St A65
STANLEY 72 Broughton Rd A25
STANLEY 11-13 Pump St B43
STAR 2 Back Hope St B70,*B70*
STAR 207 Cross La C9
STAR 10-12 Ford La A74,*A76*,B11
STAR 6 Gold St C32,C33
STAR 77 Greengate A22
STAR 125 Greengate A24,*A24*
STAR 47 Lissadel St C52,*C52*

STAR 1 Market St A75
STAR 55a Martha St B51,*B48*
STAR 15 New Bailey St A44
STAR 38 North George St A77,*A77*
STAR 85 Oldfield Rd B32
STAR 442 Regent Rd B27,*B28*
STAR & GARTER 192 Chapel St A7
STAR BREWERY 99 Bury St A56
STATION 207-209 Cross La C9,C10
STEAM ENGINE 67 Arlington St A68
STONEMASONS 29 Muslinet St B37
STOWELL SPIRE Howard S C60,A72
STRAWBERRY GARDENS Pendleton C17
STRUGGLERS REST 4 Toft St B16,C61
SUMMERVILLES Bank La C55
SUN 223 Gt Cheetham St E B73,*B73*
SUN Pendleton C17
SUN 123 Phoebe St B47,*B76*
SUN 28 Quay St A38
SUNNYSIDE 124 Ordsall La B11
SWAN Bolton Rd C54
SWAN 390 Eccles New Rd C59,C60,*C59*
SWAN (WITH TWO NECKS) Chapel St A17
SWAN WITH TWO NECKS Eccles New Rd C59
TALBOT Chapel St A10
TALBOT 22 Crowther St B43,B44
TALLOW TUB 110 Chapel St A11
TANKARD Ford La A74
TANNERS 14 Oxford S B46,*B47*,C12
TATTON 50-52 Tatton St B51,*B51*,B11
THATCHED HOUSE 297 Broad St C19,*C19*
THATCHED HOUSE 114 Eccles Old Rd C63,*C63*
THISTLE 32 Cannon St A70
THREE CROWNS 40 King St A47,*A46*,B52
THREE DOVES Chapel St A17
THREE HORSE SHOES 34 Coke St B75
THREE LEGS OF MAN 63 Greengate A20,A21,*A20*,A24,*A34*
THREE PIGEONS 293 Bolton Rd C53,C54,*C54*
THREE TERRIERS 5 Union St C49,*C49*
TOM TINKER White Cross Bank B34
TOWER 275 Broad St C23,*C23*
TOWN HALL Bexley Sq A62
TOWN HALL 215 Broad St C22,C23,*C22*
TOWN HALL 23 Ford St A63,A64,*A64*,B10
TRAFALGAR 26 Ordsall La B8,B55
TRAFALGAR 54 Trafalgar St B68
TRAFFORD 22 Trafford Rd B55,*B55*
TRAM 151 Oldfield Rd B32,B33
TRAVELLERS 117 Greengate A18
TRAVELLERS REST 40 Mount St A69
TRAVELLERS REST 118 St Stephen St A62
TRIPEDRESSERS 10 Sackville St A60
TURF 50 Cannon St A71,B3
TURF 35 Chaney St C32
TURF 2 Eccles New Rd C55
TURF 104 Greengate A22
TURF Kersal Moor B58,B57
TURF 100 Whit La C42
TURRET CLOCK 15 Essex St B17
TURTLE 33 Gold St C33
TWO BREWERS Regent Rd B20
TWO COCKS 56 Chapel St A7
TWO GREYHOUNDS Cross La C3
TYRONE CASTLE 74 Arlington St A68,C10
UGLY DUCKLING Duxbury St C60

ULSTER 16 Corporation St A75
UNCLE TOMS CABIN Broughton Rd A27
UNICORN 10 Broughton Rd P C39,C40,*C39*
UNICORN 76 Chapel St A8,B63
UNICORN 1 Union St B63,*B62*
UNION 105-7 Liverpool St B40,B41,*B40*
UNION 1 Union St B62,B63,A8
UNION 47 West Union St B17,*B17*
UNITED 184 Regent Rd B25
UPPER SHIP Chapel St A6
VAVASOUR 160 Sussex St B63,*B64*
VICTORIA 78 Chapel St A8
VICTORIA 39 Crowther St B44
VICTORIA 28 Duke St B68
VICTORIA 134 Ellor St C27,*C27*
VICTORIA 1 Everard St B12
VICTORIA 94 Liverpool St B40
VICTORIA 9 Lyth St B18
VICTORIA 47 Silk St A73
VICTORIA 3 Tomlinsons Bdgs B4
VICTORIA BRIDGE 2 Chapel St A3
VILLAGE BLACKSMITH Greengate A21,A22
VILLAGE BLACKSMITH Oldfield Rd B32
VINE 23 Broad St C20,C44
VINE 66 Broughton Rd A25
VINE 106 Ellor St C27
VINE 2 Farrell St B65
VINE 27 Hough La B62,*B62*,B33
VINE 39 New George St B3,B4,B5
VINE Oldfield Rd B33
VOLUNTEER 180 Chapel St A16
VOLUNTEER 202 Chapel St A5
VOLUNTEER 2 Liverpool St B37,B40
VULCAN 15 Grafton St C34
WAGGON & HORSES 367 Bolton Rd C15,*C15*,C54
WAGGON & HORSES 26 Booth S A9
WAGGON & HORSES Broughton B58
WAGGON & HORSES 16 Gore S A45
WAGGON & HORSES Greengate A18
WAGGON & HORSES 2 Sandywell St A29
WALLNESS 29 Wallness L C14,*C14*
WASHERWOMANS 2 Railway St C45,A46
WASHINGTON HOUSE 50 Cannon St A71
WATERLOO 93 Greengate A22,*A22*,A19
WATERLOO 3 New Bridge St A28
WATERLOO 10 Picton St A57
WATERSIDE Salford Quays B56
WAVERLEY 145 Eccles New Rd C57,*C56*,B52,C63
WEASTE Edward Ave C62,A21,B15
WEAVERS Chapel St A10,A12
WEAVERS Cross La C3
WEAVERS 10-12 Ford La A74
WEAVERS 9 Lyth St B18
WEAVERS Salford Cross A21
WEIGHING MACHINE Broad St C21
WELCOME 18 Arlington St A68,A77
WELCOME 47 Cook St A58
WELCOME 11 Ellor St C25,*C24*
WELCOME 28 King St A47
WELCOME 136 Ordsall La B12,*B11*,B11,B54
WELCOME Robert Hall St B54,B11
WELCOME 11 West Duke S B15,A69
WELCOME 6 West Worsley St B49
WELCOME STRANGER 48 Cannon St A71
WELLINGTON 347 Bolton Rd C54
WELLINGTON 124 Broughton Rd P C40
WELLINGTON 156 Cross La C9,*C9*
WELLINGTON 97 Ellor St C26,A14

WELLINGTON 11 Ford La A74
WELLINGTON 23 New Bailey St A43,*A42*
WELLINGTON 120 Regent Rd B19,B20,*B19*,B21
WELLINGTON St Simon St A32
WELLINGTON 73 St Stephen St A61,A62
WELLINGTON 239-43 Whit La C43,*C43*
WHEATSHEAF 141 Broad St C19,C20,*C19*,C38
WHEATSHEAF Chapel St A10
WHEATSHEAF 137 Chapel St A12
WHEATSHEAF 76 Ordsall La B9
WHEATSHEAF 299 Regent Rd B27,*B28*,C25
WHIT LANE TAVERN Whit La C42
WHITE BEAR 24 Broughton Rd A25
WHITE BULL Chapel St A7
WHITE BULL Deal St, Chapel St A11
WHITE HART 17 Queen St A49
WHITE HART 6 West Worsley St B49
WHITE HORSE 57 Clarence St B67
WHITE HORSE Gilda Brook Rd C63
WHITE HORSE 79 Hilton St B72
WHITE HORSE 59 West Union S B17
WHITE LION Broken Bank B3
WHITE LION Chapel St A
WHITE LION 180 Chapel St A6
WHITE LION Cook St
WHITE LION 16 Hampson St B15
WHITE LION 16 Wood St A38
WHITE SWAN Back Cross St A36
WHITE SWAN 299 Bolton Rd C54,*C54*
WHITE SWAN 25 Cannon St A71
WHITE SWAN Chapel St A17
WHITE SWAN Eccles New Rd C59
WHITE SWAN 1 Miller St A19
WHO'D HAVE THOUGHT IT Sidmouth St A57
WIDOWS REST 433 Eccles New Rd C58
WIGAN ARMS 18 Sidney St B5,B6
WILLIAM IV 79 Bury St A55
WILLIAM IV 10 East Ordsall La B7
WILLIAM IV 34 Gravel La A34
WILLIAM IV 9 Lamb La A59,B53
WILLIAM IV 221 Robert Hall St B53,B54,*B53*,A59
WILTON 143 Cross La C8,*C8*
WINDMILL 83 Arlington St A68
WINDSOR BRIDGE 24 Windsor C12
WINDSOR BRIDGE TAVERN 4 Broad St C21,*C21*,B32
WINDSOR CASTLE 15 Windsor C11,*C11*,A4,C21
WINSTON Churchill Way C38
WOODBINE 283 Liverpool St C61,*C61*,B17
WOODMAN Belvedere Rd C38,*C38*,C37
WOODMANS HUT 11-13 Pump St B43
WOODMANS HUT 43 Queen St A49
WOOLPACK 347a Broad S C16,*C16*
WOOLPACK 12 Hopefield A74
WOOLPACK Meyrick Rd C38,C16,C20
WORSLEY HOTEL 69 West Worsley St B50,*B50*,C38
YEW TREE 2 Brunswick St A65,*A66*
YORK MINSTER Bexley Sq A63
YORKSHIRE GREY 3 Cross St P C29
YORKSHIRE GREY 41 Ravald St A51,A52
YORKSHIRE HOUSE 7 Browncross St A42
YORKSHIRE STINGO TAVERN 17 New Bailey St A44

IN CELEBRATION OF

20
19
SHARJAH
WORLD BOOK
CAPITAL
الشارقة
عاصمة عالمية
للكتاب

World Book Capital is a book about the beauty of imagination and the richness of learning. It invites children around the world to imagine cities in which books, reading, and knowledge are everywhere. It is designed to trigger their curiosity about living in such cities and to learn more about the cities which have previously been crowned World Book Capital.

I authored this book to promote a love of books and literacy in children, and to celebrate reading as a powerful medium in reinforcing our interconnectedness and in building bridges of understanding and mutual respect.

الشــارقة، الإمارات العـربية المتحدة
www.kalimat.ae

World Book Capital
Text © Bodour Al Qasimi, 2020
Illustration © Denise Damanti, 2020

First published in 2020 by Kalimat Group
Second Edition 2021
ISBN:978-9948-25-166-8

تمت الموافقة على المحتوى من قبل المجلس الوطني للإعلام المرجع: MC-02-01-3569416
التصنيف العمري: 9-6

مجموعة كلمات
KALIMAT GROUP

World Book Capital

By Bodour Al Qasimi

Illustrated by Denise Damanti

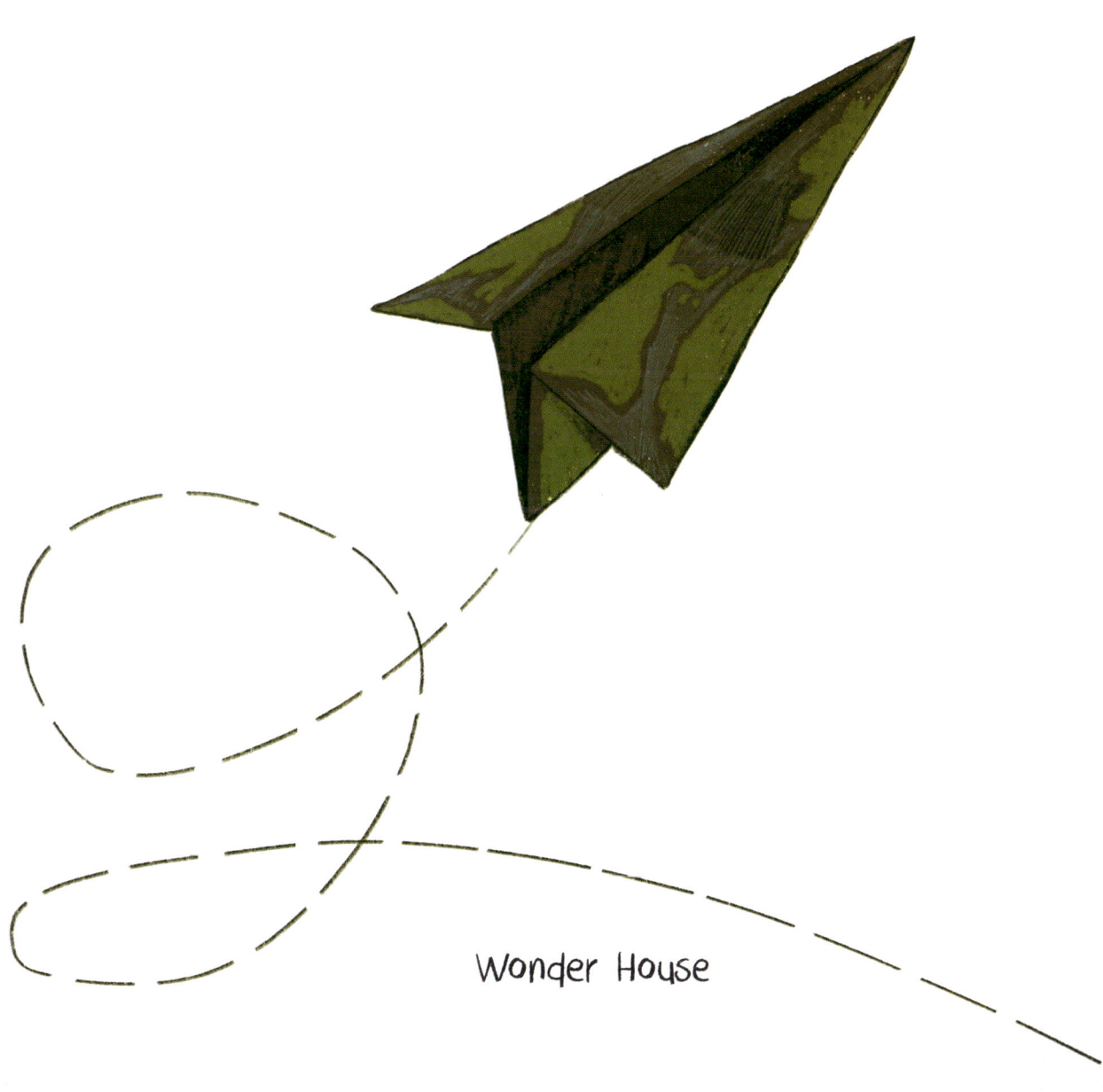

Wonder House

Imagine a city unlike any other city.

Imagine a city whose heartbeat
is unlike any other heartbeat.

Imagine a city whose streets are decorated
with books and knowledge...

Where people ask, "What are you reading?"
instead of, "How are you?"

Where libraries are everywhere.

And bookstalls on all streets.

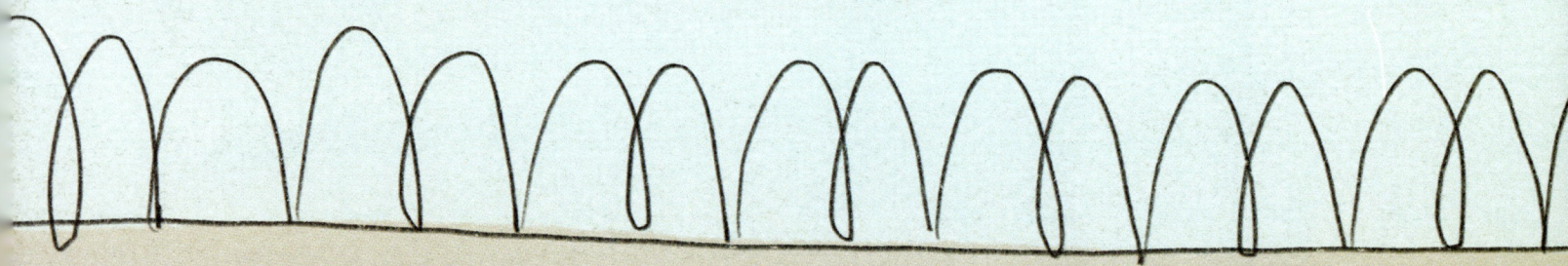

Where stories are told at park benches
and playgrounds.

On beaches and in shopping centers.

In museums and amusement parks.

Does such a magical place exist?

Yes, it does.

In fact, many cities around the world
match with this description.

The whole world celebrates these cities
as The World Book Capital.

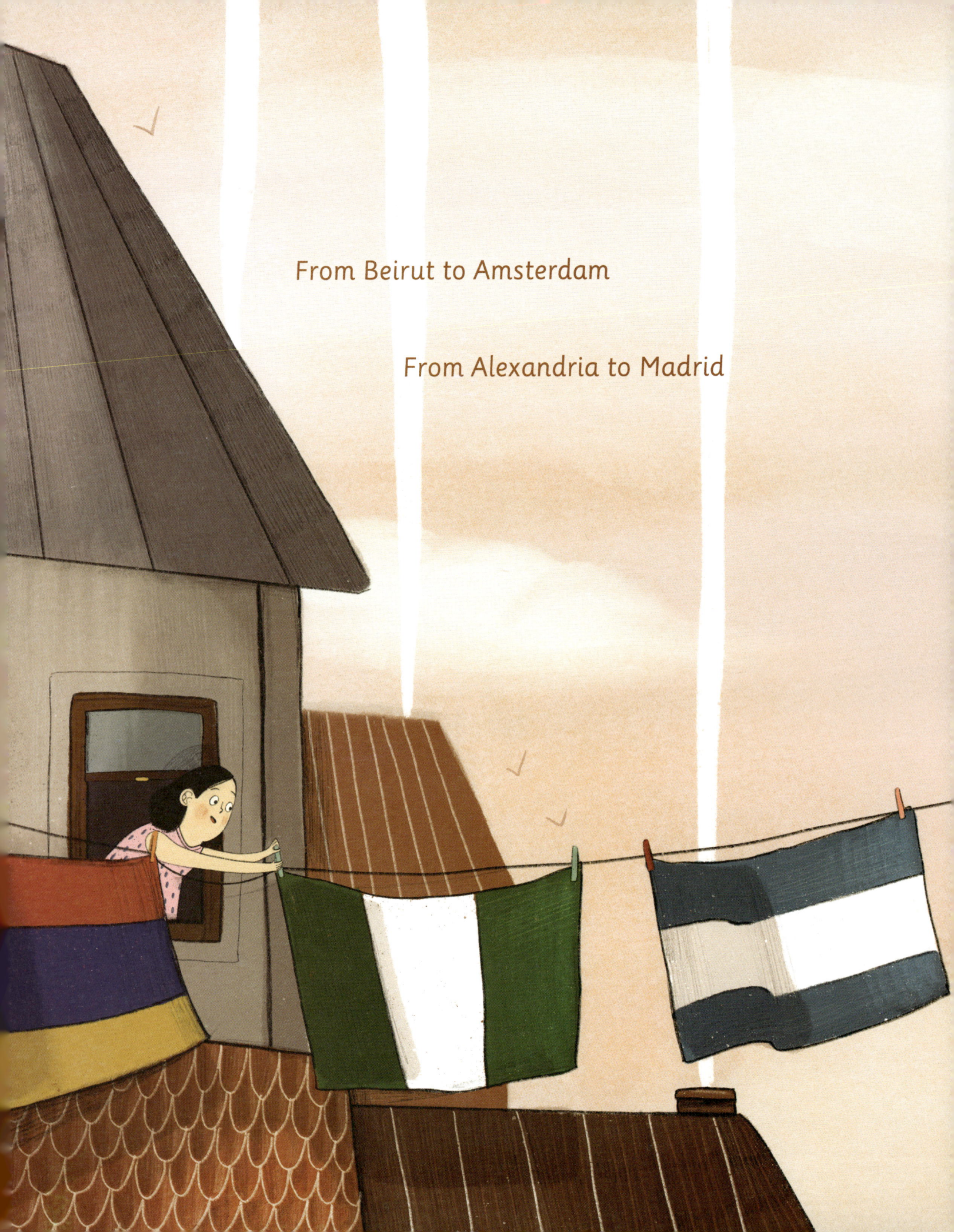

From Beirut to Amsterdam

From Alexandria to Madrid

From Athens to Port Harcourt

And from Sharjah to Buenos Aires!

All of these cities have placed books
and reading on their maps.

They have created generations of readers and thinkers who will build their own future.

Imagine how the world will be like if all of
its cities were similar to these.

Do you know one of the World
Book Capital cities?

2001
Madrid, Spain

2002
Alexandria, Egypt

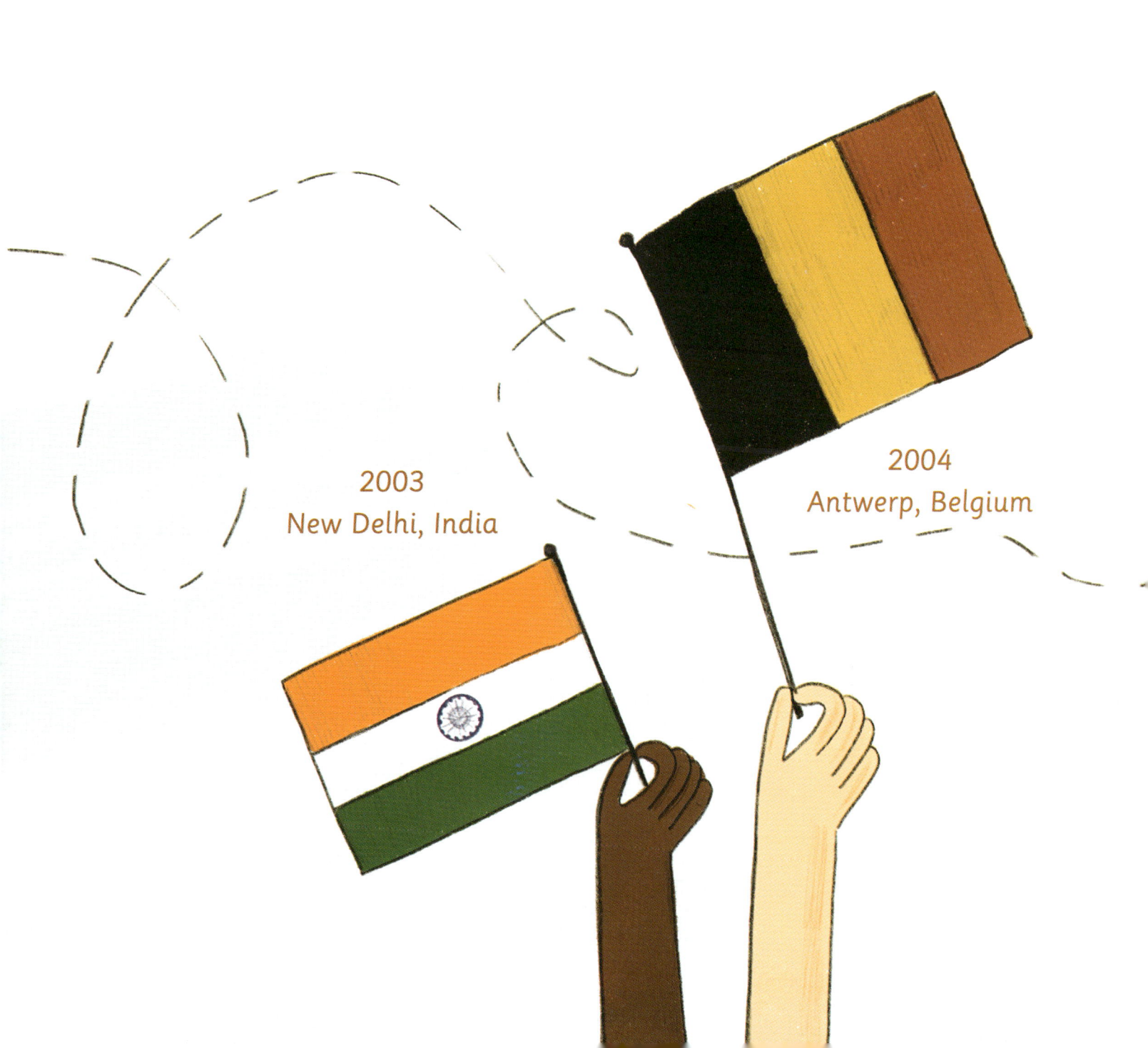

2003
New Delhi, India

2004
Antwerp, Belgium

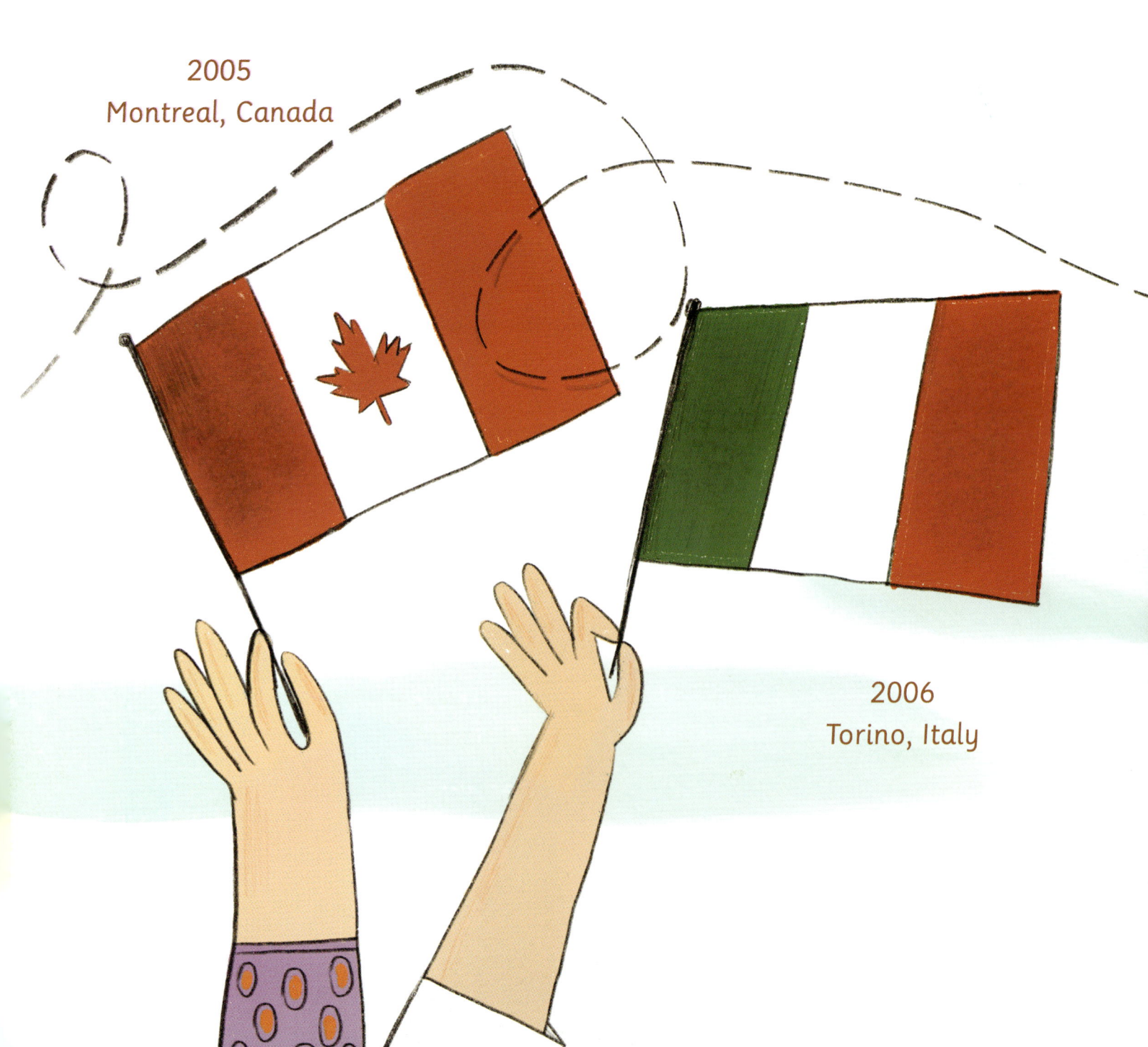

2005
Montreal, Canada

2006
Torino, Italy

2007
Bogota, Colombia

2008
Amsterdam, Netherlands

2010
Ljubljana, Slovenia

2009
Beirut, Lebanon

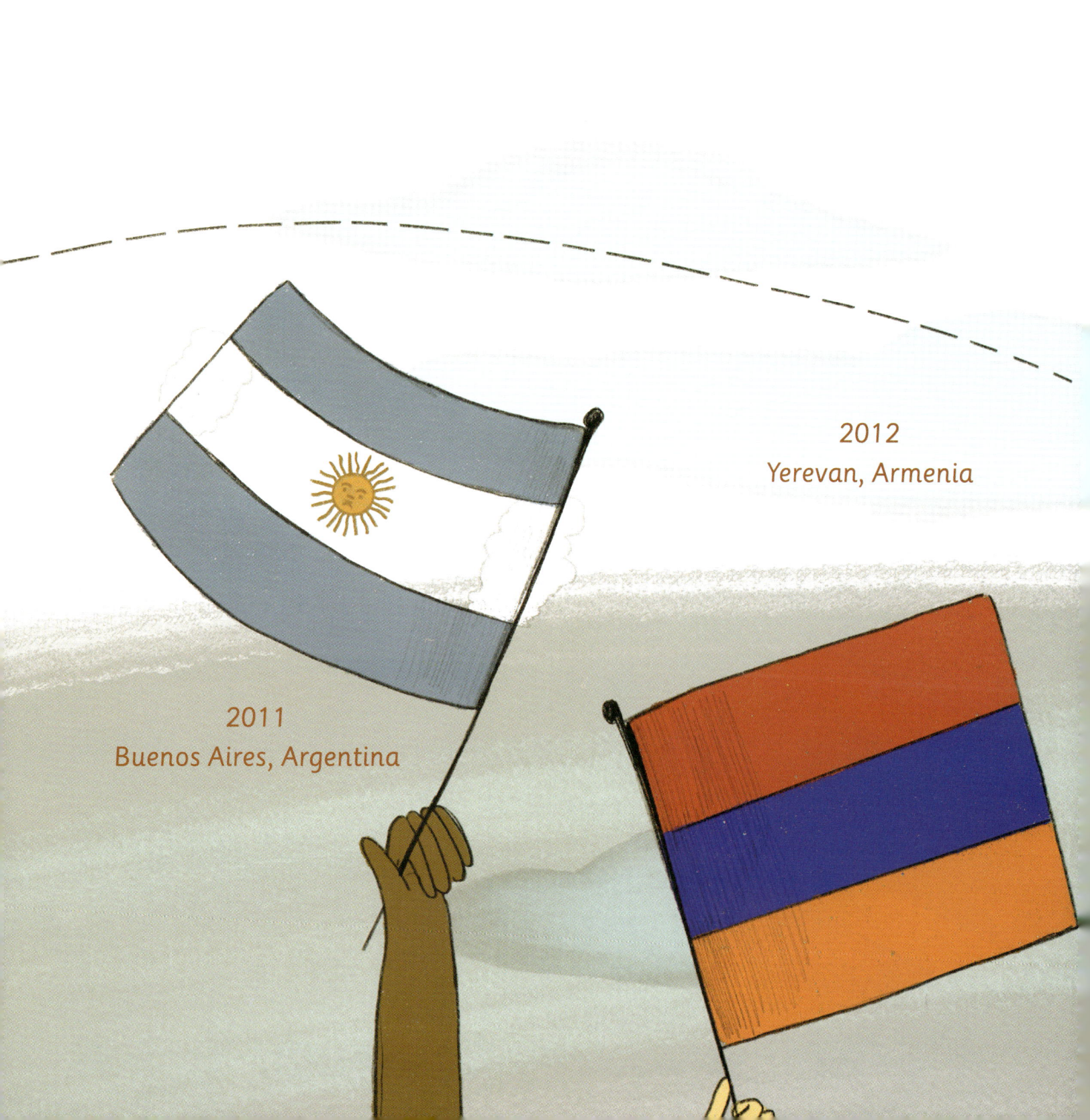

2012
Yerevan, Armenia

2011
Buenos Aires, Argentina

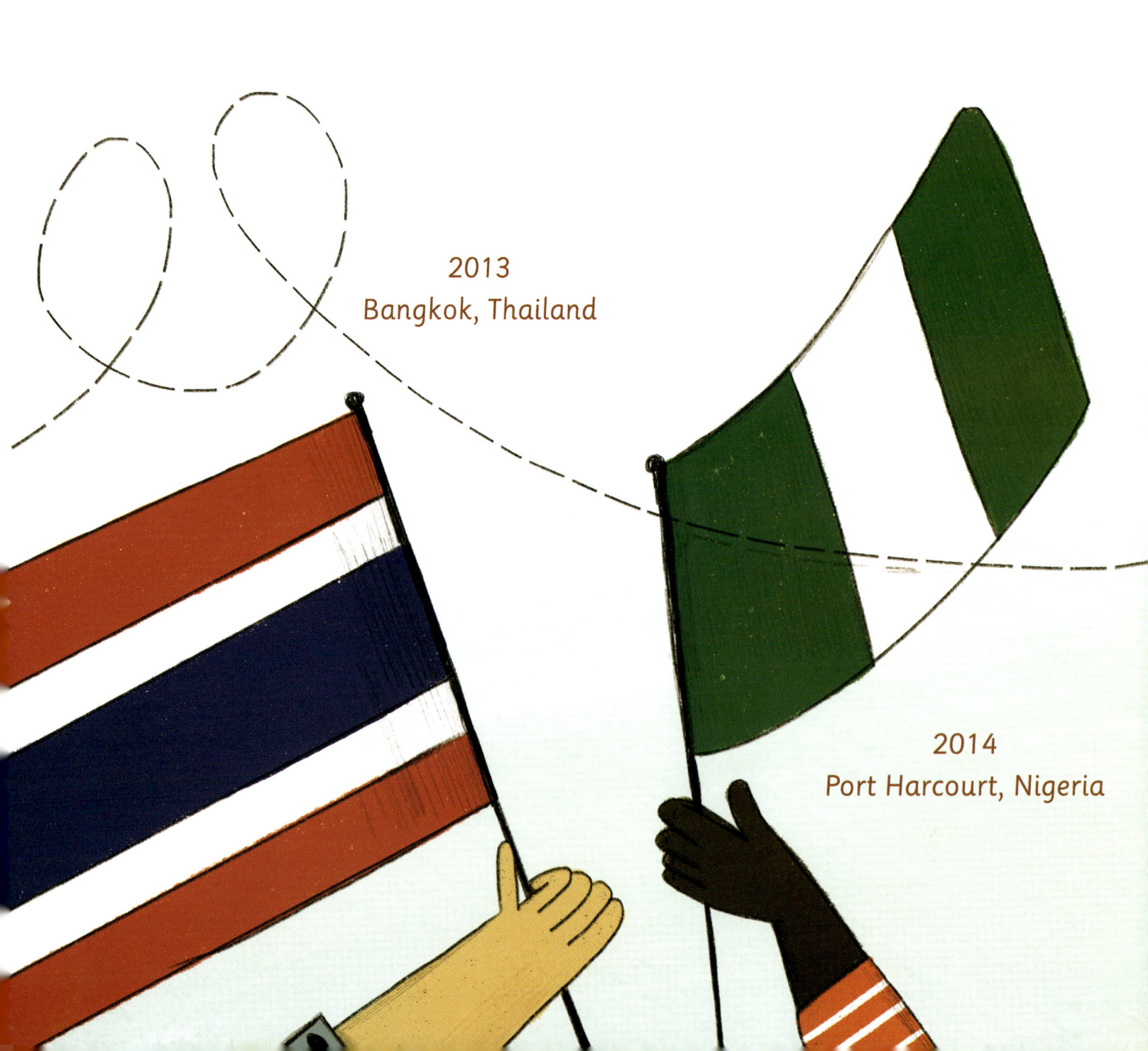

2013
Bangkok, Thailand

2014
Port Harcourt, Nigeria

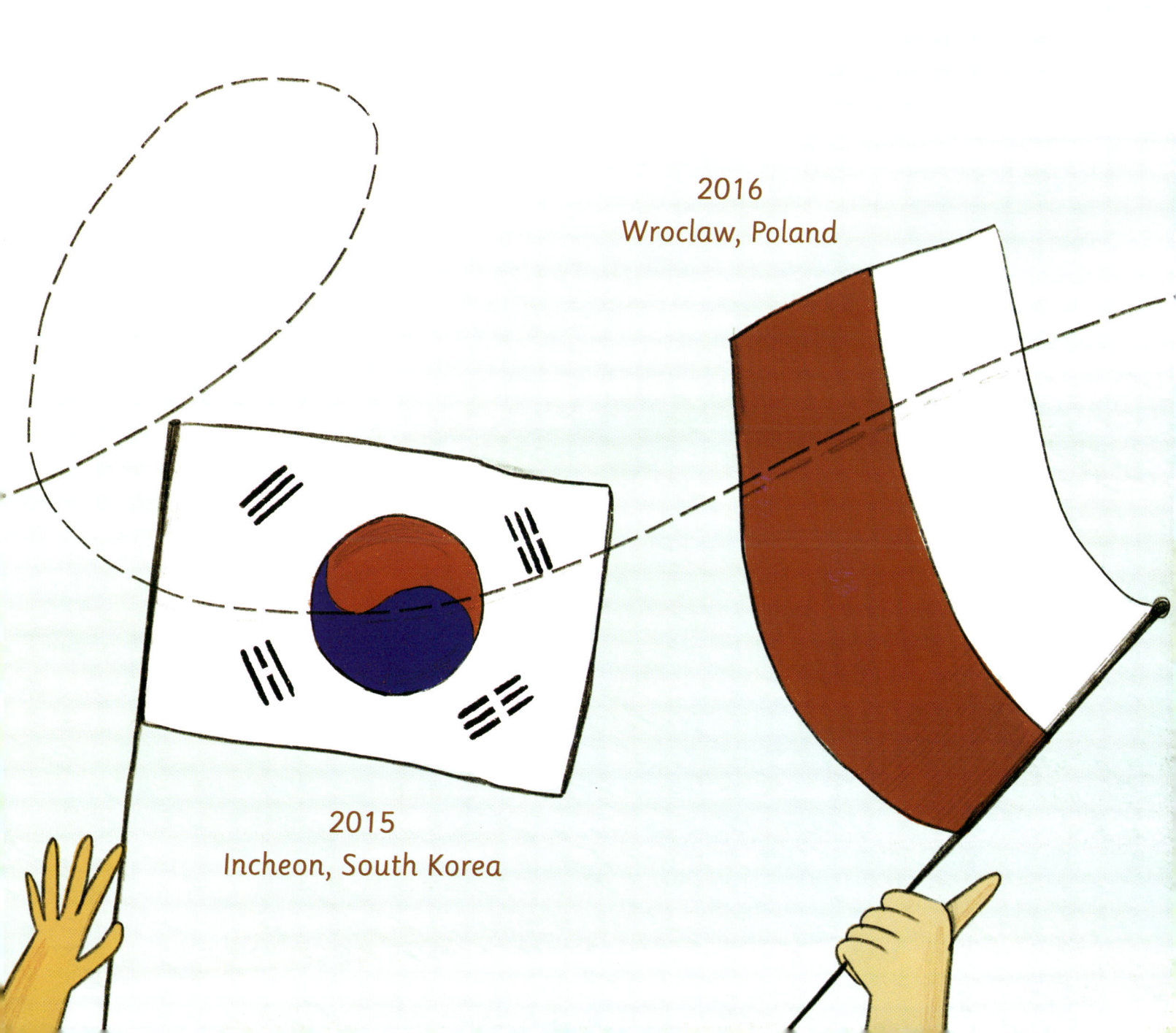

2016
Wroclaw, Poland

2015
Incheon, South Korea

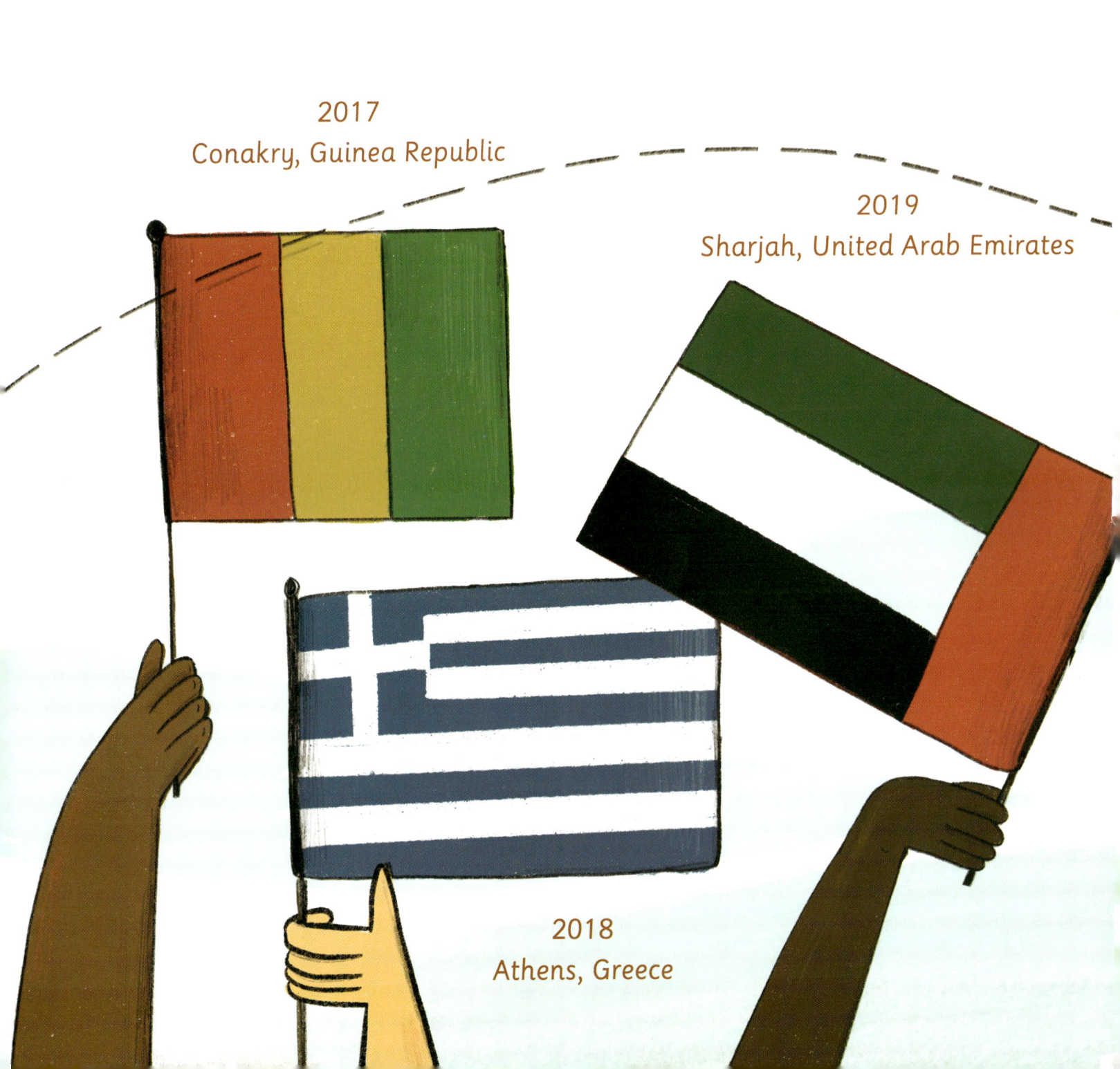

2017
Conakry, Guinea Republic

2019
Sharjah, United Arab Emirates

2018
Athens, Greece

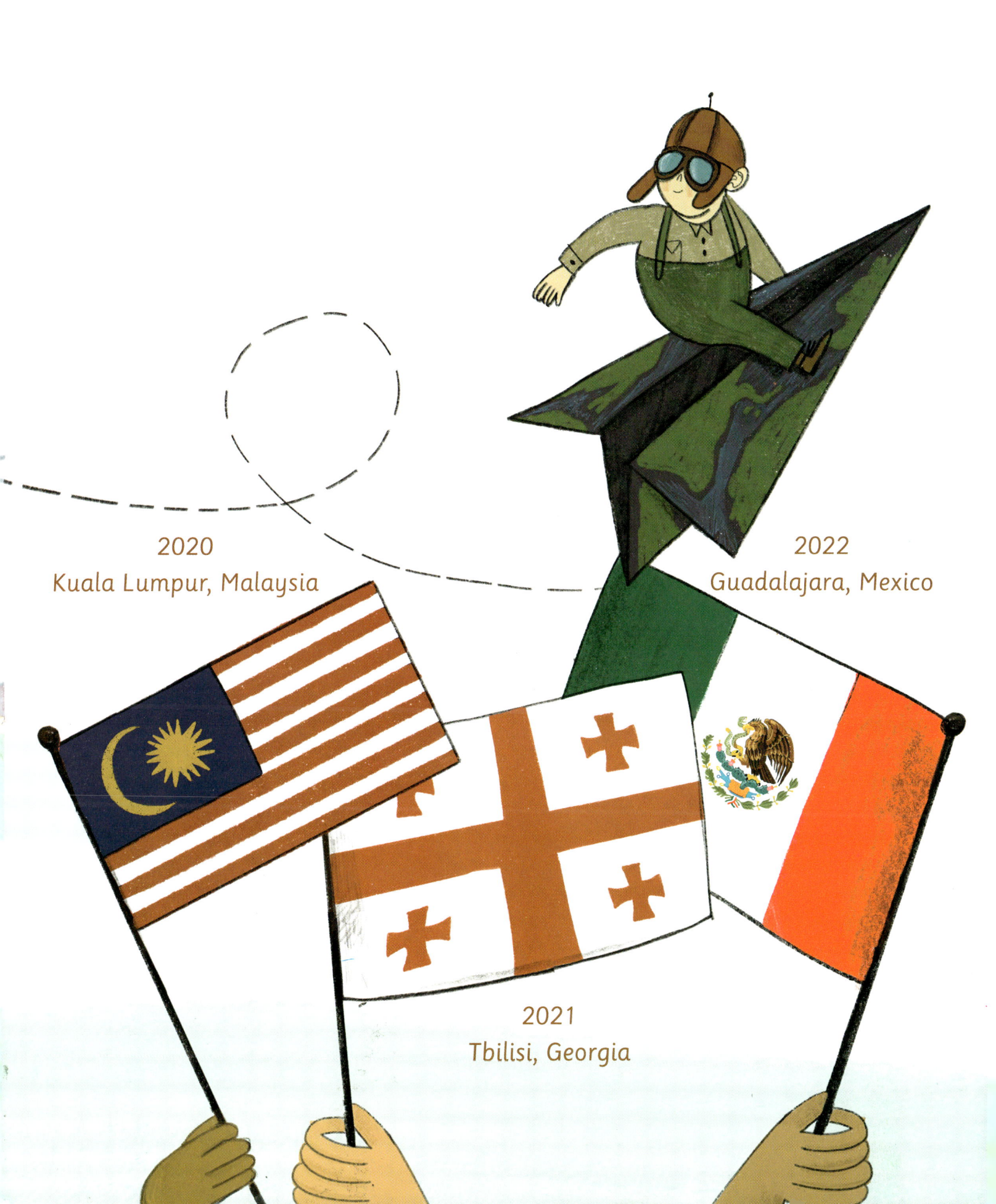

2020
Kuala Lumpur, Malaysia

2022
Guadalajara, Mexico

2021
Tbilisi, Georgia